WOMEN SURVIVING

Maria Luddy and Cliona Murphy

POOLBEG

A Paperback Original
First published 1989 by
Poolbeg Press Ltd.
Knocksedan House,
Swords, Co. Dublin, Ireland.

© The Contributors 1990

ISBN 1 85371 064 4

All rights reserved. No part of this publication may be reproduced or transmitted in any form or by any means, electronic or mechanical, including photography, recording, or any information storage or retrieval system, without permission in writing from the publisher. The book is sold subject to the condition that it shall not, by way of trade or otherwise be lent, re-sold or otherwise circulated without the publisher's prior consent in any form of binding or cover other than that in which it is published and without a similar condition including this condition being imposed on the subsequent purchaser.

Cover design by Pomphrey Associates
Typeset by Print-Forme,
62 Santry Close, Dublin 9.
Printed by The Guernsey Press Ltd.,
Vale, Guernsey, Channel Islands.

Contents

"Cherchez la Femme" The Elusive Woman in Irish History
    Maria Luddy, Cliona Murphy   1

The Limits of Female Autonomy: Nuns in Nineteenth-Century Ireland
    Caitríona Clear   15

Prostitution and Rescue Work in Nineteenth-Century Ireland
    Maria Luddy   51

Breadwinners and Providers: Women in the Household Economy of Labouring Families 1835-6
    Mary Cullen   85

Workhouses and Irish Female Paupers, 1840-70
    Dympna McLoughlin   117

Life for Domestic Servants in Dublin, 1880-1920
    Mona Hearn   148

"The Tune of the Stars and Stripes:" The American Influence on the Irish Suffrage Movement
    Cliona Murphy   180

Aspects of Women's Contribution to the Oireachtas Debate in the Irish Free State, 1922-37
    Mary Clancy   206

Fullness of Life: Defining Female Spirituality in Twentieth-Century Ireland
    Margaret MacCurtain   233

Suggestions for further reading   264
Notes on Contributors   274
Index   276

Acknowledgements

The editors and contributors would like to thank the following: the Sisters of the Good Shepherd convents in Belfast, Limerick and Waterford; the Sisters of Mercy in Limerick and Galway; the Sisters of Our Lady of Charity of Refuge in Dublin; the Sisters of Charity in Cork and Milltown, Dublin; the Faithful Companions of Jesus, Limerick; the Dominican Sisters in Galway and the Little Company of Mary, Limerick for allowing access to their records. For access to the Irish Poor Law Records thanks are due to Mr Jarlath Glynn, assistant county librarian, Wexford. Mr Joe McEvoy of St James's Hospital, Dublin, Ms Aoife Leonard, then archivist with the Kerry County Library, Tralee. Mr Chris O'Mahony, archivist in Limerick, Ms McCarthy in Cork city, Mr Kavanagh of Newbridge library, Mr Trevor Parkhill of the Public Records Office, Belfast and the county librarians and their deputies in Galway, Wicklow and Clare. Thanks to Padraig Lenihan for the maps. We would also like to thank Jo O'Donoghue at Poolbeg for her enthusiasm and interest in all stages of this work.

The editors would also like to thank Tom Dunne for his encouragement and assistance.

For our sisters: Eileen, Geraldine and Catherine

"Cherchez la femme": The Elusive Woman in Irish History

Maria Luddy, Cliona Murphy

The idea for this book was arrived at early in 1988 after numerous meetings of the Irish Feminist History Forum. The FHF was established in February 1987 and acts as a group where those interested in women's history, particularly that of Irish women, can share their thoughts and findings with other members. Much of the work carried on and debated within the forum is original and we, as editors, suggested to a number of members that they write articles on their current interests and research. We were anxious to bring this work to as broad a range of readers as possible, to show that not only do Irish women have a history but that it is a history which is vibrant and worth recording. The theme of this book, women surviving, suggested itself for a number of reasons. First of all we intended to focus on women, or groups of women, who had previously received little or no attention from Irish historians and to show that it is possible to reconstruct their history from surviving records. As the articles were written it emerged that the women under discussion were themselves "survivors" continually adapting to and exploiting the situations in which they found themselves. The "woman as passive victim" ideology, which tended to dominate earlier writing of women's history did not ring true. These women are active agents in the historical process. They had to be active and manipulative in order to survive or have their cause survive. Being imaginative and inventive was important whether one was a pauper, prostitute, nun, servant or suffragist.

Over the last twenty-five years a revolution has taken

place in the study of women's history. Women's studies centres have been appearing in universities all over the United States and in Britain and women's history is finding a home in these centres. It is also being taught in an increasing number of history departments and other courses by now, at least in the United States, frequently make some gesture towards women's history in the course bibliography.

The development of a philosophy of women's history has been one of the results of this proliferation of research, publication and teaching. It has moved from a position of seeing women as victims continually being oppressed, to what Gerda Lerner has called "compensatory history"[1], including only "famous" or "extraordinary" women in the historical process. This involved fitting women into the accepted and standard outlines of political history. In Ireland we can see such history in many of the early biographies which have appeared on women like Maud Gonne or Constance Markievicz. Indeed for many Irish people they are the best known, and perhaps the only, Irish women who have any historical presence. Again, to use Lerner's phrase, there is "contribution history", which emphasises women's contribution to political and social movements. This can be seen in most of the examinations which have been made into the Ladies' Land League, for example, where the questions asked revolved around the women's contribution to the male run Land League and their efforts were judged by male standards which generally denigrated their contribution and ignored the autonomous and radical implications of their work.[2]

These types of writing are important if only in showing that certain women did have a history. However, the shortcomings of these approaches are that they are concerned with only a minority of women, those who worked closely with male dominated organisations and those who had the luxury to be active, and the questions asked centred on the implications of the women's involvement as they affected the political concerns of men. Using these approaches meant that the majority would continue to be absent from history and women would be viewed within "a male-defined conceptual framework."[3] Therefore the question which occurred to a number of historians of women was how to have a legitimate women's history which was not an afterthought following the ground rules laid down by two centuries of male historians.

Two variables seem to be crucial in determining the future of women's history and establishing its framework. These are concerned with the sources used by historians and the concept of periodisation in history. It has been claimed that writing the history of women is necessarily limited by lack of sources. The present work illustrates what use can be made of sources which are relatively accessible and known to historians but which are used here in a new and imaginative way. Material such as the Poor Law Minute Books, household manuals, newspapers, interviews, the annals of various convents and the more traditional census records, parliamentary papers and debates, and institutional records are shown to reveal a variety of information about women's lives.

Periodisation, established in the nineteenth century, set down signposts through history which included such eras as the Middle Ages, Renaissance, the Enlightenment and so on. But it must be, and has been, asked, whether these mean anything to women. Joan Kelly convincingly argues in a classic article that women did not have a Renaissance.[4] The revolution of 1789 in France did not grant liberty and equality to women. Many of the developments of civilised society such as democratisation are seen as progressive but they are often progressive only for men and generally imposed greater constraints on women. The great Reform Bill of 1832, for example, extended the franchise to a large number of men but the phrasing of the Bill rejected the terms "man" or "men", which could conceivably be interpreted to include women, for "male person" which definitely excluded women.[5] The Reform Bill of 1867, though still denying the vote to women, allowed paupers and lunatics the vote under certain circumstances. Many suffragists saw this as not only illogical but also insulting.

Traditional interpretations of historical events are cast in universal terms and would seem to include women. In Irish history some of the significant dates of the last century are the 1800 Act of Union, 1829 Catholic Emancipation, 1845-9 the Great Famine, 1867 the Fenian Rising, 1879-82 the Land War, the various Land Acts from the 1870s, the turn of the century Gaelic and Literary Revival and in this century the 1916 Rising. These are events in Irish history with which people are familiar but the significance of these events for women has never been investigated. Seen from this perspective they could very well be viewed as less progressive and dramatic than is commonly believed. At the very least any investigation focussing on women's perspective would ask different questions and stress the dichotomy of experiences which exist between the impact of events on men's and women's lives. Ignoring this denigrates the importance of women's own experiences and their place as agents in society.

Although much work remains to be done in relation to women in Irish history it is possible, from work already completed, to formulate a list of significant events and dates for Irish women. Thus, the foundation in Dublin in 1815 of the Sisters of Charity, a congregation which devoted itself to work in the community and whose establishment in Ireland was unprecedented, paved the way for the development of active religious communities which allowed women to engage in practical social work. It is significant that in 1800 there were 120 nuns in Ireland and over 8,000 in 1901.[6] The winning of educational rights for women equal to those offered to men and beginning with the opening of the Ladies' Collegiate School in Belfast in 1859, the Queen's Institute and Alexandra College in Dublin in 1861 and 1866, were of significant importance for a number of middle class women.[7] Until education could become a means of acquiring a livelihood which allowed an independent existence, and until it stimulated the intellectual capacities of women, it prepared them only for a role as wife and mother and excluded them from participation in public life. With the advances made in education from the 1850s the expectations of women were raised and it was those who benefited from such advances who dominated the movements which called for a political voice for women.

The implementation of the Contagious Diseases Acts of 1864, 1866 and 1869, which were enforced in Cork, Cobh and the Curragh, allowed for the forcible detention and inspection of women thought to be prostitutes. The Acts attempted to control the spread of venereal diseases amongst the soldiery. Since there was no legal definition of what constituted a prostitute, all women who appeared in public were potentially vulnerable to detention. The impact of these Acts is only beginning to be studied in this country but evidence reveals the extent to which women were idealised in Irish society and how male perceptions of woman's "proper place" circumscribed her life.[8] 1876 saw the establishment of the first suffrage society in the country with Anna Haslam's Dublin Women's Suffrage Society from which were to develop the large number of suffrage societies which eventually won the right to vote. The Women's Poor Law Guardian Act of 1896 and the Local Government Act of 1898 allowed women to vote and sit as councillors and Poor Law guardians.[9] Such a list is, of course, incomplete and shows that the research and scholarship completed to date still covers only a minority of women, generally the middle and upper classes.

Such "re-vision" questions the whole basis of traditional historical enquiry and begs the question whether women can have a legitimate place in history. If the answer is yes, as it must be, it requires a radical re-conceptualising of what is considered historically important.

Women's experience has differed in each century, and has been shaped by class, culture, religion, marital status, opportunities to work, prevailing patriarchal beliefs about women's "nature" and so on. Not only has women's experience differed markedly from men's but women themselves do not form a homogeneous, undifferentiated mass and groups and individuals must be studied separately. The study of women's history means re-evaluating, re-organising and re-interpreting our knowledge of the past. In the last twenty-five years scholarship, from other countries, has revealed the value of women's experience which is different and distinct from that of men and often reveals how traditional historical, mostly male, perceptions of what exactly that experience was differed from the realities of women's lives.

The problem of creating an inclusive historical view has received much attention from social historians. Earlier debates which questioned whether to mainstream or retain women's history as a separate discipline proved unsatisfactory. The current debate about the place of women's history has led to the concept of "gender history."[10] This attempts to unify the workings of political and economic forces stressing the interrelationships of men's and women's lives and should lead to an understanding of the lives of both sexes by utilising an inclusive historical perspective.

Observing the developments which have taken place in this area, particularly in the United States, the question which prompted itself was what of the situation of women's history in Ireland? It must be said that Irish social history in general has been less well served by historians than political and nationalist history. It is indicative of a particular bias that women's history is not taught at undergraduate level, nor indeed at any other level on any systematic basis. That such history does and did not form part of the education of many Irish people leaves a gap in their appreciation of the role which women played, and still play, in the community and ignores their very great contribution to the formation of Irish society. We are beginning to see the emergence of women's studies courses in this country but on a very small scale and such courses do not form part of the core curriculum in any departments of our universities.[11] Until these pioneering courses are integrated into the curriculum they are in danger of being regarded as a peripheral activity pacifying the interested parties without taking them, their work or their students seriously.

And what is history in Ireland? A narrative account of the doings of men, largely carried out by men, written by men and taught by men. How many of the male historians in history departments in Ireland, or indeed elsewhere, take a good look at themselves and their departments and their subject matter? What is the ratio of male to female undergraduates? And how does this ratio reverse itself as one proceeds up the academic ladder? Where do all the enthusiastic female undergraduates go? Does their disappearance have any link with the invisibility of women in history? It is problematic for the discipline of history that the women who manage to hang in there and become professional historians are the ones who write women's history. Does this make it an inferior history in the eyes of the men or at the very least a separate history? — a history which sounds vaguely familiar, if only a reversal of the norm, a history researched and written by women, taught by women to women and read by women. How many men will read this book? Should we care? Yes, certainly. Why be so critical of the male historians only to go out and repeat the same mistakes? It is the duty of the newest wave of women historians to contribute to the field of history and not allow themselves to be separated into their own little ghetto. But in order to do this there will have to be some inclination on the part of male historians to accept change and accept that there is emerging a "new" history of Ireland.

In this collection we have new research in Irish history carried out from a different perspective. Besides showing that there is a history of Irish women and that scholarly work is being done on this we want to show that it is not just the history of the oppressed "other". All the articles have the women firmly planted within their own historical period. They are not living in a separate dimension as one might have supposed from either reading the traditional textbooks in Irish history or the books which are relegated to the discreet corners of bookshops under the label of "Feminist

Studies". Their lives are firmly connected to, and dictated by, the political, social, demographic and economic happenings of the time. They are a part of history, not on the fringes of it.

A number of themes run through these articles. The majority of contributors are concerned with the social and economic role of women in the period 1800-1937. Women's political activity is also encompassed and the importance of a spiritual dimension to their lives is examined. Throughout the aim has been to show the diversity of women's lives. Through case studies on individual women and on specific topics related to women we can begin to understand the very great contribution which they made to Irish history. Such particularism is the keynote to beginning the inclusion of women in Irish historiography.

The various employment opportunities available to women are noted in a number of articles. What is obvious from all these studies is that women have always worked. The ability to find remunerative employment depended upon numerous conditions which are discussed by the contributors. Women worked on small holdings to maintain a family, they engaged in begging, hawking and a multitude of other enterprises to support themselves, they worked "respectably" as domestic servants, they engaged in the outcast occupation of prostitution and were most "respectably employed," though generally in an unpaid capacity, as nuns in the many caring occupations those women engaged in.

It cannot be asserted that Irish women formed a homogeneous group. It would be naive to consider that some great "sisterhood" of women existed in either the nineteenth or twentieth centuries. The poor working women noted in Cullen's article and the paupers of McLoughlin's study had different life opportunities and experiences from those, for example, of nuns, which are noted in Clear's article. The study of suffragists and the women who were elected to the Dáil and Senate emphasise not only the differences which could exist between the various "classes" of women regarding their backgrounds and opportunities but also show clearly how women's response to society and their participation in it on a public or private level was shaped by that background.

Caitriona Clear, in a wideranging discussion, describes the establishment of religious congregations in Ireland over the nineteenth century, detailing the practical forces which allowed convents to function and revealing the limits of all female institutions in overcoming the patriarchal boundaries set by male church leaders. The establishment of convents undoubtedly gave some women the means to attain a certain degree of control over their own lives and offered them an opportunity to engage in socially useful work, work which was denied to the majority of Irishwomen. The compromises made along the way go some way to explain why Catholic female religious never attained any degree of political strength in Irish society. It is arguable whether nuns, as women, needed to express any degree of "public" power. Could it be possible that the values expressed through the work of these women, those skills of nurturing and caring, give rise to questions about the assumptions traditionally held about the importance of "power"? Is it adequate to use male norms of power as a standard by which to judge the work of women? Was their role much more important and valuable on a human level than dealing in politics? As Clear observes many of the skills used by nuns and women are generally undervalued until they are absent.

Maria Luddy investigates the extent of prostitution in nineteenth-century Ireland and the attempts made, primarily by lay women and female religious, to rescue the "fallen". Here are juxtaposed two very different aspects of women's lives. The ideology of the "good woman" is revealed strongly in this article and is shown to have shaped the response of middle-class women, and society in general, to prostitution. Rescuers were products of their own time and even if their philosophy was never radical it was clearly innovative, offering shelter to the most "outcast" of society's members. Here too we can begin to see prostitutes as real people. The harsh realities of life, it is argued, forced women into prostitution and it is seen as a viable option in a society which offered few opportunities to women to support themselves adequately. Her analysis of the entrants to Magdalen asylums shows them to have had some control over their own lives, echoing McLoughlin's findings regarding the women who entered workhouses.

Mary Cullen's article reveals, through an analysis of the family budgets of labourers, the extent to which women contributed to the household economy in pre-Famine Ireland. It is obvious that a working partnership existed between husband and wife. Whether women earned money or not they contributed to the household economy by their labour either in raising fowl or working on the family's small plot of land. They could also supplement the family's income by engaging in weaving and spinning. Women also contributed in a non earning capacity as child rearers. The loss of a woman's earnings or her inability to contribute in some form could plunge the family into destitution. But even in these instances the family devised strategies for coping with distress. The most popular of these strategies was begging, an occupation in which women played the leading role.

Dympna McLoughlin's study focuses on pauper women within the workhouse and uses workhouse minutes in a new and creative way. While succinctly describing the administrative structure of that system she reveals how women continually adapted to it, with their tendency to ignore and even circumvent its strictures to suit their own needs. Not only does she provide us with an exciting look at the everyday lives of pauper women but she also raises questions regarding our understanding of domestic life and the place of women within such scenes of "domesticity". Her analysis also provokes thoughts about the place of children in Irish society, a topic which has not yet received adequate treatment in Irish history. Poor and pauper women were specifically governed by their physical circumstances and their need for survival; the examination of a pauper culture reveals the existence of an opposing middle-class culture which functionaries of the Poor Law system generally espoused and which they tried to enforce upon their charges, obviously unsuccessfully. Her paper raises questions about the traditionally accepted dualism of the male/female spheres in society and about the ideology of separate spheres, an essentially middle-class creation which sought to impinge on the lives of poor women.

Mona Hearn in her article on domestic servants focuses attention on women in the most common occupation open to them. She analyses where these women came from, their conditions of employment and how they related to their employers. Domestic service was widely regarded as the only fitting occupation for many women from the lower classes and this was of course in keeping with the traditional role expected of women, bound to the domestic sphere where their lives were controlled and limited. However, Hearn makes it clear that a paradoxical relationship existed between employer and servant. These domestic servants had some little power over their employers and were apt to gain the best of their situation through the emotional and economic bonds they formed with them.

Cliona Murphy adds an international dimension to the study of Irishwomen at the beginning of the twentieth century when she reveals the impact American suffragists had on the Irish suffrage movement. Here she shows that Irishwomen, though living on the edge of Europe, were not isolated in their activities and gained emotional and intellectual support from their sisters in other countries. Though relying on such international support for their cause the Irish movement was autonomous and had its own particular character. She charts also, in outline, the main problems which plagued the Irish suffragists and captures the vibrancy of the movement with its schisms and diversity.

Mary Clancy analyses the role Irishwomen played in the parliamentary process after the formation of the state. It is evident here that women's contribution to debate and legislation within the Seanad and Oireachtas was formed by their own backgrounds and the prevailing patriarchal structures of society. It is significant that on issues relating to the welfare of women and children some women representatives were vocal and sought to influence the direction of legislative initiative. The notable contribution of Jenny Wyse-Power to political life reveals how a background of involvement in women's issues influenced her outlook. It is also seen that the political sphere of the 1920s and 30s was a sphere defined in male terms. Women, particularly if they were interested in women's issues, faced numerous obstacles not least of which was the desire of many public representatives not to discuss in any detail "sensitive" issues such as prostitution or divorce. The difficulty in overcoming such reticence and strictures is evident.

Margaret MacCurtain adds further international perspectives by looking at the life and work of Edel Quinn in Ireland and Africa. She first notes the pervasive importance of religion to women, an aspect echoed in a number of other contributions to this volume, and offers comparison with the spirituality expressed by Peig Sayers and Edel Quinn. In examining the devotional practices of these women she places them firmly within the context of their own contemporary worlds and explores the meaning of spirituality in their lives.

This collection revolves around women living and working amid all the complexities that made up Irish life in the period. Should we have expected radicalism, innovative critiques of society and women's place in it from these women under investigation? There were indeed women of radical intent in Irish society but that is the subject for another volume. Our intention is to cover a broad range of women in society, the ordinary rather than the exceptional, to show how groups of Irishwomen and individuals responded to society and the realities of their everyday existence.

There has been to date little or no theoretical debate regarding the nature of women's history in Ireland, partly due to the lack of an adequate research base. This volume, we trust, will encourage such debate and discussion and will spur others to investigate other aspects of women's history. The field of study is wide open. There is no lack of sources and what is needed essentially is both the desire to discover and the willingness to disseminate information. Some areas which spring to mind for further study are women on the margins of society: "outcast women" such as vagrants or criminals; further investigation into women's working lives is necessary. We need a comprehensive study of the family and women's place in it. There is a need to study those forces, cultural, social, economic and religious, which shaped women's existence over different periods. We hope this book is a beginning.

NOTES

1 Gerda Lerner, *The Majority Finds Its Past: Placing Women in History* (New York, 1979), especially pp 145-80.
2 See for example F.S.L. Lyons, *Ireland Since the Famine* (Glasgow, 1974), the standard textbook on Irish history which barely mentions the Ladies' Land League. For fuller treatments see T. W. Moody, *Davitt and Irish Revolution 1846-82* (London, 1981) and R. F. Foster, *Charles Stewart Parnell: The Man and His Family* (Sussex, 1979). See Dana Hearne's introduction to Anna Parnell's *Tale of a Great Sham* (Dublin, 1986) for a feminist analysis of the League.
3 Lerner, *op. cit.*, p. 148.
4 Joan Kelly, "Did women have a Renaissance?" in idem, *Women, History and Theory: The Essays of Joan Kelly* (Chicago, 1984), pp 19-50.

5 Martin Pugh, *Women's Suffrage in Britain*, 1867-1928 (London, 1980). See also the introduction in M. J. Boxer and J. H. Quataert (eds.), *Connecting Spheres: Women in the Western World, 1500 to the Present* (Oxford, 1987), pp 3-17.
6 Tony Fahey, "Nuns in the Catholic church in Ireland in the nineteenth century," in Mary Cullen (ed.), *Girls Don't Do Honours: Irish Women in Education in the 19th and 20th Centuries* (Dublin, 1987), p. 7. See also Caitriona Clear's *Nuns in Nineteenth Century Ireland* (Dublin, 1987).
7 Anne V. O'Connor, "The revolution in girls' secondary education in Ireland 1860-1910", in Cullen, *op. cit.*, pp 31-54.
8 Maria Luddy, Women and philanthropy in nineteenth century Ireland (Unpublished Ph. D Thesis, N. U. I., 1989), pp 275-86.
9 To date nothing has been published on the effects of these Acts for women in Ireland. For a contemporary view see Isabella M. S. Tod, "The place of women in the administration of the Irish Poor Law," *Englishwoman's Review*, 15 October 1881, pp 481-9; idem., "Municipal franchise for women in Ireland," *Englishwoman's Review*, 15 July 1887, pp 289-91. Anna M. Haslam, "Irishwomen and the Local Government Act," *Englishwomen's Review*, 15 October 1881, pp 221-5. "Women Poor Law Guardians in Ireland," *Englishwoman's Review*, 15 October 1896, pp 256-8.
10 Joan W. Scott, "Gender: a useful category of historical analysis," *American Historical Review*, 91, (1986), pp 1053-75. Gisela Bock, "Women's history and gender history: aspects of an international debate," *Gender and History*, vol. 1, no. 1, (Spring 1989), pp 7-30.
11 At the time of going to press the extra-mural department of University College Dublin offered a number of evening courses under the title "Women's Studies". Women's history is also taught in UCD.

The Limits of Female Autonomy: Nuns in Nineteenth-Century Ireland

Caitriona Clear

Women's invisibility in history is double-edged. Lacking, as a rule, access to vital sources such as money and education, women leave few records of any kind for the historian. As well as this, the kind of unpaid work which women perform is of its nature invisible, the everyday reproductive and maintenance work which is rarely noticed and usually assigned a secondary status. The majority of women workers in nineteenth-century Ireland are no exception to this rule, but the historian of one particular group of women workers, nuns, is at first pleasantly surprised. Few contemporaries failed to notice these women and to comment upon the teaching, nursing and social work which they performed. Histories of particular congregations and biographies of founders are by no means thick on the ground, but they exist, providing us with more information about nuns than is available about any other group of women workers of the period.

Their comparative visibility is not the only way in which nuns differ from the majority of their female counterparts in nineteenth-century Ireland. Living and working together in groups ranging in size from three to over a hundred, women religious are in stark contrast to the general run of women workers at this time. As the century progressed, factory work for women became almost totally confined to the north-east and to the large cities, which meant that the experience of working together under similar conditions was a rare one for Irish women workers. Domestic service, which was the most common paid occupation for women according to the census figures from 1851, was more often than not a solitary or semi-solitary occupation, and the rates of pay and wages varied from one place to the next. Women working in their own homes experienced widely divergent conditions, depending upon the income and indeed the character of the breadwinner. Their work in nineteenth-century Ireland did not, for the most part, lend itself to the development of a shared work identity among women, which partly explains the comparatively low level of female trade union activity towards the end of the century. Nuns, however, had a common identity as women religious in the Catholic church, and the various congregations into which they were subdivided—Presentation, Mercy and many others—had very strong identities of their own. Most of these congregations, native and foreign, were founded by women, women who were respected, even revered, not only by their followers, but by priests, bishops and Catholic lay people.

Convents, furthermore, are all-female institutions, governed on a day-to-day basis by women. Nuns were removed from the domestic authority of fathers, husbands and brothers, at a time when economic change was reinforcing such authority. They were, moreover, active religious in a church which was undergoing a renewal and consolidating its economic and political power. The organisations run by nuns—the congregations themselves, and many of their projects—survive to the present day.

It is also true, however, that nuns were members of one of the largest and most consistently male-dominated organizations in the history of the western world, the Roman Catholic Church. On the face of it, female religious had high visibility, optimum conditions for the development of gender-based solidarity, and a freedom from domestic roles which entailed no loss of social status, at a time when most contemporary opinions insisted that women's proper sphere was the home. An exploration of the position of nuns in the Catholic Church in nineteenth-century Ireland will help us to discover the extent to which these apparent advantages over other women workers resulted in a stretching of the limits of female autonomy laid down by the society of the day.

Nuns' Position in the Church

The question of authority over women and the proper exercise of such authority was debated at length by the supporters and opponents of the Inspection of Nunneries Bill at mid-century. "On Monday the chivalry of Ireland will array itself in united protest against the coward assaults made by the fanatics of England upon the timid and shrinking inmates of the nunneries", ran a report in the *Freeman's Journal* of Saturday June 11, 1853. Opponents of the Bill portrayed themselves as protectors of their womenfolk: "A father's feeling in defence of his daughter—a brother's in defence of his sister, is not blunted because that daughter or that sister may have dedicated her life to the service of religion and the teaching of the poor." Convents were "sanctified retreats": "the peace of that home she would not change for the throne of an empress." [1]

Supporters of the Inspection of Nunneries Bill (which never passed into law) claimed that women were often detained against their will in convents, and that these institutions removed females from the authority and protection of their menfolk, subjecting them to the tyranny of "unnatural" all female institutions. The Bill's opponents at the meeting in June 1853 did not refute the notion that women needed male protection, as their comments above would suggest, and there was loud applause for a Mr D'Arcy, T.C., when he hinted that inspection of convents, if it came into force, would set a dangerous precedent:

> Under its provisions there was not a house in the Empire that might not be entered. They might enter by force the dwelling of the father who had a disobedient daughter— they might hear her complaints and order her redress in defiance of parental authority. [2]

Dominick Murphy, in his 1865 work on nuns in Ireland,

shied away from the "timid and shrinking" label applied to nuns by some of the opponents of the Nunneries Bill. Instead he emphasised the social utility of female religious, depicting them as intelligent women who provided essential services effectively and inexpensively. He went so far as to question the rule of enclosure which prevented active religious like the Presentation from going outside their convents, and his admiration and respect for nuns is evident. Even he, however, found it necessary to call attention to the rules and customs which governed houses of religious, describing the checks and balances build into the hierarchical chain of command in the Church. Convents selected superiors, but these superiors were answerable to the local bishop to a greater or lesser extent; convents' independence was limited. This will be discussed in greater detail; staying with Murphy for the present, it is significant that he did not neglect the question of authority over women. Regulations which sprang from centuries-old canonical tradition guaranteed the stability and security of convent life, just as the sober dress worn by nuns deterred them from "the besetting weakness of their sex."[3]

The eighteenth and nineteenth centuries saw the foundation of hundreds of new religious congregations of women throughout the Catholic world. These congregations were for the most part responses to the evangelicalism of the time and to the social dislocation which was a result of economic change. Most of these groups began as groups of lay people who were motivated by a strong religious impulse to carry out work of various kinds among the poor. The Congregation for the Propagation of the Faith, in Rome, was the central body responsible for approving the rules and constitutions which aspiring religious congregations were obliged to adopt. These were usually drafted by interested priests versed in canon law, and passed on to Rome for approval. It was with evident relief that somebody in the Propaganda Fides, as the central body was also known, made the following comment about the constitutions of the Sisters of Mercy congregations in 1840:

> Constitutions cannot be said to be complete when they lack those positive prescriptions for observation of rule which are so necessary for religious communities, especially of women, whence to remove doubt, disquietude and perplexity of soul in subjects, and to moderate within certain limits the authority of superiors.[4]

This canon lawyer obviously believed that women religious were in special need of solidly-rooted rules and regulations; his fear that superiors might abuse their power was a common one, which applied equally to male religious communities, but in this context it throws up echoes of the contemporary fear that women placed in authority over other women would have a natural tendency to tyranny.

As religious in the Catholic Church nuns were automatically entitled to a certain amount of respect from bishops, priests and lay Catholics, and as tireless workers and able administrators in nineteenth-century Ireland they earned this respect. Cullen, archbishop of Armagh from 1848 to 1852 and of Dublin until he became Cardinal in 1866: rarely had any negative comments to make about nuns; he claimed in 1852 that they were "the best support to religion",[5] acknowledging their key role in the disciplinary drive over which he presided. Three priests, writing in the 1860s, 1880s and early 1900s praised nuns unstintingly.[6] No churchman, however, challenged (on paper at any rate) nuns' position on the bottom rung of the ecclesiastical ladder. Females are barred from ordination and therefore from entering into the mainstream of the power structure of the Church. Writing in 1884, Addis and Arnold made the following comment about abbesses:

> these powers (i.e. the powers of property and patronage traditionally allowed abbesses) are included within that capacity of a ruling and possessing property which every truly civilised state recognises no less in women than in men, but when ... any exercise of authority bordering on episcopal power is in question, the abbess is no more than any other woman.[7]

In other words, abbesses—traditionally the most powerful women religious in the Church—might not have been religious at all, for all the real authority that their state of life conferred upon them. As for abbesses, so too for nuns in nineteenth-century Ireland.[8]

Religious communities of women are as old as the Church itself, and concern on the part of popes and bishops about how best to control these communities has an equally long history. The quite extensive powers enjoyed by medieval abbesses were cut back in the eleventh century, and the other religious congregations were brought increasingly under control also. Modifications of the power and the status of women religious reached a culmination in the third session of the Council of Trent, 1563-6. It was decreed that strict enclosure should be essential to the female religious life; the Church was alarmed at the plethora of female congregations set up in the zeal of the Counter-Reformation. Bringing these congregations under strict control was an integral part of a wider disciplining drive which embraced regular and secular clergy also. Religious orders of priests have, however, certain advantages over those of women; as ordained ministers of the Church they enjoy higher jurisdictional status than do women religious,[9] and are therefore less prone to episcopal interference.

The seventeenth and eighteenth centuries saw, as already mentioned, the development of a new wave of women religious. These congregations performed socially useful work, and many of them, such as the Daughters of Charity of St. Vincent de Paul, did not observe enclosure but managed, nonetheless, to survive.[10] It was left to individual bishops to enforce papal directives on the control of women religious, and they did not always do so.

In Ireland the major growth and development of the new kind of female religious congregation took place from the late eighteenth century onward, and the multiplication of houses of nuns coincided with administrative changes in the Church itself, which increased the central control of Rome and tightened up the organisation of the Church in Ireland.

Before exploring nuns' position in the nineteenth-century Church in Ireland, we must first look at the basic questions of how many nuns there were, and how convents were distributed throughout the country.

Numbers and Distribution

The number of nuns in Ireland increased eight-fold between 1841 and 1901, despite a near halving of the Catholic population in the same period. In the post-famine decades the rate of increase in their number from one decade to the next never fell below twenty per cent.[11] At the beginning of the century there were eleven convents in Ireland. Growth was slow but steady in the first half of the century; immediately after the Famine the number of houses of women religious stood at 91. The next half century saw an acceleration in growth, and in 1900 the number of convents stood at 368. The average size of convent was also larger than it had been a century, or even fifty years, earlier.[12]

These convents were not, however, evenly spread throughout the country. Seventy-three per cent of all convents in Ireland in 1864 were situated in the ecclesiastical provinces of Dublin and Cashel, an area corresponding to Munster and south and east Leinster, including Dublin. Over two-thirds, or seventy per cent of convents, were concentrated in these provinces in 1900 also. The foremost agricultural and commercial Catholic regions boasted the highest number of convents throughout the century. As might be expected, a map of convent distribution for 1850 shows a dense concentration of convents south of an imaginary line from Dublin to Galway, most of the important provincial towns having at least one convent, and the cities considerably more. The map for 1900 shows an increase in the number of convents north of this line in the second half of the century, though parts of the west and north-west are still as sparsely populated with convents as they had been fifty years earlier. Even in 1882 there were almost three times as many convents per head of the Catholic population in the south and east of the country as there were in the west and north-west.[13]

The Catholic commercial and professional middle classes were the chief suppliers of money to found and maintain convents. The Loreto convent founded in Navan in 1833 was set up with £1,000 which a business person had entrusted to the local bishop some years previously, for this purpose. In Carlow town three years later, a Mercy convent was founded with £7,000 donated by a local shopkeeper.[14] Amounts provided depended on the donor; there was no fixed sum. Four Presentation nuns from the Sexton street convent in Limerick were sent to a famine-stricken Castleisland in 1847, with money provided by a Miss Wallace of Limerick: there were obviously no able or willing donors in the town of Castleisland itself. The same was true of Swinford, six years later, when the local priest was obliged to appeal publicly for funds to establish a convent of the Sisters of Mercy in this town which had been badly affected by the Famine.[15] The St Louis convent in Bundoran was founded in 1870 with money provided by a Monaghan businessman, and the Mercy convent set up in Kinvara in 1878 was largely founded with money from outside the area.[16] A community of nuns was a voluntary organisation, and usually insisted on being assured subsistence for a short period at least, before it settled in an area. This explains why convent density was lower in the less prosperous parts of the country, throughout the century. The initiative to set up convents came very often from philanthropic lay people, sometimes prompted by the religious congregation in question, or by the bishop, and sometimes not. A convent of Ursulines settled in Ennis in 1829, but problems with the bishop of Killaloe forced them to move to Galway in 1829.[17] There is also evidence that Presentation nuns had a short-lived stay in the same diocese in the 1820s, but that similar difficulties forced them to leave. Local people had, obviously, put up the money to establish both of these convents, certainly that of the Presentation, as this congregation did not run pay schools, in this period at any rate,[18] and would not therefore have been able to raise money for a foundation in the hope of recouping it through fees.

Some congregations, however, did have ample resources of their own with which to establish houses, but these too relied on long-term financial support. The Sacred Heart nuns, a French congregation, managed to found a convent in Roscrea in 1842 where the Brigidines had originally failed to do so.[19] The boarding school set up by the French nuns was their long-term financial support, but they had enough resources to tide them over until the school began to pay for itself. Another French congregation, the Faithful Companions of Jesus, settled in Oughterard in 1843 and set up a free school there. In 1845, however, they moved to Limerick to set up a pay school, as plans to establish a pay school, from which the nuns could support themselves, in Oughterard had come to nothing because there were hardly any prospective paying pupils in the area. In Limerick they started building a three-story convent and school out of their own resources, almost as soon as they had obtained permission from the bishop to establish a convent in the diocese.[20] Abundant internal resources gave some congregations the freedom to choose where to go, a freedom which was not shared by all convents, and one which was modified by the need to seek episcopal approval. The Sisters of Mercy were dismayed upon their arrival in Charleville in 1836 because there did not seem to be any middle-class in the vicinity, and therefore no prospect of support "for the sisters or for the poor." The convent building was so damp that the curtains and bedclothes had to be wrung out each morning. The foundation survived—a new convent was provided, and long-term support eventually established.[21] The Presentation nuns who settled in Castleisland in 1847 did not even have a convent for the first few years; the four sisters who had been sent from Limerick lived in the presbytery vacated by the priest and the curate for them. Any money which the nuns had was spent on famine relief, one died of consumption and another returned to Limerick in poor health, and only a last minute injection of funds by a Michael Harnett of Liverpool saved the convent from dissolution.[22]

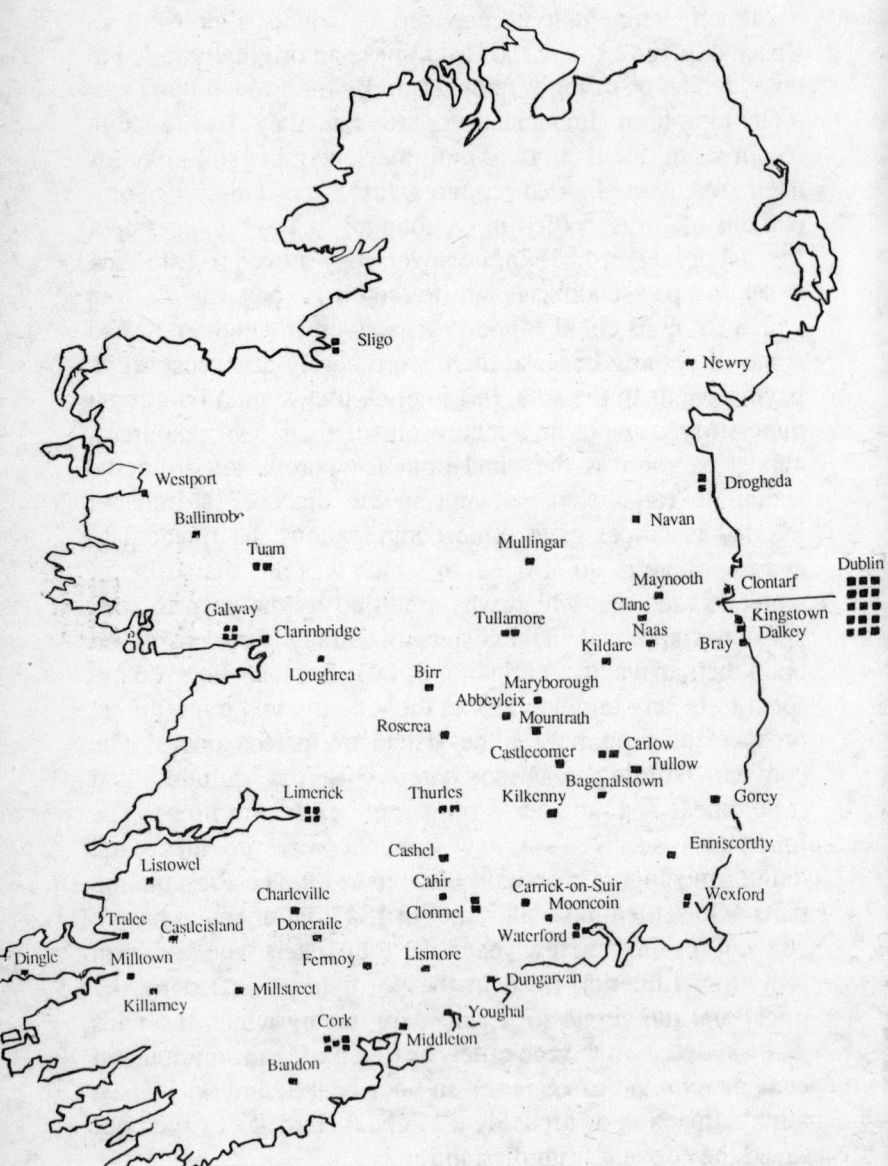

Distribution of Convents in Ireland 1850
Map 1

Distribution of Convents in Ireland 1900
Map 2

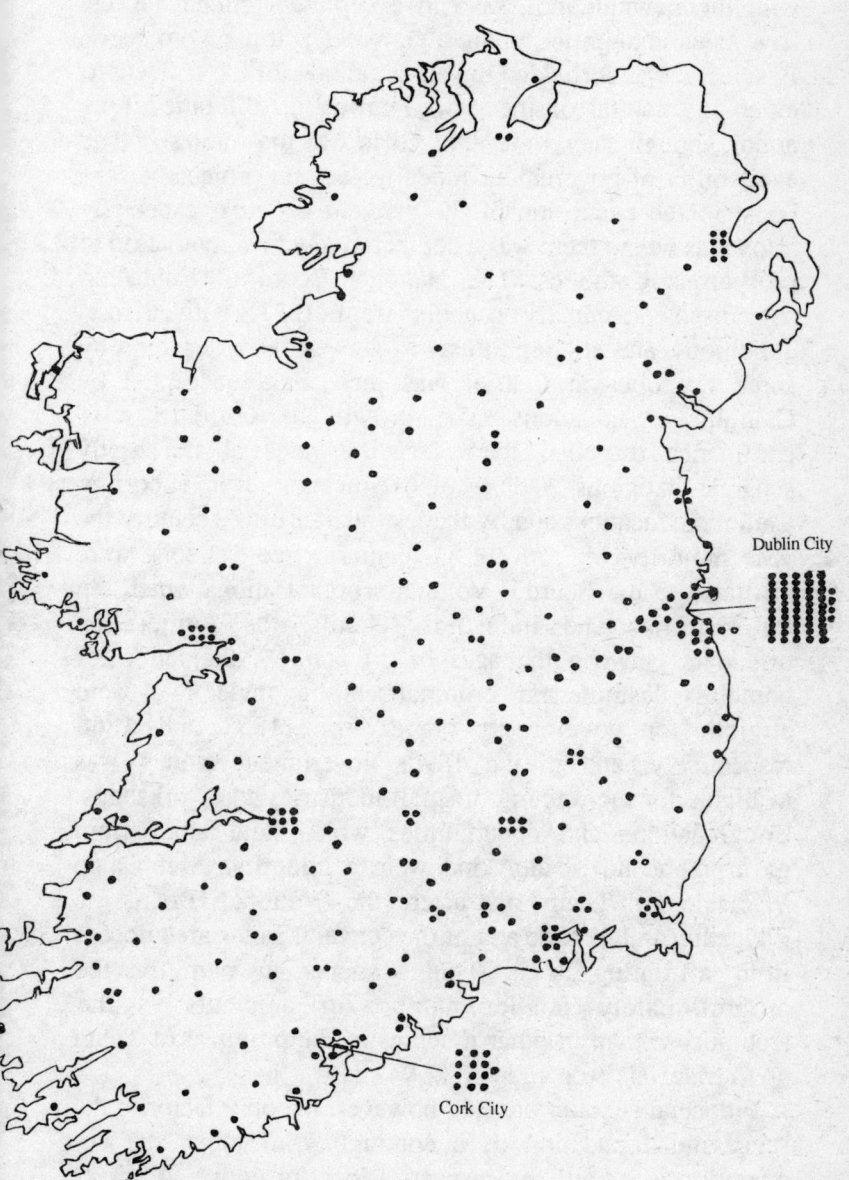

Newspapers of the period are dotted with small items about bequests to convents, and donations also. Dowries, or the sums of money which entrants brought to the convent with them, would not, save in exceptional circumstances, have been enough to maintain convents and their projects.[23] Besides, it was forbidden under canon law for the convent to touch the capital of the dowry during the lifetime of its donor, though they were allowed to use the interest.[24] The availability of government funds for certain projects gave a boost to the expansion of the convent network, especially into areas where there was a comparatively low population of prosperous Catholics. The National Board of Education subsidised elementary schools from 1831, with certain conditions, and although this was viewed with suspicion by some Catholics at first, it was increasingly accepted by Catholic organisations. The growth of Catholic self-confidence dispelled fears that the rules about strictly separate religious and secular education would corrupt Catholic education, and by the last quarter of the century the vast majority of convent elementary free schools were affiliated to the Board.[25] Voluntary organisations which ran reformatories and industrial schools—the former for offenders between the ages of 14 and 16, the latter for homeless, destitute and "criminal" children under 14— were eligible for government grants from 1858 and 1868 respectively, and in the 1890s government money was available for the running of small industries and workshops. Congregations and communities which held aloof from government aid of any kind were a minority. Archbishop MacHale of Tuam distrusted the National Board of Education and forbade any of the convents in his archdiocese from affiliating to it. This accounts in part for the proportionately smaller number of convents in the archdiocese than in other dioceses in the province of Tuam up to MacHale's death in 1882.[26]

Financial support was not, however, the only factor in the successful foundation of a community of nuns; the co-operation, goodwill and respect of local bishops and priests was also vital. This is clearly illustrated in the story of the foundation of the modern female religious congregations in Ireland.

Nuns in the Church in Nineteenth-Century Ireland

All the modern female religious congregations in Ireland were set up between 1776 and 1875. In this period many congregations were introduced to the country from Britain and from continental Europe. The gradual dismantling of the Penal Laws from the middle of the eighteenth century added to the political power of Catholics, and the sense of collective identity of a disadvantaged majority intensified the crusading zeal of an evangelical age. Rivalry with Protestants for the saving of the souls of an ever-growing poor population sharpened the missionary impulse of middle-class Catholics, an impulse which was boosted by the ultimate victory of Catholic Emancipation in 1829.

The setting up of the first of the new wave of Irish female congregations pre-dated Catholic Emancipation by several decades. Nano Nagle's Sisters of the Charitable Instruction of the Sacred Heart of Jesus were founded in Cork in 1776; this was the culmination of over twenty years' work with the poor of the city. Nagle had invited the Ursuline nuns from France to Cork in 1771 to take over the running of the free schools which she had set up, but their rule of enclosure prevented them from operating four of the five schools then in existence. Supported by the bishop of Cork, Nagle set up her own congregation, a non-enclosed sisterhood which would not only teach in the schools, but would also carry out visitation of the old and sick and other missionary work among the poor which Nagle and her associates had been doing for years.

Though already common on the continent, this kind of sisterhood was without precedent in Ireland. The Poor Clares, the Carmelites and the Dominican nuns, all of whom had come to Ireland in the first half of the seventeenth century—another era of Catholic revival and retrenchment—were enclosed religious orders with solemn vows rather than the simple vows proposed by Nagle for her sisterhood. Suppressed from time to time under the Penal Laws, these orders had not, for the most part, developed any regular or systematic work projects, although many individual convents were running schools and orphanages by the early nineteenth century—such activities were not seen as essential to their religious life. Nagle's was the first female congregation in the country to have a specific *social* purpose which found expression in concrete projects, and it was therefore in some demand. Branches were set up in Killarney, Kilkenny and Waterford, before the end of the eighteenth century, and this put a strain on resources, human and financial. Nano Nagle died in 1784; she did not live to see the sisterhood which she set up changed to a religious congregation. Simple vows and freedom to go outside the convent were discouraging recruits and donations. The Presentation nuns were formally approved in 1805, with solemn vows and enclosure. This was a considerable modification of Nano Nagle's original scheme, which had envisaged sisters being able to go outside the convent and to work with the poor in their own homes, indeed it was commonly said of Nagle herself that there was not a garret in Cork city with which she was unfamiliar. Enclosure limited the Presentation congregation to the running of free schools.[27]

In Dublin city, a sisterhood founded by Teresa Mulally had been running free schools for the Catholic poor simultaneously with Nagle's projects. In 1794 this group was incorporated into the organisation which later became the Presentation congregation.[28]

In 1810 Dr. Murray, later to become archbishop of Dublin, approached Mary Aikenhead, a woman who had been carrying out missionary and social work among the poor of the city, and asked her if she would be interested in setting up a religious congregation. The model for this congregation was the Daughters of Charity, whose work and way of life Murray felt was suitable to conditions in Dublin. Aikenhead and two of her associates accordingly went to the Institute of the Blessed Virgin Mary convent in York to carry out a novitiate, as the IBVM rule was similar to that of the Daughters of Charity. In 1815 the first convent of the Irish Sisters of Charity was set up in Dublin, and the following year the deed which defined the congregation as one with simple vows and no rule of enclosure was drawn up and in due course approved by Rome.[29]

Dr Murray also approached another wealthy woman long associated with charitable activities in Dublin, Frances Ball. He suggested that she lead a new congregation, similar to the Institute of the Blessed Virgin Mary, in Ireland, and she agreed. After a novitiate in the York convent, Loreto Abbey, a pay school with a free school attached, opened in Rathfarnham in 1821.[30]

Nagle, Aikenhead and Ball were all members of the Catholic upper-middle classes; Teresa Mulally was a milliner who used a small inheritance to fund her projects, the other three were heirs to fortunes. All had overtly religious motivations for their work prior to setting up congregations. Only Nagle, although receiving the support of the bishop of Cork, actually founded a congregation on her own initiative, and this, as we have seen, was radically altered after her death. In the case of Aikenhead and Ball the initiative came from a prominent churchman, though both women had long been attracted to religious life. Mulally never became a religious herself, and indeed it has been suggested that she was not very happy about certain aspects of her group's way of life after it had been transformed into a sisterhood.[31] Though there is no doubt that all of these founders were strong characters with ideas and abilities of their own, in all cases the crucial action which determined the eventual shape of their congregations was taken by a priest or bishop. The same was true of Catherine McAuley's group. Like Nagle, Aikenhead and Ball, McAuley was heir to a large fortune, which she used to set up her original projects in Dublin in the 1820s—a hostel for unemployed working-class women and a free school. McAuley and a group of other women lived in community, and like the other founder figures, she had a strong religious motivation for her work. It seems, however, that McAuley did not intend to set up a religious congregation at all, in fact, that she intended not to do so, because she disliked the idea of superiors and subjects. The suspicion, and indeed hostility, of local clergy in Dublin was aroused by her obviously religiously-minded group, the Institute of the House of Mercy, which was not however a religious congregation and therefore, not subject to local ecclesiastical control. Dr Murray, archbishop of Dublin by this time, seems to have persuaded McAuley that rules, constitutions and a religious identity approved by Rome would ensure the permanence of her projects by guaranteeing the cooperation of the local clergy and thus encouraging a steady stream of recruits. By the time the constitutions of the Sisters of Mercy were approved by Rome in 1840, the congregation, which took simple vows and did not observe enclosure, was well established in Ireland, with several convents throughout the country.[32]

The eventual shape of Nagle's sisterhood, and the fate of McAuley's secular institute, to say nothing of the setting up of the Irish Sisters of Charity and the Loreto nuns, underline the decisive nature of outside ecclesiastical intervention in the establishment of a female religious congregation. The story of Margaret Aylward and the Sisters of the Holy Faith shows how difficult it was for a woman to set up a religious congregation without this intervention. Aylward, a rich Waterford woman, had come of age in the heady Catholic-revival atmosphere of the early nineteenth century. In the early 1830s she had carried out an unsuccessful novitiate in the Irish Sisters of Charity.[33] For the next thirty years she tried to set up a religious congregation, eventually succeeding in 1867, when the Association of the Ladies of Charity, an anti-proselytising organisation which she had founded in mid-century in Dublin, became the Sisters of the Holy Faith.[34] It followed the by now familiar pattern of simple vows, no enclosure.

The Brigidines and the Sisters of St. John of God appear at first glance to be exceptions to the general rule; founded in 1807 and 1870 respectively, neither has a female founder figure comparable to Nagle, Aikenhead or McAuley. The Brigidines were set up in Tullow by Dr Delaney, bishop of Kildare and Leighlin, and its founding members were drawn from the parochial schools of the diocese. Papal approval was extended in 1840, by which time the congregation was well established in the diocese of Kildare and Leighlin. Apart from the aforementioned unsuccessful foundation in Roscrea, this congregation was confined to the Kildare and Leighlin diocese for the remainder of the century.[35] Dr Furlong, bishop of Ferns, set up the Sisters of St John of God in Wexford, to teach in the National schools and to nurse in the Union hospitals. Like all the other modern congregations, with the exception of the Presentation, these two took simple vows, and were free to go outside the convent in the exercise of their duties.[36]

Are these two congregations really different from the others? The change from secular group to religious congregation, from energetic and religious project leader to founder, has been portrayed in the histories and biographies as a logical sequence of events, but it has been shown that the intervention of bishops was, in all cases, crucial in diverting the socially aware and essentially religious energy of these Catholic Irishwomen into canonically approved channels. In this way these organisations were brought under the control of the Church, their leaders subjected to the Church's discipline and their, in many cases considerable, resources of expertise and confidence harnessed by a church which was increasing its political and economic power. Aylward appears at first glance to have been the odd-one-out; she, after all, wanted to set up a congregation, but was frustrated in this effort for almost three decades. Her experience can be seen as the other side of the coin from, for example, that of McAuley; if churchmen were eager to control and to shape existing women's organisations, they were also wary of women's organisations which had, like Aylward's, a definite religious identity in mind and a well thought out programme of work to go with it. It is true that female founders of congregations had a strong impact on the kind of work which their successors performed; Nano Nagle is associated with teaching the poor, Mary Aikenhead with a variety of charitable works, Frances Ball with teaching, Catherine McAuley with hostels for unemployed girls, schools and various other works, but none of these women, however strong their personalities, had any more than a consultative voice in the framing of the rules and constitutions which would bring this work firmly under the control of the huge male-dominated organisation that is the Roman Catholic Church.

On the day-to-day basis, the power of bishops over congregations and specific communities varied from one congregation to the next. Staying with the native congregations for the moment, however, it is instructive to look at the two largest and most widely distributed ones, the Presentation and the Mercy. In 1900 the two congregations, taken together, made up 58 per cent of all the convents in the country, taking both native and imported varieties into account.[37] The Presentation had a head start on the Mercy, of course, and in 1840 the former alone made up 55 per cent of all convents in Ireland. By the end of the century, however, the younger congregation had far outstripped the older, because of the greater versatility which its non-enclosed status permitted it. The Presentation nuns were confined to running free or national schools. This, like the broadly based charitable work of the Sisters of Mercy, was in great demand, but there is another reason for the extraordinary popularity of these two congregations.

The question of the direction, or proper government of female congregations was undecided throughout the nineteenth-century. "Let women govern women" Leo XIII declared in 1900, when he decreed that the primary control of female orders and congregations was vested in the elected superiors-general of these congregations, where such superiors-general existed. This decree reflected a strong body of opinion through the nineteenth century which favoured such a step, but the question was left undecided until Leo's decree.[38] In the confusion, local bishops were free to make their own interpretations. Besides, Leo's decree made provisions only for those female congregations which already had centralised structures and elected superiors-general. Many congregations did not have such structures; the Presentation and Mercy did not. Douglas street convent in Cork city and Baggot street convent in Dublin are considered the founding houses of each congregation respectively, but they are not mother houses in anything other than sentiment. From the time of their foundations, each Presentation and Mercy convent was directly subordinate to the authority of the bishop of the diocese. Neither congregation had a centralised structure. Any links between convents in different dioceses were informal ones and carried no administrative weight.

There is nothing inherently better about centralisation, but even its alternative—de-centralisation—demands some level of organisation, some thread linking all branches. Neither the Presentation nor the Mercy possessed even such a basic form of unifying organisation. Therefore, the two largest and most widely distributed congregations of women in Ireland lacked the machinery for effective corporate action. This very lack, indeed, must be seen as one of the reasons for their numerous branches and wide dispersal. Bishops liked to know exactly where they stood with the congregations under their control, and with the Presentation and the Mercy there was no doubt whatsoever of the bishop's authority. It can also be suggested that bishops liked to be in control of congregations. A comparison between the Sisters of Mercy and the Irish Sisters of Charity is instructive. There is no reason on the face of it why the Sisters of Mercy should have been more popular than the older congregation. Both had the same degree of flexibility, both had strong female founder-figures, both began in the capital city, and the same person, Dr Murray, had a key role in the founding of each. The Irish Sisters of Charity was, however, centralised in structure, with a mother-house and superior-general. Murray encouraged this, as he also did in the Loreto congregation. The Loreto nuns did not manage to preserve their centralisation.

Rathfarnham was supposed to be the mother-house or Generalate, but foundations from this convent to Navan in 1833, Fermoy in 1853, and to Letterkenny, Omagh and Killarney in subsequent years were forced to cut all links with Rathfarnham, in each case by the local bishop.[39] The bishop no doubt believed that his authority was threatened by the centralisation of this group, and because the whole question of the government of female congregations was left undecided until 1900, he was able to use his authority unchallenged. The Sisters of Charity do not seem to have had any such experience, but their branches were not at all as farflung as, nor their numbers even comparable with, those of the Sisters of Mercy. As early as 1840 the Sisters of Mercy— then only twelve years old—had twice as many convents as the older congregations which resembled it, and by 1900 the Irish Sisters of Charity only constituted 7.1 per cent of all convents in Ireland, and over half of these—16 out of 26— were concentrated in the Dublin archdiocese.[40] Delaney urged the Brigidines to preserve "unity and harmony" among all their convents,[41] but this was not the same as providing them with, or encouraging them to develop, a centralised structure, and besides, the congregations remained confined to one diocese for the remainder of the century, so this unity was not tested by being exposed to a variety of episcopal attitudes. Perhaps the unsuccessful Brigidine foundation to Roscrea, in the diocese of Killaloe, failed for reasons apart from the financial? Could it have been that this congregation did not transplant well because of the ambiguity about its government?

When native congregations with centralised structures were not proof against interference, it is no surprise that foreign congregations were also vulnerable. The Sisters of St Louis, a French congregation, were invited to Monaghan town in 1859; they arrived and set up a reformatory and a school, but two years later, in 1861, they were forced by the bishop, Dr Nally, to break all ties with their mother-house in France. As the alternative was abandoning all the projects which they had set up, the small group of nuns decided to stay in Ireland, a decision which the French mother-house saw as a betrayal.[42] The Good Shepherd nuns also belonged to a centralised congregation but this did not stop Dr Butler, bishop of Limerick, from introducing modifications in their way of life; in 1861 he prevented a novice in the Limerick convent from following the usual custom of going to France for the period of her novitiate. By so doing he forced the reluctant agreement of the Mother-General in France that Ireland be made a province of the congregation, with its own subsidiary Provincialate, or mother-house, in Limerick.[43] Some degree of centralisation was preserved in this case, although the Mother-General's natural desire to preserve the unity of her command across national boundaries was frustrated. By making Limerick a Provincialate Butler was interfering with the centralisation of the congregation as a whole, and reinforcing his own control over the convent.

The Dominican nuns in Galway, however, stood fast against archbishop Cullen in 1851 when he tried to insist that their convent go under the direct authority of the bishop of Galway, like the Presentation and Mercy convents in the city. The nuns wished to remain under the authority of their own Mother-Provincial, herself answerable to the Father-Provincial of the Dominican order of priests. The Galway nuns wrote to Pius IX, who ordered an investigation which ruled in the nuns' favour.[44] But this convent was in many ways exceptional, having been in Galway for over 200 years at this stage, and what is more, belonging to an order which was centuries old and whose canonical status was secure. Their success in this matter suggests that it was sometimes possible for nuns to bypass local ecclesiastical authority and appeal directly to the peak of the structure, but what raw sisterhood, on whose rules and constitutions the ink was barely dry, would have had the expertise or indeed the confidence to do this? The sheer novelty of this non-enclosed mode of living for women religious in Ireland made it immediately prone to interference.

Besides, it is worth pointing out that the Galway Dominican convent did not send out any Irish branches for the remainder of the century. Congregations which were centralised were not, on the whole, very popular with bishops, as the Good Shepherd case illustrates, and also the case of the Faithful Companions of Jesus. When this congregation came to Limerick in 1845 they had, according to their annals, been "well warned" of the bishop, Dr Ryan's, indifference to them, and the founder Madame d'Houet, who was 63 years of age and quite frail, was obliged to journey by coach to Ryan's summer residence in Kilkee to obtain his permission to settle in the diocese.[45] It was not only bishops fearful of administrative headaches and conscious of their own authority who shied away from centralisation; others in the church seem to have objected to it in principal. When Margaret Aylward asked the advice of Fr St Leger about setting up a congregation, he told her that her idea was a sound one, provided the congregation was "on the same footing as the other convents, dependent upon the bishop and subject to no other authority."[46] Fr St Leger was a Jesuit, and assuming he approved of the spirit and structure of his own organisation, why was he not encouraging a similar structure in a female religious congregation?

There is, of course, ample evidence of respect and often friendship between convents and bishops and priests. Some bishops were very generous to convents, regularly heading the subscription lists, giving donations to particular projects, and visiting the convent. However, the lack of clarity on the issue of jurisdiction meant that different bishops had different interpretations of the extent of their power over convents. Congregations which were organised on a diocesan basis were particularly at risk, as the case of the Mercy *Guide* illustrates. In 1864 a group of Mercy nuns decided to compile a guidebook of all Mercy convents which would, they hoped, regularise the activities of all existing communities, and serve as a reference book for the new ones which were springing up all over Ireland at the rate of at least one per year. Accordingly, invitations were sent from Limerick to all Mercy convents to send representatives to a meeting at which the project would be discussed.

Sisters of Mercy from the dioceses of Cork, Cloyne, Dromore, Ross, Killaloe, Achonry, Kilmacduagh, Kerry, Ardagh and Clonmacnoise, Cashel and Emly, and of course, Limerick itself, attended the meeting. Others, the Limerick annals report, "had to content themselves with good wishes and prayers, not being able to obtain permission from some bishops to attend." The bishop of Elphin, for example, forbade permission on the grounds that he himself intended "compiling customs" for the Sisters of Mercy in his diocese, when he could find the time to do so.[47] Some bishops obviously saw this meeting as a threat to their authority over convents in their areas, others did not.

The women who headed convents, especially new foundations, were usually chosen by the founding convent for their strength of will and negotiating ability, and stories of strong-willed Superiors outwitting bishops abound in convent lore. The first Superior of the Limerick Mercy convent was despaired of for some time due to her natural timidity: "she will do all interior and exterior work, but to meet on business, confer with the bishop, conclude with a new subject, you might as well send the child that opens the door."[48] Priests also had to be dealt with, and on a more day-to-day basis; they were depended upon to say mass and hear confessions. A new community found it expedient to stay on good terms with the local clergy, especially if the nuns were complementing the clergy's role by running schools and visiting the people. Catherine McAuley recommended, in the 1830s, that members of the Carlow convent stop wearing veils because the local priest objected to them; "You know he has strange notions and must be humoured," she wrote.[49] Fr Peter Daly of Galway city at first provoked the same indulgent attitude from her: "You would like him very much," she wrote to a friend in 1840, the year the Mercy convent was founded in Galway, "though he is the greatest master we have ever had."[50] "The greatest master," it is obvious from the context, is a reference to Daly's "bossy" ways. Daly had two parishes in Galway city, he was chairman of the Corporation, the Gas Company and the

Harbour Board, he owned the Lough Corrib Steamship Company and he had a huge personal fortune.[51] In short, he was the kind of priest-cum-local-politician-and-gombeen-man that Cullen was working so hard to try to eradicate at the time. The newly-founded Mercy convent entrusted their accounts to Daly, who refused to return their account book to them in the late 1840s, "so for a time, strained relations existed between the Sisters and their Guardian." In 1855 Dr MacEvilly, bishop of Galway, gave the sisters permission to take Daly to court; it turned out that he had spent £4,000 of the convent's money in building a church.[52]

MacEvilly was no doubt pleased to see Daly brought to heel; he was far too powerful a priest for any bishop to accept, especially in the reforming atmosphere of the 1850s. It was MacEvilly who described the sisters as "having been left completely at his (Daly's) mercy."[53] The convent was certainly in a vulnerable position, and not least because it was obliged to obtain the bishop's permission before embarking on litigation to recover what was rightfully theirs. Suppose MacEvilly had been an associate of Daly's, or even anxious to avoid scandal? His predecessor, Dr O'Connell, had noted in a letter to Rome in 1848 that Daly had embezzled £1,250 of the Presentation funds.[54] Why hadn't Daly been brought to court on this occasion?

Convents usually struggled to maintain good relations with all and sundry; such diplomacy seems to have been essential to their survival. The opposition of the local priest was one reason why Sr M Francis Clare Cusack left Knock in 1882, though in this case the priest was the last in a long line of bishops and clergy who harassed her. The autobiography of this woman who was known as the Nun of Kenmare is bitter in tone, and it is easy to understand why; as Liam Bane points out, none of Cusack's opponents ever stated exactly why they wished to be rid of her.[55] Cusack was originally, up to 1881, a member of the Poor Clare community in Kenmare. She wrote literary, historical and polemical works, on subjects as diverse as St Patrick and women's work. During the period of the Land War she wrote several tracts supporting the Land League and the Ladies' Land League. Her writings in general were an important source of revenue for the convent which also operated a school.

In 1881 Cusack left Kenmare and the Poor Clares to set up a new religious congregation, the Sisters of Peace, which she proposed to base in Knock, where no religious community of women existed. She was duly given permission to leave Kerry, and proceeded to Dromore, the diocese in which she had been professed. Dr Leahy, the bishop there, formally transferred her to Tuam. On her own account, she received her first indication that all was not well when, en route to Knock and passing through Dublin, Cardinal McCabe forbade the Poor Clares in Harold's Cross to shelter her for more than one night. His opposition to her seems to have been transmitted to MacEvilly, at this stage archbishop of Tuam, and as mindful as ever of central authority. He tried to go back on the permission which he had given Cusack to settle in his diocese, but eventually relented, so as not to cause scandal. Cusack managed to set up her congregation in Knock, along with a kindergarten and an industrial school, but opposition at parish and diocesan level wore her down. In 1881 MacEvilly requested her to cut all links with the Sisters of Peace and to leave Knock. She did so. The Pope, in a private interview the following year, gave her permission to bring her congregation to the USA, and commended her scheme for setting up homes for immigrant girls there. However, the opposition of the American bishops and priests was corrosive, and she resigned as Mother-General of the Sisters of Peace in 1888.[56]

Cusack had powerful supporters in the church who constantly urged her to vindicate herself publicly, which she eventually tried to do in her autobiography. In it she reproduces letters from archbishop Croke of Cashel, one of her staunchest supporters, and Bishop Bagshawe of Nottingham. MacEvilly said he was appalled at her "extraordinary conduct" but his correspondence does not cast any light on this conduct.[57] Her projects were by no means radical; they belonged to the long established tradition of missionary work.[58] Could it be that Cusack's action in leaving the Poor Clares—a congregation with solemn vows—was canonically irregular? Contemporary authorities state that it is permissible for a religious to move from one congregation to another only if both congregations are on the same canonical footing.[59] If this was the reason why Cusack was opposed, why then had she been given permission to leave the Poor Clares in the first place? Were the bishops in question equally vague about whether her actions were correct? Did Cusack's outspokenness on political and social issues during the Land War—she was a tireless pamphleteer—alienate those bishops, like McCabe, who believed that women had no business getting involved in politics? Or was it that Cusack's own persistence and perseverance in the face of opposition alienated those who believed that the vow of obedience incorporated a vow of humble silence in the face of inexplicable and apparently unjust treatment?

Cusack herself claimed that she was unpopular with Irish and Irish American bishops and priests because she published works about the causes of social problems in Ireland, and suggestions for their solution. It was indeed unusual for a nun in nineteenth-century Ireland to speak out on social ills and their prevention or cure. This is odd, when we consider that nuns were the single largest body of "social workers" in the country at that time, the largest group of workers sharing a common identity who were in daily contact with the casualties of the social system, from cradle to grave. Convents' dependence upon the rich for donations and recruits no doubt inhibited nuns from condemning, for example, slum landlordism and starvation wages, but it need not have deterred them from making comment of a socially conservative nature, like Cusack's, and suggesting reforms which would not have been repugnant to their support base, the Catholic middle class. Neither did nuns venture into public and systematic observation of women's role in society[60] despite their constituting one of the largest groups of women workers in the country and being, themselves, the biggest single group of women who worked with other women in the fields of education, training, "protection" and "rescue". This was a period when women's work and women's role were hotly debated in literature, in the periodical press, and from the 1860s, in parliament; the perceived "problem" posed by the untrained unmarried middle-class women was attracting as much attention as the perceived "problem" of the pauper women under the Poor law system. Some women in Britain and in Ireland were involved in this debate on one level or another; Irish nuns were not. Nor did they have an alternative forum of their own in which to discuss these and other issues, drawing on their unique experience in the fields of social work in general and work with females in particular. The feeling of working together for a common goal, the crusading zeal, the everyday sisterhood which existed between convents of the same and of different congregations, beams forth from the pages of the annals, and from letters. But this did not find formal, regular expression in the form of regular get-togethers and discussions on the work. Given their lack of a central organisation it is surprising that congregations like the Presentation and the Mercy and many others held onto their distinct identities at all; the control exercised by bishops and the arbitrary interpretations of their power, saw to it that the preconditions for central co-ordination, discussion and active reflection would not develop.

As well as this, convents were very busy, and the pressure to set up new projects and to found new branches added to an already heavy workload. A two or three-project convent was common—63 per cent of all convents ran more than one project in 1900.[61] The mid-century defenders of convent life would have described convents as havens, but hives of activity would have been more apt. Community life, it is true, set aside certain times for recreation, for prayer and for meditation, all of which may have enabled the average nun to unwind after a day's work. Communities, however, had to find within themselves resources to staff the project(s), to perform the administrative work of the latter and of the convent itself, and to carry out the day-to-day domestic tasks of the convent.[62] Ironically, convents were usually smallest where convents were most scarce, and demands heaviest. In the diocese of Achrony—roughly, north Mayo—in 1882, the average size of convent was eleven nuns, while in the diocese of Cloyne (east county Cork), in the same year there was an average of twenty-four.[63] The Mayo diocese had a much higher density of unemployed and underemployed Catholics than the Cork one, and therefore much greater scope for the missionary and social work for which nuns were so highly valued. Seventeen Presentation nuns ran schools for one thousand children in Drogheda in 1864, while in the same year seventy Loreto nuns in Dublin ran schools for 310 children.[64]

The move into the hospitals of the Poor Law Unions, spearheaded by the Limerick Sisters of Mercy in 1861,[65] increased the demands on the human resources of convents. By the end of the century nuns were working in over eighty workhouse hospitals, and the number grew from year to year.[66] The congregation involved was, in most cases, the Sisters of Mercy, but the Daughters of Charity, the Sisters of St Louis, the Congregation of Mary, the Poor Servants of the Mother of God and the Sisters of St John of God also performed this work. None of these congregations had been set up specifically as a nursing congregation, though nursing had, it is true, been seen as one of the activities which they should carry out if required. Nuns were highly valued as workers for a number of reasons. They embodied modern Catholicism, at once triumphalist and socially useful, and this pleased the ever-growing number of Catholic Poor Law guardians. Nuns cost less than lay nurses; it was common for perhaps four nuns to work for two salaries, and they never complained about pay. Besides there was, as O'Riordan was quick to point out, a certain logic, as far as many middle-class Catholics were concerned, in using largely voluntary labour to staff institutions which were paid for out of ratepayers' money—often thought of as "charity" by those who paid it.[67] The nuns, like mothers of families and other unpaid domestic workers, were working for no personal gain and were working until they dropped. The flexibility demanded of them and the amazing adaptability which they displayed meant that convents came under constant pressure to take on new areas of responsibility. One of Catherine McAuley's maxims could have applied to almost any female religious congregation in nineteenth-century Ireland: "If a person about to enter a convent were asked; what duties will be assigned you, what rules will you be obliged to observe? She would reply, 'I do not know exactly, I am going to become a religious, and therefore to do whatever I shall be desired to do.'"[68] Mary Aikenhead was more blunt, if half in jest, when she admonished a potential Sister of Charity who spoke of bringing her Latin bible to the convent with her: "We are ignorant women and do nothing but spin and obey," she is reputed to have said.[69]

Fahey has described the work of nuns in Ireland at this time as having more in common with the enthusiastic amateur than the professional.[70] This is no doubt true, and it need not devalue the work; there is, after all, nothing to prove that professionalisation and the specialisation of various fields of work which came about in the nineteenth century was necessarily a good thing. Nuns' flexibility did not make their work less valuable of itself. However, their willingness and ability to turn their hand to anything was at its height at a time when such ability was respected less and less in the world of formal, paid work. Nuns, like women in the home, were menders and fixers, tireless workers who seldom complained, doing all for "love" and asking no recognition in the form of increased authority or say in certain matters directly concerning their work. "You can switch a Sister of Charity on to anything" a Fr Vaughan commented in 1899.[71] The more a nun "switched on to" (or was switched on to, Vaughan's comment suggests that it is somebody else who is working the controls) the more she was expected to do in the long run, and the less time and energy she had for switching off the day-to-day practicalities and onto the larger context of her work.

Visibility, solidarity and survival—these are the concepts

which can be applied to nuns in nineteenth-century Ireland, but with important qualifications. "Going about their work noiselessly and calmly" earned Dublin nuns the praise of their archbishop towards the end of the century.[72] Nuns' work was, certainly, visible in the form of schools, hospitals, orphanages and other institutions; education, health care and social work are society's essential maintenance tasks which, like women's nurturing work in the home, are noticed only when they are neglected. Nuns commanded attention but this attention usually bounced back off themselves and the objects of their work to reflect credit upon the church and the Catholic middle-class. "O! such a country is too good to continue in slavery!" was O'Connell's comment on the work of Irish nuns in the 1840s; he used them as a potent argument for Repeal of the Union. Around mid-century the normally prosaic archbishop Cullen drew a parallel between the Blessed Virgin's role in the redemption of the human race and nuns' regenerative work among the Irish Catholics. Some thirty years later Fr Burke, the famous Dominican preacher, drew attention to nuns' sacrifices on behalf of the Irish people, using them to bolster his own brand of Catholic nationalism.[73] Kelly points out that in the last decades of the century Catholic nationalist Poor Law unions were indignant at any criticism of nuns' management of workhouse hospitals, seeing this as a direct criticism of Irish Catholics.[74]

For all this shining visibility, nuns appear hardly at all in the *Irish Ecclesiastical Record* of the period, and this was the official journal of the Catholic church in Ireland. The occasional reference to these vital agents of the propagation of modern Catholic practice slips through, but this is all. The index refers to subjects as diverse as the ring worn by nuns and nuns as hospital nurses, but when these are investigated they invariably turn out to be documents from Rome, not native contributions.[75] It could be argued that the *Record* was intended primarily for secular clergy, but the fact that documents relating to nuns were printed in it in the first place implies that they were seen to be of some relevance. There was, moreover, no similar publication for or by Irish nuns.

Visible but not vocal, nuns were an Irish Catholic variation on the theme of the ideal Victorian female. Her existence was to be a source of inspiration to her menfolk, but she was not allowed to have a voice in matters which directly affected her. Nuns were at a double disadvantage, as females in a church which does not allow women any say in decisions about faith and morals or any more mundane matters, and as women without votes in a society where parliamentary politics were becoming increasingly popular.

The fragmentation, diocese by diocese, of many congregations, and the limits placed upon nuns' freedom of movement and action meant that the feeling of common identity, which undoubtedly existed, never developed into a concrete expression of solidarity. "Divide and rule" worked well in hindering meaningful co-operation and co-ordination, and in smothering voices raised in dissent. We cannot state confidently that Cusack was the only one of her kind in nineteenth-century Ireland. We know her story only because she put it down on paper for us. Concannon's history of the Poor Clares in Ireland, published in 1928, mentions her only in passing and does not refer to the controversy which surrounded her. The *Record* refers to her only once, on the occasion of the publication of her life of St Patrick in 1871. Obviously her "extraordinary conduct" and the equally "extraordinary" treatment which she received did not send parish priests rushing to their writing-desks to pen letters to the "Notes and Queries" section of the *Record,* and no bishop put pen to paper either. D'Alton's 1928 history of the archdiocese of Tuam does not refer to "the wretched nun of Knock" as MacEvilly called her, at all, but then D'Alton hardly refers to nuns in any context. The story of Daly's embezzlement of convent funds is left out of the Galway Mercy convent's centenary record, and Degnan's history of the Mercy convents founded in Catherine McAuley's lifetime, though it refers to Daly, does not mention it either.[76] Examples of similar gaps in the secondary sources could be multiplied; certainly these sources give nuns a visibility which surpasses that of most women workers of the period, but they tell only part of the story, the part which does not rent in two the seamless robe of Irish Catholicism's triumphal march from penal days to prosperity to political power.

All of the female religious congregations founded in Ireland since 1776 survive to the present day. All, that is, except Cusack's abortive foundation in Knock, which nonetheless resurfaced in the USA. However, the Sisters of Peace were not allowed to recognise Cusack as their founder until Vatican II, because of her departure from the religious life and eventual abjuration of the Catholic religion. It obviously suited the church to allow this congregation to continue in its useful work once Cusack had been removed and her congregation tailored to fit in with requirements. Nothing quite so dramatic happened to the other Irish congregations, yet, as we have seen, all of these made their own compromises with the patriarchal power-structures of the church, as did many imported congregations forced to cut off or to modify links with mother-houses abroad. Faced with a choice between adopting the shape imposed upon them or disbanding altogether, these groups chose to compromise. It is unlikely that communities of women, headed by women, looking to female founders and working largely with females, would have been allowed to survive under any other circumstances.

NOTES

1 *Freeman's Journal*, June 11 1853; June 14 1853.
2 *Freeman's Journal*, June 14 1853.
3 Rev Dominick Murphy, *Sketches of Irish Nunneries* (Cork, 1865).
4 Quoted in Sr Bertrand Degnan, *Mercy Unto Thousands* (Dublin, 1958), p. 279.
5 Peadar MacSuibhne, *Paul Cullen and His Contemporaries*, 5 vols., (Naas, 1961-77), iv, p. 50.

6 Murphy, *op. cit.* Rev Thomas Burke, O.P. *Ireland's Vindication: Refutation of Froude and Other Lectures, Historical and Religious* (London, c.1872); idem. *On Faith and Fatherland* (Glasgow, c.1874). Monsignor O'Riordan, *Catholicity and Progress in Ireland* (St Louis, 1905).
7 W. Addis and T. Arnold (eds.), *A Catholic Dictionary* (London, 1884), part 1.
8 The term "nuns" is used throughout this article to refer to all women religious. In strict canonical terms, nuns are enclosed religious who take solemn vows, rather than the simple vows taken by the majority of women religious in nineteenth-century Ireland. I have chosen to use the popular term "nuns" to refer to all women religious, whether these are strictly speaking nuns or not, because of its common usage, and also because "sisters" implies a familial relationship, and "women religious" is too cumbersome.
9 *New Catholic Encyclopaedia*, 15 vols., (Washington, D.C., 1966), ix, p. 681; xiv, pp 491-2. (Hereafter *NCE*). Mary Daly, *The Church and the Second Sex* (London, 1968), pp 63-4.
10 *NCE*, iii, pp 470-3.
11 Tony Fahey, Female Asceticism in the Catholic church: a case study of Nuns in Nineteenth-century Ireland (Unpublished Ph.D thesis, University of Illinois, 1981), p.56.
12 Unless otherwise stated, all information on the numbers relating to convents and nuns is taken from the *Catholic Directory* (Dublin, 1840-64), and *Irish Catholic Directory* (Dublin, 1865-1900), censuses of the period and the following secondary works, in order of publication: S. Atkinson, *Mary Aikenhead: Her Life, Her Work and Her Friends* (Dublin, 1879); A Member of the Order of Mercy, *Leaves from the Annals of the Sisters of Mercy* (New York, 1881); Helena Concannon, *The Poor Clares in Ireland* (Dublin, 1929); Margaret Gibbons, *Life of Margaret Aylward* (Dublin, 1928); idem, *Glimpses of Catholic Ireland in the Eighteenth-Century* (Dublin, 1932); R. Burke Savage, *A Valiant Dublin Woman: The Story of George's Hill* (Dublin, 1940); Brigidine Convent, *Gleanings from the Brigidine Annals* (Naas, 1945); Degnan, *op. cit.*; T. J. Walsh, *Nano Nagle and the Presentation Sisters* (Dublin, 1959); Sr Mary Pauline, *God Wills It: The Centenary Story of the Sisters of St. Louis* (Dublin, 1959); A Loreto Sister, *Joyful Mother of Children: Mother Mary Francis Teresa Ball* (Dublin, 1961).

13 The *ICD* from 1882 included data from the censuses on Catholic population.
14 Loreto Convent, Navan, *One Hundred Years of Progress* (Navan 1933), p. 5; Degnan, *op. cit.* pp 196-7.
15 Ms Annals, (PLC); Mary P. Cryan, The Sisters of Mercy in Connacht (Unpublished M. A. thesis, University College Galway, 1963), p. 143.
16 Sr M. Pauline, *op. cit.*, pp 189-90. Sr M. de Lourdes Fahy, *Education in the Diocese of Kilmacduagh in the Nineteenth-Century* (Gort, 1972), p. 98.
17 Walsh, *op. cit.*, pp 242-4.
18 Later in the period Presentation convents occasionally ran pay schools, for example, they were running a Young Ladies' School in Clondalkin in 1864, *CD*, 1864, returns for Dublin.
19 Gibbons, *op. cit.*, (1932), pp 373-6.
20 Ms, History of the coming of the Society to Ireland (FCJL).
21 Degnan, *op. cit.*, p. 302.
22 Ms annals (PCL).
23 For a discussion on dowries see Caitriona Clear, *Nuns in Nineteenth-Century Ireland* (Dublin, 1987), pp 86-99.
24 All information on this is taken from L. Fanfani and K. O'Rourke, *Canon Law for Religious Women* (Iowa, 1961). For information on bequests see William J. Walsh, "The Law in its relation to religious bequests," *Irish Ecclesiastical Record,* xvi, (1895), pp 593-618; Donal Kerr, *Peel, Priests and Politics* (Oxford, 1982), pp 123-51.
25 In 1860 seventy-five per cent of convent free schools were connected with the Board, and the number continued to grow. Walsh, *op. cit.*, p. 216.
26 As the *ICD* noted "this is the only diocese in Ireland in which none of the schools conducted by the religious Orders are under state control or derive public grants for their support," *ICD*, 1882, p. 198. The situation was soon to change under the new archbishop, MacEvilly.
27 All information on Nano Nagle and the origins of the Presentation Order from Walsh, *op. cit.*, Murphy, *op. cit.* and *Annals of South Presentation Convent, 1802-1825* (published by South Presentation, Cork, n.d., for private circulation).
28 Burke Savage, *op. cit.*
29 Atkinson, *op. cit.* Religious congregations which did not observe enclosure took "simple vows"; the older religious orders took

"solemn vows." This is a canonical distinction, *NCE*, xiv, pp 756-8.
30 A Loreto Sister, *op cit.*
31 Walsh, *op. cit.*
32 Degnan, *op. cit.*; A Member of the Order of Mercy *op. cit.*
33 Aylward was one of a group which left the Sisters of Charity in 1833. For more information on this see Gibbons, *op. cit.*, (1928); A Member of the Congregation of the Sisters of Charity, *Life and Work of Mary Aikenhead* (Dublin, 1924); Atkinson, *op. cit.*
34 Gibbons, *op cit.* (1928).
35 Brigidine Convent, Tullow, *op. cit.*
36 *Religious Orders and Congregations* (Dublin, 1933).
37 *ICD*, 1900.
38 Fahey, *op. cit.*, p. 42.
39 A Loreto Sister, *op. cit.*
40 *CD*, 1840; *ICD*, 1900.
41 Brigidine Convent, Tullow, *op. cit.*
42 Sr M. Pauline, *op. cit.*
43 Ms, Synopsis of annals (GSCL).
44 Ms, History of the Dominican convent of Jesus, Mary and Joseph (Dominican Convent, Galway).
45 History...... (FCJL).
46 Gibbons, *op. cit.* (1928), p. 57.
47 Ms, Annals, (MCL).
48 A Member of the Order of Mercy, *op. cit.*, pp 284-5.
49 Degnan, *op. cit.*, p. 285.
50 Letter from Catherine McAuley to Superior, Mercy Convent, Baggot St., Dublin, 1840, transcribed in Ms annals of Mercy Convent, Galway.
51 Liam Bane, John MacEvilly, 1816-1902 (Unpublished M.A. thesis, University College Galway, 1979) p. 216.
52 Annals, (MCG); Bane, *op. cit.*, pp 217-20.
53 *Ibid.*, p. 308.
54 Dr O'Connell to Rev. Mullins, Rome, 6 September 1848. (Galway Diocesan Archives).
55 Bane, *op cit.*
56 All information on Cusack taken from M. F. Cusack, *The Nun of Kenmare: An Autobiography* (London, 1889); Irene Ffrench Eager, *The Nun of Kenmare* (Cork, 1970); Bane, *op. cit.*, pp 352-7.
57 Cusack, *Autobiography*, appendices.

58 See note 60 below.
59 Addis and Arnold, *op. cit.*, pp 698-9.
60 Cusack is one exception. See her *Woman's Work in Modern Society* (London, 1874) and "Woman's place in the economy of creation," *Fraser's Magazine*, 11, (1874), pp 200-7.
61 For a more detailed treatment of trends in the work of nuns see Clear, *op. cit.*, pp 100-34.
62 Lay sisters usually performed this domestic and maintenance work. These sisters had inferior status in the convent. See Clear, *op. cit.*, pp 86-99.
63 *ICD*, 1882.
64 *CD*, 1864.
65 Annals (MCL). See also *Limerick Chronicle*, Dec. 1860-Jan. 1861.
66 Patricia Kelly, From Workhouse to hospital: the role of the Irish workhouse in medical relief to 1921 (Unpublished M.A. thesis, University College Galway, 1972), passim and appendix.
67 O'Riordan, *op. cit.*, pp 399-400.
68 *Maxims and Counsels of Mother McAuley* (n.p., n.d.).
69 A Member of the Congregation of the Sisters of Charity, *op. cit.*, p. 174.
70 Fahey, *op. cit.*
71 *ICD*, 1900, chronicle of events for 1899.
72 *ICD*, 1899, chronicle of events for 1898.
73 Cryan, *op. cit.*, p. 1; *Freeman's Journal*, 21 May 1853; Burke, *op. cit.*
74 Kelly, *op. cit.*, pp 173-4.
75 Very Rev. P. J. Canon Hamell, *Index to the Irish Ecclesiastical Record 1864-1917* (Dublin, c. 1918).
76 Degnan, *op. cit.*

Abbreviations
CD Catholic Directory
ICD Irish Catholic Directory
PCL Presentation Convent, Sexton St., Limerick
FCJL Faithful Companions of Jesus Convent, Laurel Hill, Limerick.
GSL Good Shepherd Convent, Limerick
MCG Mercy Convent, Newtownsmith, Galway
MCL Mercy Convent, St. Mary's, The Parish, Limerick.

Prostitution and Rescue Work in Nineteenth-Century Ireland

Maria Luddy

Like many aspects of women's history the history of prostitution and rescue work has been a neglected area of study for Irish historians. This article outlines briefly the level of prostitution in Irish society but is concerned principally with the attempts made by lay and religious organisations to rescue "fallen women". An analysis of the subject reveals much about society's attitudes towards prostitutes and also reveals how women generally were viewed by society. Throughout the nineteenth century there was little public discussion of prostitution; prostitutes were judged as social outcasts and many of the philantropists who worked in the field of rescuing "fallen women" seem to have accepted prostitution as an inevitable feature of society. There were no campaigns directed at the social causes of prostitution, and rescue work, carried out mainly by women as a strictly voluntary occupation, was done out of the public eye. Prostitutes themselves can be described as an historically "invisible" group, having left us no records of their own. We can only use official sources such as police reports and the registers of rescue homes when trying to understand a prostitute's existence. There is no doubt that engaging in prostitution was a hazardous enterprise, with the dangers of disease, pregnancy, social ostracism and violence being common. However, it is naive to think that all women who engaged in prostitution were victims. Though their lives were harsh they did make choices even if those choices were limited by the lack of other economically viable means of earning a livelihood. The preliminary survey provided in this article of those women who entered rescue homes will show that they played some role in shaping their own lives and deciding their own futures.

Extent of Prostitution

One impressionistic account of prostitution in Irish cities, from the earlier part of the century, comes from evidence gathered by William Logan in a trip he made to Ireland in 1845.[1] From a "philanthropic gentleman" he ascertained that Cork contained eighty-five regular brothels and 356 public prostitutes. In addition to these women there were thought to be one hundred "privateers" who operated from houses not designated as brothels. Logan was also informed that there were 1,700 prostitutes operating in Dublin at the same time. In Belfast he quoted Dr Edgar as saying that 236 prostitutes lived in brothels in that city.[2] The concrete evidence of police statistics provides a more accurate picture of the situation. The earliest figures, for Dublin, come from the Dublin Metropolitan Police statistics and cover the years 1838-1899. These figures account for arrests and convictions of women accused of soliciting; they do not record the number of re-arrests so the number given is obviously higher than it should be. On the other hand it is unlikely that the police arrested every prostitute who operated within the city.

Table 1. Arrests for prostitution in the Dublin Metropolitan District, 1838-1899.[*]

Year	Total number arrested	Discharged	Convicted
1838	2,849	439 (15.41%)	2,410 (84.59%)
1839	2,888	345 (11.95%)	2,543 (88.05%)
1840	3,556	401 (11.28%)	3,155 (88.72%)
1841	3,733	588 (15.75%)	3,145 (84.25%)
1842	3,968	560 (14.11%)	3,408 (85.49%)

Year	Total number arrested	Discharged	Convicted
1843	4,086	508 (12.43%)	3,578 (87.56%)
1844	4,468	613 (13.72%)	3,855 (86.28%)
1845	4,394	640 (14.57%)	3,754 (85.43%)
1846	4,054	647 (15.96%)	3,407 (84.04%)
1847	3,819	809 (21.18%)	3,010 (78.82%)
1848	4,05	915 (22.57%)	3,139 (77.43%)
1849	4,293	997 (23.22%)	3,296 (76.78%)
1850	4,650	1,168 (25.12%)	3,482 (74.88%)
1851	No records available		
1852	4,298	1,237 (28.78%)	3,061 (71.22%)
1853	3,527	1,044 (29.6%)	2,483 (70.4%)
1854	No records available		
1855	3,333	1,202 (36.06%)	2,131 (63.93%)
1856	4,784	2,140 (44.73%)	2,644 (55.26%)
1857	3,104	1,377 (44.36%)	1,727 (55.63%)
1858	2,528	1,078 (42.64%)	1,450 (57.35%)
1859	2,733	221 (8.08%)	2,512 (91.91%)
1860	2,815	304 (10.79%)	2,511 (89.2%)
1861	2,359	147 (6.23%)	2,212 (93.76%)
1862	2,824	127 (4.49%)	2,697 (95.5%)

Year	Total number arrested	Discharged	Convicted
1863	2,993	105 (3.5%)	2,888 (96.49%)
1864	3,241	41 (1.26%)	3,200 (98.73%)
1865	3,933	32 (0.81%)	3,901 (99.18%)
1866	3,848	125 (3.24%)	3,723 (96.75%)
1867	3,220	27 (0.83%)	3,193 (99.16%)
1868	3,836	133 (3.46%)	3,703 (96.53%)
1869	3,152	25 (0.79%)	3,127 (99.2%)
1870	3,255	32 (0.99%)	3,193 (99%)
1871	2,196	27 (1.22%)	2,169 (98.77%)
1872	1,920	4 (0.2%)	1,916 (99.79%)
1873	2,057	6 (0.29%)	2,051 (99.7%)
1874	1,522	9 (0.59%)	1,513 (99.4%)
1875	1,462	6 (0.41%)	1,456 (99.58%)
1876	2,015	11 (0.54%)	2,004 (99.45%)
1877	1,672	5 (0.29%)	1,667 (99.7%)
1878	1,393	15 (1.07%)	1,378 (98.92%)
1879	1,102	3 (0.27%)	1,099 (99.72%)
1880	1,009	9 (0.89%)	1,000 (99.1%)
1881	975	1 (0.1%)	974 (99.89%)

Year	Total number arrested	Discharged	Convicted
1882	785	2 (0.25%)	783 (99.74%)
1883	1,146	1 (0.08%)	1,145 (99.91%)
1884	1,202	5 (0.41%)	1,197 (99.58%)
1885	1,600	6 (0.37%)	1,594 (99.62%)
1886	1,563	6 (0.38%)	1,557 (99.61%)
1887	1,413	10 (0.7%)	1,403 (99.29%)
1888	1,407	11 (0.78%)	1,396 (99.21%)
1889	1,355	9 (0.66%)	1,346 (99.33%)
1890	1,077	1 (0.09%)	1,076 (99.9%)
1891	948	8 (0.84%)	940 (99.15%)
1892	684	3 (0.43%)	681 (99.56%)
1893	583	7 (1.2%)	576 (98.75%)
1894	753	4 (0.53%)	749 (99.46%)
1895	699	20 (2.86%)	679 (97.13%)
1896	681	15 (2.2%)	666 (97.79%)
1897	556	28 (5.03%)	528 (94.96%)
1898	806	14 (1.73%)	792 (98.26%)
1899	494	7 (1.41%)	487 (98.58%)

* Source: *Dublin Metropolitan Police Statistics*, 1838-1900.

As is evident from table 1 the figures are high, with 2,849 arrests in 1838 increasing yearly to a maximum of 4,784 in 1856. From 1868 the number of arrests gradually decreased reaching a low of 494 in 1899. Not all of those women arrested were actually convicted of prostitution and generally, in the earlier period, an average of 18 per cent were released without being charged. From the 1870s only about 1 per cent were discharged. Under the Dublin Police Act of 1842 all that was necessary for conviction was for a policeman to state that a woman was known to him as a prostitute and he had seen her approach males. It is unclear from the available evidence what standards were used to allow a woman go free. In some instances, for those freed, an assurance by some person known to the woman of her future good behaviour was given. It is interesting to note that the greatest number of arrests occurred during the famine years with an annual average of 4,123 women being taken into custody from 1845 to 1849. This may have resulted from an influx of poorer women into the city who had no other possible source of income. It appears also that in the earlier part of the century very few prostitutes ended up in prison. In 1851, for example, an average of one woman per month was sentenced to Grangegorman Female Prison on conviction of being a "common night walker." The sentence was usually a month in prison or a fine of between one and two shillings.[3] This had changed quite dramatically by the 1870s, due no doubt to the vigilance of the police, when for example, in the month of February, 1879, forty-one women were sentenced and fined for the same offence. The most common sentence at this stage was a fine of twenty shillings, a not insubstantial sum, or fourteen days in prison. It is interesting to note that of these forty-one women only four had not been previously imprisoned.[4]

The police statistics also provide a breakdown of the ages of those convicted. Throughout the period, 1838-1899, over 60 per cent of convictions were for women aged between 20 and 30 years. In 1838 twenty of those convicted were between the ages of ten and fifteen years. For the remainder of the period the average annual number of convictions for this age group was ten. For the whole period also the illiteracy level of those convicted averaged 99 per cent. The picture which emerges of the "common prostitute" reveals her to have been poor and uneducated and ranging in age from twenty to thirty years. Most women appear to have given up the occupation by the time they reached their forties; many indeed may have contracted illnesses or died by this stage. It is probable also that prostitution was engaged in by most of the women as a temporary occupation, many abandoning it once they married or secured enough money to keep themselves.

The figures available also detail the number of known brothels which existed within the city. In 1838, for example, there were 402 such establishments. The highest number recorded comes from 1845 with 419; by 1853 the number had declined to 207; in the 1870s it averaged about 96 per year and in the 1890s about 80.

A more general picture of prostitution throughout Ireland for the years 1870 to 1900 can be gained from looking at the criminal and judicial statistics of the period. Dublin had the greatest number in 1870 with 3,255 women arrested, this had dropped to a low of 431 by 1900. If the figures given for arrests and the number of alleged prostitutes (that is women who were charged with other offences but were known to be prostitutes) are taken together then Dublin had 11,526 arrests in 1870, and even taking account of the fact that re-arrests were not recorded, it is still a very high figure. For the country in general the combined total for 1870 is 15,537 arrests, this had dropped to 3,626 by 1900.[5] Some of the reasons for this remarkable drop in numbers can be summarised briefly. The activities of the White Cross Vigilance Association, established in Dublin in 1885, whose members patrolled those areas noted for prostitution and often harassed brothel keepers by keeping vigil outside their establishments, may have had some impact. The increased vigilance of the police, who in many instances were forced to act by the WCVA, and the introduction of the Criminal Law

Amendment Act of 1885 also helped to reduce the vice. Also there was an increase in the numbers of refuges, homes and clubs whose function was primarily preventative, providing shelter to those who were thought likely to end up on the streets.[6] Given these figures it is hardly an exaggeration to say that prostitution was a sizable problem within Dublin during the last century, and that problem was not confined to the major cities.

Towns which housed garrisons also provided their quota of prostitutes. Mason, in his parochial survey, noted the immorality which existed in Athlone and the Protestant rector commented that prostitutes

> ...infest the streets, as well as the hedges and ditches about the town, not only to the destruction of the moral(ity), of the present as well as the rising generation, but even in violation of common decency; to such a pitch is depravity risen, that vice does not hide its deeds in darkness, but boldly stalks abroad in open day.[7]

The Tipperary town commissioners first recorded the problem in 1877, with the opening of a new military barracks, when they recommended that summonses be issued to the "ladies of the night". The commissioners got little support from the military authorities in curtailing the vice but continued to wrestle, unsuccessfully, with the problem.[8] The police seem generally to have turned a blind eye to prostitutes unless they created a public nuisance. Some attempts to curtail the vice came instead from clergymen. Again in Tipperary pressure from the local clergy on the town commissioners to clean up the streets resulted in a bounty being paid to nightwatchmen at the rate of five shillings for every successful conviction of a prostitute.[9]

Similarly, in 1876 the Catholic priests in Cork city, determined to close down the brothels in St Finbarr's parish, acted without police aid.

> There was one street which contained probably 12 or 14 houses of ill fame, and the priests determined to clear out

the whole nest; it was in a back lane or alley; we took public action; we called on the people of our confraternities to assist us; and by bringing public opinion to bear upon the question, all these houses were shut up.[10]

The Rev Henry Reed, who provided this information declared the success of the action in ridding Cork of brothels; other evidence, however, reveals that such activity only drove the problem underground.[11]

In the case histories of prostitutes, often published in the annual reports of rescue agencies, they were portrayed as women whose lives were destroyed by sexual experience. Rescuers never accepted that women could choose prostitution as a viable means of earning or supplementing an income. For rescuers, the passage to prostitution was forced upon the woman. A "virtuous" woman was first seduced, and thus shamed, after this, due to abandonment by her seducer, she continued as a "privateer" and finally became so degraded that she took to the streets. Logan, in his study, states that prostitutes came usually from the lower classes "... low dressmakers, and servants; manure collectors, who are sent very young to the streets for that purpose, have also furnished their quota."[12] He also claimed that some individuals sold their daughters and other relatives to brothel keepers. Prostitutes, he noted, were not accepted into brothels unless they were well recommended, usually by another prostitute, and paid eight shillings per week to their mistresses for board; any other money they made was for their own use. [13]

For the poorer prostitutes conditions could be miserable. The "Bush" was a wooded place near Cobh, Co. Cork, where "... 20 to 25 to 30 women...lived...all the year round under the furze...like animals."[14] Many prostitutes also followed soldiers around from one depot to another. Dr Curtis, who gave evidence to a select committee on the operation of the Contagious Diseases Acts, stated "they (the prostitutes) are always moving about from Fermoy to Kinsale, and the garrison towns...and sleeping under forts, and behind the barracks."[15] The "Wrens of the Curragh" were a notorious band of prostitutes who lived primitively in makeshift huts on the perimeters of the Curragh army camp in Co. Kildare. The number of women living in these conditions varied but up to sixty women were stated to live there at any one time. Many of these were undoubtedly prostitutes but it is probable that some, at least, were also involved in long standing common law relationships with some of the soldiers, since it was the practice of the army authorities at this time not to recognise soldiers' marriages unless they were living in married quarters in the camp. Even living in such conditions there was a certain bond of solidarity amongst the fifty or sixty women who occupied the "nests". The women pooled their meagre financial resources and lived off it. The "colony" was also "open to any poor wretch who imagines that there she can find comfort." "The poor women who followed soldiers to the camp were …made as welcome amongst the wrens as if they did not bring with them certain trouble and an inevitable increase to the common poverty."[16] These women appear to have been badly treated by the local population and Charles Dickens, writing of a visit he had made to the area in the 1840s, stated that it was "…quite common for the priest, when he met one of them ('wrens') to seize her and cut her hair off close." Similarly local shopkeepers would not serve them in their shops.[17] Their outcast status is evident from one contemporary comment; a market was held in the camp and it was stated the women "were allowed to approach and make their purchases 'just like other people'."[18]

There were also prostitutes who made a good living at the trade and catered for a better class of client than the ordinary soldier. The area around St Stephen's Green in Dublin was noted as a place where the "upper class" prostitute operated.[19] Evidence from the commissions on the effects of the Contagious Diseases Acts notes the existence of prostitutes who would not deal with soldiers and who considered themselves to be of a "better class" than women who did. It is impossible to assess how the women themselves felt about their occupation. For some it may have been freely chosen; for others a necessity. Despite the dangers of disease, pregnancy and social ostracism involved, a large number of women took it up.

Rescue Work

In the nineteenth century at least twenty-three asylums or refuges were established to rescue and reclaim "fallen women." The title "Magdalen asylum," used by many refuges, reveals the influence of religious symbolism using Mary Magdalen as the model of repentance and spiritual regeneration. Of these asylums at least fourteen operated in Dublin,[20] most others being attached to convents, especially those of the Good Shepherd sisters, the Sisters of Charity and the Mercy nuns. Six of the Dublin asylums were run by religious congregations or Catholic clergymen, the rest had Protestant clergymen as trustees, governors or committee members. In these latter institutions the laity played a greater role. Throughout the century there was a direct link between institutional religion and the asylums, strongest in those refuges run by female religious. While there were certain similarities between the organisation of lay and religious asylums the differences were important and they will be treated separately here.

Lay Asylums

The earliest refuge established was the Magdalen Asylum in Leeson Street, Dublin, which opened in 1766. Lady Arbella Denny, who founded this home, had become interested in rescue work while involved in the reform of the Dublin Foundling Hospital.[21] There she came across unmarried mothers who had been abandoned by their families and were forced to give up their children. In this asylum, it was stated that the women would be sheltered

> from Shame, from Reproach, from Disease, from Want, from the base Society that has either drawn you into vice, or prevailed upon you to continue in it, to the utmost hazard of your eternal happiness.[22]

The organisation and ethos of the Magdalen Asylum was taken up by other refuges which appeared in Ireland later on in the eighteenth and nineteenth centuries.

"Penitents," as these "fallen women" were called, most often gained entry by making their own way to an asylum. One reason given for rejecting penitents was the lack of room available in the institution, and many of the homes certainly catered for small numbers and had limited funds. However, judging from some of the reports, it appears that a number of asylums also operated on a discriminatory basis. In those institutions under lay control penitents were more acceptable if they were "...young, unskilled...and not hardened in the ways of vice."[23] The Magdalen Asylum in Leeson Street took in Protestant women who were under twenty years of age, or were expectant mothers, and the stated aim of the home was to afford protection to young women after a "first fall."[24] The committee of the Rescue Mission Home in Dublin aimed for the "reformation of a better class, socially, of young women than those in other homes."[25] The attitude of the committee of the Dublin Midnight Mission and Home towards prostitutes was quite different. Its members, who appear to have been male, went into the streets to gather prostitutes, usually after midnight meetings. They accepted all "penitents" and if there was not enough room in their own establishment they found other places of refuge or lodgings for the women immediately.[26] The majority of asylums did not discriminate on a religious basis and accepted women of all religious persuasions; in practice, however, Catholic women tended to go to the religious run asylums and Protestants to the lay homes.

The policies of some of the lay Magdalen philantropists seem to have excluded the admission of hardened prostitutes. From the case histories provided in the annual reports, many of the women appear not to have been prostitutes at all. Many were described as "seduced" women who on abandonment by their seducers and families turned to the asylums for protection. It was also probably easier to reclaim young and "seduced" women than hardened prostitutes and the greater the success rate claimed by the asylums in the reform of penitents the more justification they had for their existence and the greater their claim for public support, on which the lay asylums depended, particularly in their earlier years. The reports of these asylums included case histories of young, vulnerable females in an attempt to engage public sympathy and to open purses. The only requirement common to all these institutions in allowing entry was the expressed desire on the part of the "penitent" to reform. After that, asylums selected women to suit their own facilities. Almost no public opposition to the establishment of these refuges is evident, though some objections were raised in 1813 regarding the opening of the Dublin Female Penitentiary, on the basis that a public asylum could only encourage prostitution by providing the vice with publicity and that there were sufficient refuges within Dublin already to cater for reform.[27] Generally these charitable efforts were well supported by the public initially but public interest usually waned after the first years of an institution's existence.

What was life like for the women who entered these institutions? Once within the walls of a refuge the penitents were generally issued with a uniform, one outfit for Sundays and another for everyday wear. In some institutions the women were separated into different classes. In the Dublin Female Penitentiary the classification was carried out with reference "...to their (the inmates) former education and habits of life,"[28] suggesting a social rather than moral classification. The institutions were "...designed to comfort and relieve the distressed soul who has happily perceived the error of her ways and loathes her former vileness."[29] There was a seemingly contradictory attitude expressed towards the women accepted. In many of the reports the belief that the women, in themselves, were not evil is expressed. Rather it was the keeping of bad company or other harmful influences which led them astray. The Female Penitent Refuge in Summerhill wished to remove the young female "...from the contagious influence of her former associates."[30] In the reports available for the Dublin Female Penitentiary the blame for the fall into vice was credited to abuse by seducers.[31] In one Catholic refuge the early neglect of prayer or the sacraments was seen as depriving the "...young girl of the only means of withstanding successfully the seductions of the world, and of forming habits of caution and restraint."[32]

Within the institutions, however, responsibility for their actions was laid firmly on the shoulders of the women themselves. A strict regime was followed in the asylums which stripped the women of their former identity and moulded a new one for them. Penitents were forbidden to use their own names or to speak of their past. In the Magdalen asylum in Leeson Street the penitents were given a number and known as Mrs One, Mrs Two etc. In religious run asylums they were given the name of a saint.[33] But even in rejecting their past the penitents were never allowed to forget that they had sinned. Their daily life was made up of prayer, labour, recreation and silence. This programme of reform and dicipline made no allowance either for maternal feeling. The children of penitents, it seems, were usually sent for adoption which is unsurprising as these children were direct evidence of "sin" having been committed. Within all the asylums there was an exaggerated rejection of the penitent's past. "Until the penitents forget the past," as one report stated, "nothing solid can be done towards their permanent conversion."[34] All contacts with their past life were broken, they could not write or receive letters without the matron first reading them, they were rarely allowed visitors and if they were they had to meet them with the matron present. The control these institutions attempted to exert over the women even extended to selecting topics of conversation; "...all occasions which might give rise to improper mental associations are...carefully guarded against...all light and trifling conversation is strictly inhibited."[35]

Within the asylums the inmates had to do a certain amount of work. A policy of religious instruction coupled with vocational training was normally followed. To effect reform and rehabilitation the home inculcated a sense of guilt in the penitents and united this with lessons in sobriety and industry. The conversion of the inmates depended on them being constantly employed; an idle life was considered to be prejudicial to their good. The inmates, it was stressed, were changed by work — industry allowed "...the mind to be tranquillised and made the penitents more amenable to religious instruction."[36] The aim of the work was not only to keep the inmates busy but also to train them new occupations once they had left the asylum. In the Female Penitent Asylum the women were taught

> ...to weep incessantly over their sins, and pray without intermission for their pious benefactors, their time being usefully filled up in washing and working for the public, and no opportunity was lost to refit them to fill, at some future date, their proper station in society."[37]

All the asylums engaged in needle and laundry work. Although the main reason given for engaging in such work was the desire to discipline the penitents and to give them a trade, such work was also a vital source of financial support for the institutions. The Dublin Female Penitentiary earned 11 per cent of its annual income in this way in 1815, compared to 27 per cent from subscriptions and donations. By 1824 the income derived from subscriptions and donations had dropped to 9 per cent whilst that from laundry work had increased to 55 per cent.[38] The pattern of becoming almost self-supporting through laundry work occurred in all of the asylums. Generally, subscriptions dropped after the first few years of an institution's existence and it had to rely on the laundry for financial support. Penitents did receive some money for their work, usually when they left the refuge. In the Magdalen Asylum in Leeson Street this amount varied from a few shillings to, at most, £7, but conditions regarding behaviour and length of stay in the homes had to be fulfilled before the money would be paid.

In these lay run establishments women stayed for a period of up to three years. When leaving after this time they were usually placed in domestic service if they did not return to their families or friends. By the middle of the century the Dublin by Lamplight Institution also provided some women with the funds to emigrate. However, if a penitent left of her own accord, as many of them did, or was dismissed for any reason, she was not helped by the committee.

It is difficult to assess how successful these institutions were in reforming or rescuing their inmates. Clearly claims made regarding the rehabilitation of the penitents in such annual reports as have survived, should be treated with caution. In the Magdalen Asylum, Leeson Street, the total number of inmates from 1767 to 1784 was 251. The committee claimed a reform rate of 52 per cent or 130 of the women and a failure rate of 32 per cent or 90 inmates. The remaining 16 per cent were resident in the home when these figures were compiled.[39] In the Dublin Female Penitentiary from 1813-17 the success rate claimed was 37 per cent, it was 42 per cent from 1818-20 and from 1823-25 it was 33 per cent.[40] The Magdalen Asylum in Limerick was run by a Miss Reddan until the Good Shepherd Sisters took it over in 1848. It is only one of two early refuges for which a complete list of penitents can be found. From May 1828 to June 1843 the total number of penitents was 218. Of these 47 were placed in situations and 34 were restored to friends or returned home. All of these penitents would have been seen as reclaimed and if we include the five deaths which occurred in the home, the ultimate redemption, 39 per cent of the women were considered rescued.[41] The Magdalen asylum, in Townsend Street, Dublin, was also operated by a lay woman until the Sisters of Charity took it over in 1833. Of the 96 women who left the asylum while it was under lay control, a total of 52 would have been deemed reclaimed; again, this included women who returned to their families or friends, secured situations or died while in the home. The failure rate for this refuge was approximately 46 per cent.[42] The Rescue Mission Home in Dublin claimed a very high success rate of 65 per cent in 1899.[43] This home was very selective in choosing its inmates and the figure may indeed be accurate. However, these samples are too small to make any generalisation about the successes of the asylums and since these refuges did not investigate the fate of their inmates it is possible that some of the women may have eventually returned to their former lifestyles. Many women also left or ran away from the refuges before their allotted release date; about 11 per cent of the inmates of the Limerick Magdalen Asylum did so. It seems likely that many of the women used these homes as a temporary refuge and had no intention of reforming, an aspect which will be looked at later.

Lay women played an important role in running these establishments. All of the lay homes had male governors, patrons or committee members and they all had ladies' committees or lady visitors.[44] In many cases the ladies on these committees were philantropists who had either established the refuge or had been invited to take over its management by a male committee. Active rescue work was not generally engaged in by men, probably because their motivation could be misconstrued. These women came generally from the upper middle classes and espoused the values of their class. The ladies' committees effectively took charge of the running of the institutions. Even when men made policy decisions they were influenced by the women who did the routine work of ensuring that the homes ran smoothly. All the employees of the homes were female, usually with the exception of a male porter or carter who brought in the washing. The work these women did for the refuges covered three areas; firstly, the administration of the day to day running of the home; secondly, the instruction of the inmates in religion, reading and needlework and thirdly, the raising of funds. Groups of women generally visited the home a number of times during the week and recommended policy changes to the male governors. In the raising of funds the women mainly sought financial aid from other women. The committee of the Dublin Female Penitentiary sought money

...from all...but chiefly (looked) to their own sex, whose

bosoms must beat with corresponding sentiments of anxiety to become instrumental in rescuing an unhappy fellow creature, a sister, from temporal and possibly, from spiritual destruction.[45]

Although, as we have noted, subscriptions generally decreased after an initial period of enthusiasm: over the first ten years of its operation women averaged 52 per cent of subscribers to that home.[46] In the Dublin by Lamplight Institution they generally made up 40 per cent of subscribers.[47] Most of the lay asylums also operated repositories which were run by women where needlework or articles donated to the home were sold. The asylums also depended on a regular supply of laundry to ensure financial viability and it was women, in charge of households, who kept them supplied with such work. Without the voluntary and financial support of women it is certain that many of these refuges could not have functioned.

The women who ran these refuges were motivated by Christian charity. Although life within these asylums was difficult, those who operated them did so with a genuine measure of humanitarianism and it was obvious to these philantropists that prostitutes were certainly better off in the homes than on the streets. The function of the refuges was to provide "...a shelter from the scorn, derision and temptations of the world."[48]

All the asylums were extremely conservative in their approach to the problem of prostitution. They concentrated all their energies on saving the victim. In the earlier part of the century prostitution was an evil because it was "...injurious in its effects on society."[49] If left unreclaimed a prostitute could not "...fill with credit the character of child, wife, mother, friend."[50] A prostitute could be a corrupter of female innocence and if left unreclaimed could corrupt others. Not only was her temporal life a misery but if she continued on her way she would also lose eternal life. The principal aim of the homes was to give back to society a virtuous being. Through discipline and work the prostitute learned self-control. These philantropists believed that the causes of prostitution lay with the individual; if the woman could be reclaimed then the vice would be eliminated. Religious salvation was even more important to them than temporal salvation.

These refuges were established in response to social demands and the alarming number of prostitutes who operated openly in the city was generally given as the reason for their existence. In the nineteenth century women were not expected to be sexual beings, hence the pretence in these homes that prostitutes had no past life. The prostitute, by her "unwomanly" behaviour in displaying her availability for sexual acts, was seen as an affront to "respectable" women who were supposedly sexually ignorant. There is little evidence to show that the women who managed these asylums felt aggrieved at the sexual habits of men or frowned on the double standard of sexual morality which existed.

It was not until the initiation of the campaign to repeal the Contagious Diseases Acts that Irishwomen publicly showed their disapproval of the double standard which existed.[51] It is perhaps significant that the women who engaged in that campaign were not involved in any of the rescue societies. The function of such homes was not to question the existence of a sexual double standard, nor did the women who ran these homes express any degree of solidarity with their fallen sisters. In a sense they subscribed to the madonna ideal of womanhood which was common. They wished to elevate the "fallen woman" to an acceptable level of womanhood, to carry out her service role in society without acknowledging her sexuality.

Convent Institutions

The institutions run by nuns are of especial interest in regard to the idealised picture of women common in Ireland in the last century. In these refuges the "purest" women looked after the most "impure". As in other charitable endeavours in which they became involved, female religious provided an extensive, organised network of refuges which operated throughout the country. The Good Shepherd nuns ran homes in Belfast, Cork, Limerick, New Ross and Waterford. The Sisters of Mercy ran a refuge in Galway and Tralee and an institution in Dun Laoghaire. The Sisters of Our Lady of Charity of Refuge operated the largest asylum in either England or Ireland in Drumcondra and a branch of that congregation ran a home from Gloucester Street in Dublin. The Sisters of Charity also operated homes in Cork and Dublin. The Good Shepherd asylum in Cork appears to have been the only religious run asylum established to meet the demand for a refuge resulting from the implementation of the Contagious Diseases Acts in the 1860s, for after 1830 no lay Catholic asylum was established to look after prostitutes and those begun earlier in the century were all taken over by religious congregations.

The nuns generally took over institutions which were already in existence but which through both managerial and financial considerations had run into difficulties. For example, the Magdalen asylum in Townsend Street, Dublin, was run by a Mrs Ryan, a niece of archbishop Troy, from 1798. By the 1830s Mrs Ryan, through illness, was unable to control the penitents under her care. As a penance for unruly behaviour the penitents were not allowed to change the straw on their beds and to ensure that this rule would be kept Mrs Ryan had the ticken, which held the straw, nailed to the bed posts. When the Sisters of Charity entered the asylum they found that, as a result of Mrs Ryan's action, the beds were crawling with maggots. [52]

The Sisters of Charity also took over a Magdalen Asylum in Cork in 1846 which had been established in 1809. A letter from the Rev. Mother to Mary Aikenhead records that there was

> ...not a sound bit of timber in the place...rusty locks...no cutlery...very dirty...nothing in the house...the wash(room) is low and dark, when the water is taken from the troughs they (the penitents) are up to the ankles in it...the women are there without shoes.[53]

The nuns had to build a new washroom and with thirteen penitents in the home refused to take in any more until they could be adequately looked after. It was a very practical move to hand the institutions over to the nuns because they had the personnel, commitment, organisation and financial support which many of the lay Catholic organisers lacked.

All the religious congregations insisted on having complete control over the asylums and once they had gained this control ran efficient homes.[54] Convent asylums were larger and catered for more individuals than the lay run establishments. Most of the lay asylums put between 30 and 50 women through their homes annually with room for perhaps 40 penitents at the most. Some of those refuges run by religious could house 100 to 150 inmates at a time. None of the religious run asylums published annual reports but the majority did keep registers of their inmates. These documents provide fascinating details about the women who entered these refuges and it is worth looking at them in some depth.

The general impression gained from reading any of the contemporary literature published about the asylums is that they were virtual prisons and that the women who entered them were unlikely ever to leave. The evidence of the registers disproves this. Tables 2 and 3 provide a detailed breakdown of the inmates of seven asylums run by religious congregations during the last century. Overall these asylums, for the period covered, catered for a total of 10,674 women. Of this number approximately 2,219 entered an asylum more than once. (This is underestimated as not all the registers account for repeats). The majority of women who entered these refuges did so voluntarily, approximately 7,110, or just over 66 per cent) and many women entered up to ten times. Thus entering a refuge was, for the majority of women, a matter of choice. While it is true that many such women had only the workhouse or the Magdalen asylum to turn to in times of utter distress, it would appear that the second was the favoured option of many. The length of stay in the asylums varied from one day for some women to an entire

Table 2: Inmates of religious run Magdalen asylums in 19th century Ireland.*

| Institution | Dates Covered | Total number of entrants | Number of re-entrants | Source of Entry |||||
				Voluntary	Religious	Family/Other	Police/Prison	Unknown
GSMA, Belfast	April 1851-Dec. 1899	894	266	294	130	64	-	406
GSMA, Cork	July 1872-Dec. 1899	1,749	592	902	569	167	103	8
SCMA, Cork	June 1846-Dec. 1899	1,267	?	?	?	?	?	1,267
LCR, Dublin	May 1839-Dec. 1899	2,633	434	?	211	139	37	2,246
SCMA, Dublin	Jan. 1833-Dec. 1899	1,387	?	568	520	202	35	62
GSMA, Limerick	1848-Dec. 1899	2,039	873	675	902	110	27	325
GSMA, Waterford	July 1842-	705	54	350	250	87	11	7
Totals:		10,674	2,219 (20.78%)	2,789 (26.13%)	2,582 (24.18%)	769 (7.2%)	213 (1.99%)	4,321 (40.48%)

Table 3: Departures from religious run Magdalen asylums in 19th century Ireland.*

Institution	Left Voluntarily	Expelled	Situation Work	Emigrated	Magdalen Class	Hospital	Workhouse	Lunatic Asylum	Deaths	Escaped	Home Friends	Other Convents	Unknown
GSMA, Belfast	412	69	50	17	14	40	4	3	49	11	95	14	116
GSMA, Cork	815	206	76	112	23	178	3	15	44	23	136	27	91
SCMA, Cork	1,005	23	5	6	-	24	-	6	119	1	27	10	41
LCR, Dublin	1,403	232	16	21	-	211	3	4	147	1	103	3	489
SCMA, Dublin	599	345	26	9	-	106	10	-	128	4	115	34	11
GSMA, Limerick	907	384	81	37	9	199	12	7	88	47	142	13	113
GSMA, Waterford	359	50	5	4	16	27	2	5	48	3	45	5	136
Totals	5,500	1,309	259	206	62	785	34	40	623	90	663	106	997
As percentage of total no. of entrants	(51.52%)	(12.26%)	(2.42%)	(1.92%)	(0.58%)	(7.35%)	(0.31%)	(0.37%)	(5.83%)	(0.84%)	(6.21%)	(0.99%)	(9.34%)

Abbreviations: GSMA Good Shepherd Convent Magdalen Asylum: SCMA Sisters of Charity Magdalen Asylum: LCR Magdalen Asylum operated by Our Lady of Charity Refuge, High Park, Drumcondra.
*Sources: Mss, registers of the Magdalen asylums held by the convents cited.

lifetime, of thirty or forty years, for others. It was generally women who entered in their teens or who were in their thirties or older, who remained in the homes. One woman, in the Donnybrook asylum, died in 1881 after spending nearly fifty-one years in the home. The decision to stay was made by the women themselves and although the nuns certainly did not encourage women to leave they had little choice in the matter if the woman was determined to go. It would seem from the number of re-entries that some women may have used the asylums as a temporary shelter and once they thought it possible to return to the outside world they did so. The stability of life within a refuge, the order and discipline imposed, may have given a sense of security to others and made it an attractive option to remain.

The second largest source of referral, after voluntary entries, came from religious, either priests and in some cases bishops, or nuns in other convents. Family/other referrals signifies either parents sending their daughters to a refuge, matrons from hospitals or employers sending women to a home. It seems likely that those women who were unaccounted for entered the homes of their own choice.

The homes in Dublin appear to have catered almost exclusively for women from the Dublin area. In the Good Shepherd asylum in Cork the majority of women, or 91 per cent, came from the city, 4 per cent came from the county and the remaining 5 per cent from places as far away as Dublin, Liverpool and even Scotland. The asylum in Limerick received women from the Limerick, Clare and Tipperary area generally but took in women from other parts of the country as well.

The majority of women who left the asylums did so of their own wish. Over the period 5,500 or approximately 52 per cent of the women did this. It appears that some form of permission to leave had to be granted by the nuns and a small number of women, about 1 per cent, ran away or escaped form the homes. One woman, who left the asylum in Donnybrook, at her own request, after spending four years there, was intriguingly noted in the information column of the register as "...having protestant tendencies" coupled with a bad temper.⁵⁵ Another woman in the same refuge asked and was granted permission to leave after a few weeks stating she could not survive a life in the home without smoking!⁵⁶

About 12 per cent or 1,309 were expelled from the refuges. Insubordination, violence, madness or a refusal to attend to religious duties or ceremonies were the reasons usually given for dismissal. One penitent in Donnybrook was dismissed after ten years' residence. She was described as "...extremely slothful, irreligious and (having) a shocking tongue."⁵⁷ Another woman in Limerick was expelled in 1891 after a month in the home. It was her sixth time in the refuge and the record of her dismissal states "...not to be admitted again...a very bad spirit."⁵⁸ Many penitents were also dismissed for engaging in lesbian relationships, or "particular friendships" as such were termed, with another woman in the home. Whether this involved actual sexual activity or not remains unrecorded. Nuns themselves were warned against forming "particular" attachments to other nuns because they had to devote all their energies to serving God. They may have seen intense friendships between the women under their care as dangerous because it could distract them from the purpose of their stay in the home, total self abnegation, the suppression of their own desires, and repentance. It was undoubtedly difficult for the nuns to control many of the penitents and they were probably glad to see the back of many of them. Expulsion did not mean that a penitent would not be taken back into the refuge again at a later stage. Indeed the nuns did not operate on any discriminatory basis and seem to have taken in any women who came to their doors.

In terms of rehabilitation it is easier to judge the success rate of the religious run asylums than their lay counterparts. If we take the women who were provided with situations, emigrated, entered a Magdalen class, returned home or entered another Magdalen asylum and those who died (the deaths recorded in the tables refer to those women who died while in the home) 1,919 or 18 per cent of the women would be deemed reclaimed by the nuns. This percentage, even if overly optimistic especially in regard to women who "returned to the world," is probably much more accurate than that claimed by the lay asylums. Contact with the penitents was not maintained once they had left the asylums and neither lay nor religious refuges provided any after-care services for the women.

Life in the religious run homes was similar to that in the lay run establishments. The penitents' days were made up of work, prayer, silence and recreation. In the refuge run by the Sisters of Our Lady of Charity of Refuge the penitents addressed the nuns as mother and were referred to privately as children. In public and when being instructed the title penitent was always used in order to make the inmates realise its true meaning.[59] The penitent was not treated as an adult and had no control over her life in the refuge. The nuns organised her day and took away all the responsibility of decision making. Also within this refuge the women were never allowed to be left alone for a moment. In some of the religious run homes the penitents could also join a Magdalen class.[60] Within these homes the penitents were classed in three groups, the ordinary penitents, Children of Mary and the "consecrated," which was also called the "class of perseverance." The women could move from one class to another by displaying piety and discipline. The highest class was that of the "consecrated" or class of perseverance. The women who entered this class took a form of religious vow similar to that taken by the nuns themselves. If consecrated the penitents were expected to remain in the home for life and were given special privileges within the community. They also wore a habit similar to that worn by the lay sisters.[61] The nuns' own ideal of austerity and holiness was offered as the ideal for the rescued penitents, but they could never become "real" nuns nor be totally integrated into the community. Those "consecrated" remained part of the penitent community and were, by their example of piety, thought to influence other penitents for good. Although treated as children these women could never be full members of a religious family; the nuns kept their distance from their charges. "The sisters must inspire the children (penitents) who are generally headstrong, and obstinate, with confidence, without familiarising themselves with them in the slightest degree."[62]

The nuns reached out to more penitents, numerically speaking, than did the lay women who ran the other asylums. In the annals of those convents to which asylums were attached there are many stories related of women who led a holy and penitent life within the refuges and great satisfaction was expressed by the nuns in the saving of these souls. These annals are full of anecdotes about the relationship between the nuns and the penitents. They generally refer to requests by penitents to leave and it is only the superior wit of the nun in charge which fools them into remaining.

All of the penitent asylums were in effect "total institutions." The social world of these refuges reproduced the patriarchal and class order of society in general. Women in the nineteenth-century had a carefully defined sphere of action and this can be seen clearly in the operation of the Magdalen asylums. The women who ran these refuges played out their maternal role creating homes for the penitent "child". They sought to inculcate in the penitent the correct attitudes and behaviour expected of women in that age. Penitents were trained in deference and subordination in isolated refuges which shielded them from the world, the source of possible temptation. They stressed the importance of personal guilt and that only personal discipline could lead to salvation. Any individual expression of personality or sexuality was denied to the women in these refuges and this was in keeping with what was considered correct behaviour for all women at this time. Judging from the large numbers of women who left these refuges voluntarily, it is obvious that these standards were unacceptable for many.

Using the information provided in these registers and uniting it with the information available from prison and police records it is possible to produce a general profile of the life of a prostitute. It can be taken for granted that these women were poor. Although no occupational category is listed in the asylum registers such a column was used in prison registers; the majority of women imprisoned for prostitution were accorded no occupational status. In the census registers for 1901, asylum inmates were generally listed as penitents or laundresses.[63] This latter status would have reflected their position in the refuge rather than refer to a position previously held outside the asylum. What is obvious also from these sources of information is that most of the women had migrated to large centres of population from country areas. A large percentage of the inmates of the Magdalen asylums had been born outside large towns or cities. These women had therefore migrated seeking occupations or indeed with the intention of going on the street. Being, as we have seen, almost totally illiterate there were very few options open to them. Manufacturing industry offered few opportunities in Ireland and where women found work in factories it normally proved to be a tedious, harsh and badly paid means of earning a livelihood. The largest opening for women would, of course, have been domestic service. This was not a very attractive choice for many women since the lives of domestic servants were extremely confining and they too were badly paid.[64] Prostitution, then, may have been seen as a legitimate means of securing an income. It can be argued that this occupation also allowed the women a certain degree of independence. There is no reference, in the existing records, regarding the presence of pimps in these women's lives and they may have had a greater control over their own fate than many other working women who laboured for twelve to fourteen hours a day for meagre wages.

Another interesting feature of the prison records is the recurrence of residence in the same areas of Dublin city. Moore Street, Mary's Lane and Purdon Street appear as the addresses most frequently given for arrested women. Like the "Wrens of the Curragh" they may have had their own community support networks. It was also police policy, of course, to restrict the area of prostitution to certain streets and alleys and women who removed themselves to such areas suffered less harassment from the authorities.

As we have already seen many women had given up the trade by the time they had reached forty and were most active in their twenties and thirties. Of the women who entered, and remained, in the refuges the majority had either entered very young, at sixteen or less, or were in their late thirties. It would seem then that the latter group had given up their life on the streets and purposely entered the refuges with the intention of "retiring." Unless they had saved enough money to establish a business, or had married there was very little choice for them other than the workhouse. Many of the women who entered and left the refuges on a regular basis were in their twenties and thirties and were obviously using the homes as a temporary refuge from their occupation. One other fact which emerges from the evidence of the registers is that the majority of women involved were without an immediate family. Most often both parents were dead and in some few instances parents had emigrated without taking their children with them. The home was often disrupted also by the death of one parent with the surviving parent remarrying and in a number of cases it seems that the children of the first marriage were not welcome in the new home. The disruption of the family and migration to large centres of population would have removed the woman from the constraints of family life and expectations. The need to support herself and perhaps the desire to be independent may have made prostitution a viable option in a world where there was little else a woman could do to maintain an existence.

Both nuns and prostitutes were extreme examples of what women could be.[65] The pure lifestyle of the nun was the ideal, the impurity of the prostitute an evil which had to be battled with. Within all the asylums no fundamental change in the relations between the sexes was contemplated. No serious consideration was given to the causes of prostitution, or at least there is no evidence to suggest that any such discussion took place, and the only cure seemed to be to attempt to rescue the fallen. Judging from the evidence given above it appears that the nature of a prostitute's life was a relatively complex one. Further analysis and investigation is required before the picture is complete. What is obvious is that these women, perhaps the most hidden group in Irish society, do have a history which deserves to be recorded.

Notes

1 William Logan, *The Great Social Evil: Its Causes, Extent, Results and Remedies* (London, 1871). There are numerous earlier references to women operating as prostitutes in the various inquiries made by the government into the condition of the poor. One early reference, found in official records, relates that a flourishing red light district operated in a maze of back alleys and lanes between Aungier Street and St Stephens Green. One of the occupants of this area petitioned the Lord Lieutenant in 1835 to restore order to this "...nursery of human turpitude and hotbed of depravity" where prostitutes "in a state of nudity openly and wantonly assailed the most respectable persons." The police however, claimed that there was little they could do and the area continued as a centre of vice until about 1875. Quoted in Gregory Allen, "The new police: London and Dublin," *The Police Journal*, vol. 1, no. 4, (October 1977), pp 307-8. For a recent analysis of prostitution in England see Judith R. Walkowitz, *Prostitution and Victorian Society: Women, Class, and the State* (Cambridge, 1980).
2 Logan, *op. cit.*, pp 48-52.
3 Grangegorman Female Prison, General Register, 1st January - 31st December. 1851. Prisons, 1/9/13, V16-4-2 (National Archives, Four Courts, Dublin).
4 Grangegorman Female Prison, General Register, 24th July 1879 - 30th September 1880. Prisons 1/9/13. V/16/4/14 (National Archives, Dublin).
5 See *Judicial and Criminal Statistics for Ireland*, 1871-1901.
6 For information on these organisations see Maria Luddy, Woman and philanthropy in nineteenth-century Ireland, (Unpublished Ph. D Thesis, N.U.I., 1989), chapter five.

7 Quoted in W. S. Mason, *A Statistical Account or Parochial Survey of Ireland*, 3 vols. (Dublin, 1814, 1816, 1819), iii, p. 79.
8 D. G. Marnane, *Land and Violence: A History of West Tipperary from 1660* (Tipperary, 1985), pp 72-3, 112, 117.
9 *Ibid.*, p. 72.
10 Evidence of the Rev Henry Reed, *Report of the House of Commons Select Committee on the Administration, Operation, and Effects of the Contagious Diseases Acts of 1866-69*, H. C. 1881 (351), viii, Q. 6, 206.
11 See the evidence of Dr James Curtis in *ibid.*, Q. 6, 389.
12 Logan, *op. cit.*, pp. 49-50.
13 *Ibid.* The Rev John Edgar, who became involved in rescue work in Belfast, in a lecture entitled *Female Virtue — Its Enemies and Friends* (London, 1841) stated "In a small village, where ten sisters in four families are prostitutes, I know four sisters who support their father, mother and younger brother, by the wages of iniquity."
14 Evidence of Dr Curtis, *House of Commons Select Committee ... on CDAs*, 1882 (340), ix, Qs. 11,256; 11,257.
15 *Ibid.*, Q.11,278.
16 A series of articles in the *Pall Mall Gazette* recounts their story. See, *Pall Mall Gazette*, 15, 16, 17, 19, 23 October 1867. These articles were later reprinted as a booklet titled *The Wrens of the Curragh* (London, 1867). See also Padraic O'Farrell, "Camp followers of the Curragh," *The Irish Times*, 31 January 1988.
17 Charles Dickens, "Stoning the Desolate," in *All the Year Round*, (November 1865), p. 370.
18 *Wrens of the Curragh*, p. 35.
19 Evidence of Dr R. McNamara, *House of Commons Select Committee...on CDAs*, 1881 (351), viii, Q. 6,472.
20 The figures given here are not absolute as some homes opened for short periods of time under different management and different names. Many refuges, which were not primarily for prostitutes, like the Olive Mount Institution of the Good Samaritan, which operated from 1843 to about 1860, took in "fallen women." There is some confusion also regarding refuges which existed in northern Ireland. There is a reference to an Ulster Female Penitentiary existing c. 1816. However, the 6th annual report of the Ulster Female Penitentiary dates its foundation from 1822. There is another reference to an Ulster Female Penitentiary which dates its foundation in 1835 and the

Ulster Magdalene Asylum was certainly founded in 1838. The Ulster Female Penitentiary of 1816, 1822 and 1835 may have been the same establishment reformed under new committees. The Rosevale Home, which opened in 1862 near Lisburn, may also have been a Magdalen home. One annual report of its activities is available but the description of its work is so circumspect that it is difficult to be sure of its function. For references to all of these institutions see Luddy, *op. cit.*, appendix two.

21 For the work of Lady Arbella Denny in the Foundling Hospital see J. A. Robins, *The Lost Children: A Study of Charity Children in Ireland 1700-1900* (Dublin, 1980), chapter two. For the life of Lady Denny see Beatrice Bayley Butler, "Lady Arbella Denny, 1707-1792," *Dublin Historical Record*, vol. ix, no. 1, (Dec 1946 — Feb 1947), pp 1-20.

22 Quoted in J. D. H. Widdess, *The Magdalen Asylum, Dublin 1766-1966* (Dublin, 1966?), p. 5.

23 Dublin Female Penitentiary, annual report 1814, p. 12. (Hereafter DFP).

24 R. M. Barrett, *Guide to Dublin Charities* (Dublin, 1884), part III, p. 4.

25 *Ibid.*, p. 6.

26 *Ibid.*, p. 3.

27 Luddy, *op. cit.*, chapter five.

28 DFP, annual report 1814, p. 6.

29 Quoted in Butler, *art.cit.*, p. 10.

30 Leaflet in Murray Papers, File 31/1/4. undated (Dublin Diocesan Archives).

31 DFP, annual reports 1814-16.

32 *Abstract Report and Statistical Sketch of the Magdalen Asylum, High Park, Drumcondra* (Dublin, 1881), p. 17.

33 See Bayley-Butler, *art. cit.*, and the registers of the various asylums.

34 *Abstract Report*, p. 17.

35 Asylum for Penitent Females, annual report 1831, p. 11.

36 DFP, annual report 1816.

37 Leaflet in Murray Papers, File 31/7-9, 1840 (Dublin Diocesan Archives).

38 DFP, annual reports 1812-25, financial accounts.

39 *Asylum for Penitent Females, Rules and Regulations*, (Dublin, 1785), appendix, p. 3.

40 DFP, annual reports 1812-1825.
41 Ms register of the Magdalen Asylum (GSL).
42 Ms register of the Magdalen Asylum, 1796-1967 (SCD).
43 G. D. Williams (ed.), *Dublin Charities, A Guide* (Dublin, 1902), p. 60.
44 These women were philantropists who engaged in rescue work and were always referred to as "ladies" in the annual reports. They were generally from middle and upper class backgrounds.
45 *An Appeal to the Public from the Committee of the Intended New Dublin Female Penitentiary* (Dublin, 1812), p. 20.
46 DFP, annual reports 1812-25, subscription lists.
47 Dublin by Lamplight, annual report 1868.
48 Leaflet in Murray Papers, File 33/1/20, undated (Dublin Diocesan Archives).
49 *Ibid.*
50 DFP, annual report 1816.
51 For the Irish activities of the Ladies' National Association, established in 1871 and a branch of Josephine Butler's Ladies' National Association, founded in England in 1869 to campaign against the Contagious Diseases Acts, see Luddy, *op. cit.*, pp 275-85.
52 Typescript annals of the Sisters of Charity, vol. 1, 1833, pp 277-9 (SCM).
53 Letter from M. Chantal, Cork to Mother M. Aikenhead dated 14/6/1846, File 1/13/97 (SCM).
54 It was not always an easy task for nuns to take full control of an asylum. For example, the Sisters of Our Lady of Charity of Refuge were invited from France in 1853 by the Rev John Smith to run a home established by him in 1833. These nuns had severe difficulties with Smith who refused to relinquish control of the home for many years, and who interfered constantly with the nuns' work. See Ms annals (Convent of Our Lady of Charity of Refuge, Dublin).
55 Penitent, Ms Register of the Asylum (SCD).
56 *Ibid.*
57 *Ibid.*
58 Penitent, Ms register of the Asylum (GSL).
59 *Abstract Report*, p. 25.
60 This system did not operate in those refuges run by the Sisters of Charity or the Sisters of Mercy.
61 *Abstract Report*, pp 26-7.

62 *Ibid.*, p. 25.
63 Ms census records, 1901 (National Archives, Dublin). For Lock hospital records see Mss, General registers of patients, Westmoreland Lock Hospital, 4 vols., 1816-1868 (Royal College of Physicians of Ireland, Dublin).
64 See Mona Hearn's article in this volume.
65 See Luddy, *op. cit.*, for a discussion of women in nineteenth century Ireland.

Abbreviations:
GSL Good Shepherd Convent, Limerick.
SCD Sisters of Charity, Donnybrook, Dublin.
SCM Sisters of Charity, Generalate, Milltown, Dublin.

Breadwinners and Providers: Women in the Household Economy of Labouring Families 1835-6

Mary Cullen

This paper examines the role of women in the household economy of labouring families as it emerges in the evidence given to the commission of inquiry into the condition of the poor in 1835-6. This shows that the labouring family operated as an interdependent economic unit where husband and wife—and children when they were old enough—contributed to family survival by paid and unpaid work. It establishes that the wife's contribution was a crucial one without which the economic unit could not have survived.

Labouring families adopted different strategies as their economic fortunes fluctuated. There were two main situations; in the first a family managed to live in more or less relative comfort, by its own independent labour; in the second its independent labour was not sufficient and supplementary methods had to be sought. In both situations a family continued to operate as an interdependent unit which maximised the economic potential of its different members.

In the relatively good times of survival by independent labour all able-bodied family members worked on the potato crop which provided their staple diet. All members also contributed earned income as opportunity allowed. In spite of the decline of domestic industry, in which they had been able to make substantial earnings, women still made a surprisingly large contribution to household income. This was in addition to their contribution through child rearing, food preparation and care of the home, activities to which the poor inquiry did not attach an economic value but which were vital to family survival.

When and if a family could no longer live by independent labour, a situation whose immediate cause was usually the husband's failure to get adequate employment, the wife regularly became the sole family breadwinner for the crisis period. In the economy of labouring families begging was women's work. She begged and by begging could support the entire family while it had no other resources. She could also support herself and her children over a period of months while her husband went to seek work and to try to save enough to re-establish the family at home.

Little of the evidence used here came from women themselves, and the inquiry showed little interest in their views or attitudes. It does not tell us much about how they experienced their lives or what they thought about them. It tells little directly about family relationships; about affection between wives, husbands and their children; or about autonomy and the location of decision-making and power. It does reveal a good deal about the structure of the family economy and of women's vital role in this, and, in doing so, raises questions about some of these issues.

The paper is divided into four sections; a brief discussion of the source; an examination of women's explicitly economic contribution to the day-to-day survival of a family while it supported itself by independent labour; an examination of women's contribution to family survival when independent labour failed and it had to turn to combinations of labour, begging, migration and vagrancy; and a brief consideration of some of the implications of the findings.

The Poor Inquiry as Source

The brief given to the commissioners was "to inquire into the condition of the poorer classes of your majesty's subjects in Ireland, and into the various institutions at present established by law for their relief"[1] and to suggest what further provisions might be made. In the process of carrying out this task the commissioners gathered an enormous amount of evidence about the conditions of life of the poor in

Ireland.

They divided the evidence-gathering process into two sections. The first dealt with the *extent* of destitution and the various existing systems of providing relief and their effectiveness, while the second was concerned with the possible *causes* of destitution. The allocation of a social group to either category was made on the basis of preliminary enquiries which identified the aspects of poverty widely regarded as significant.

Women greatly outnumbered men among the destitute. Seven topics were included in the examination of the extent of destitution and the existing methods of relieving it. These were: deserted and orphan children; illegitimate children and their mothers; widows having families of young children; the impotent through age or other infirmity; the sick poor, who in health were capable of earning their subsistence; the able-bodied out of work; and vagrancy as a mode of relief. The first topic obviously affected the lives of many more women than men. The second and third concerned groups comprised solely of women and children. The fourth and fifth included both women and men, but the evidence indicates there were more females than males, especially among the aged. The sixth dealt with unemployed men while the seventh showed that far higher numbers of women than men begged. These last two categories are to an extent inter-connected since many of the women counted among the vagrant beggars had husbands who were included in the able-bodied unemployed. Both these groups were relevant to the subject of this paper.

The commissioners adopted two complementary methods of gathering information. The first was the time-honoured method of asking important people in the localities for their views. A set of "statistical questions" was sent to clergy, magistrates, heads of police and "educated persons." This list immediately excluded the possibility of any woman being asked to fill in a questionnaire since there were no women clergy, magistrates or heads of police and the restrictions surrounding the education of women and girls[2] made it unlikely that any woman would qualify for selection as an "educated person" as understood by the commissioners, themselves all male establishment figures. It further excluded all men who were not members of an élite group of the well-off and privileged.

Some 7,600 questionnaires were sent out and replies were received from about 3,100 witnesses covering 1,100 parishes. Two of the questions related to the earnings of women and children. Question 11 asked "Are women and children usually employed in labour and at what rate of wages?" and question 14 asked "What in the whole might his (the labourer's) wife and four children, all of an age to work (the eldest not more than 16 years of age) earn within the year, obtaining as before an *average* amount of employment?" The fact that question 11 was confined to agricultural employment and did not include other sources of earnings limited its value for this paper. Question 14 was potentially useful but did not turn out to be so for a number of reasons: respondents' answers differed wildly from one to another and an individual respondent's answer to the first question was frequently irreconcilable with his answer to the second. The cause of much of the confusion appears to have arisen from the location and wording of question 14, which led some respondents to understand they were asked to calculate the earnings of women and children on the assumption that they obtained the same average amount of employment as men, which was of course rarely, if ever, the case.[3]

There was another problem with the statistical question method which was duly noted by the commissioners. "To obtain information sufficiently extensive in its range, and sufficiently impartial" in this way was "obviously impossible."[4] One man from a particular religious, social and economic class, however well informed, could not of his own knowledge supply full and accurate information on all aspects of the conditions of the poor in his locality. Equally important was the certainty that information on a topic as sensitive as the extent and causes of Irish poverty was going to encounter considerable problems of credibility if it was seen to come solely from clergy, magistrates, heads of police and "educated persons."

The idea of local examinations was based on the belief that the information most likely to be accurate and, equally important, most likely to be accepted as such by the greatest number of people, would be that which was seen to be agreed to by a wide cross section of Irish society. The method of achieving this was local enquiry sessions. These were to be presided over by two assistant commissioners sitting together, one Irish and one English, so that knowledge of the Irish scene and an outsider's objectivity could be combined in the conduct of the examinations. No-one else was to be allowed to preside or ask questions. Each "grade in society...each of the various religious persuasions...each party in politics" was to be present. The testimony of each class was to be given equal attention, and the examination was to take place "in the presence of all". The names of those attending and giving evidence and, as far as possible, the actual words used by witnesses were to be recorded, the latter as a precaution against misinterpretation. The assistant commissioners were to record the evidence and the impressions they themselves formed at the time. In the anticipation that there might be some conflicting evidence they were instructed to make it clear to all attending that a statement or opinion put forward by any witness and which was not challenged by anyone else would be considered to be accepted by all present as at least probably correct.[5]

Local examinations into the seven topics relating to destitution and modes of relief were held in one parish in every barony in seventeen counties; Galway, Mayo, Roscommon, Sligo, Carlow, Kildare, Longford, Westmeath, Wexford, Clare, Cork, Kerry, Limerick, Tipperary, Antrim, Donegal and Derry. Examinations into the topics identified as possible causes of poverty were held in thirty-two baronies in twenty-two counties; Galway, Leitrim, Mayo, Sligo, Dublin, Kilkenny, King's County, Louth, Meath, Queen's County, Wicklow, Clare, Kerry, Limerick, Tipperary, Waterford, Armagh, Cavan, Tyrone, Fermanagh,

Down, and Monaghan.

The evidence found most useful for this paper came from the baronial examination into labourers' expenditure and into the earnings of women and children, and from the parochial examinations concerning the able-bodied out of work and vagrancy as a method of relief. The first two provided most of the information about women's contribution to the economy of a family living by independent labour. The second two revealed the nature and extent of women's contribution when a family could no longer so survive.

One strength of the local examinations as a source was their structure as laid down by the commissioners. The fact that witnesses from the various religious, political and class affiliations presented their evidence in each other's presence gave some confidence that information which was seriously inaccurate would have been challenged and have failed to find its way into the agreed consensus view on any topic. The efforts of the assistant commissioners at many of the examinations to establish general patterns agreed by all present were particularly useful. Where there was an explicit consensus it seemed safe to take this as a reasonably accurate approximation to the reality. Where no explicit consensus was forthcoming it was difficult to generalise on the basis of the testimony of the individual witnesses. These often contradicted each other, or used hyperbolic language, or their version diverged significantly from the consensus reached at the same examination.

Another strength was that the commissioners were concerned with the situation of the "average" or "typical" labourer rather than with extremes of either poverty or prosperity. While the number of baronial examinations was relatively small yet their geographical distribution covered much of the country and their objective was to find the general pattern of labouring families' household economy. This, of course, was what was needed to assess the extent and pattern of women's contribution.

Thirdly, the local examinations did in fact provide a considerable amount of information on women's economic activity. By using the agreed consensus views, and the opinions formed by the assistant commissioners themselves, it was possible to identify a pattern of women's economic contribution which was essentially similar in all parts of the country where examinations took place. It was possible to identify the main components of women's income-generating activity and the proportion of total family income their earnings constituted.

Having said this it must also be said that the evidence for women's contributions was not always readily recognised. The major reason for this was the paradigm of family economy underlying the structure of the report itself. The evidence was collected and presented within a frame of reference which saw the labourer-father as the family head and provider. All family income was regarded as his no matter which member of the family actually earned it. Since the English common law gave a husband a legal right to his wife's earnings there was, strictly speaking, no factual inaccuracy in this. As Blackstone explained, this depended on the fact that, in the eyes of the law, "the very being and existence of the woman is suspended during the coverture, or entirely merged or incorporated into that of the husband...it follows, that whatever personal property belonged to the wife...is absolutely vested in the husband."[6] The resulting ambiguities created problems in identifying women's contributions. It was, for example, under the heading "labourer's income" that the most detailed evidence of his wife's earnings was found. This sort of ambiguity is a recurring problem when searching for evidence of women's activity in source material compiled within terms of a patriarchal paradigm.

Women's Economic Contribution While the Family Lived by Independent Labour

At nineteen of the baronial examinations into "labourer's expenditure" an agreed budget showing, in varying degrees of detail, the estimated yearly income of the typical labourer in the area was drawn up. These calculations of "labourer's earnings" were the source which revealed the pattern of women's contributions and its importance to balancing the family budget. Those compiled in the baronies of Kells Upper and Lower, and Moyfenragh in County Meath, Talbotstown in County Wicklow, Portnahinch in Queen's County (Laois), and Dundalk Upper in County Louth were the most detailed and will be considered first. In all these baronies separate budgets for the yearly income and the yearly expenditure of both constantly employed and occasionally employed labourers were drawn up. In Kells, Portnahinch and Talbotstown the budgets for the occasionally employed were further subdivided according to the amount of employment the labourer obtained during the course of a year. These carefully itemised budgets were particularly useful for establishing the extent and value of women's contributions. They were based on a family of husband, wife and three or four young children.

1. Barony of Kells, Co. Meath

SUNDRY GAINS

Produce of 3 roods conacre potato ground, 45 barrels eating potatoes at 3s 4d plus 15 barrels small potatoes used for pig and seed	7	10	0
Profit on pig	1	10	0
Total	£9	0	0
Deduct rent of 2 1/2 acres conacre tilled and manured by farmer at 7 per acre	4	7	6
	4	12	6
Remaining 1/2 rood rent free, being manured by pig manure mixed with ditch earth, bog stuff etc.			
Add net produce of fowls in eggs and chickens	0	10	0
Earnings of wife and children by field work, manufacture, gleaning, etc.	0	10	0
Total	£5	12	6

BUDGET FOR LABOURERS CONSTANTLY EMPLOYED

INCOME				EXPENDITURE			
Sundry gains as above	5	12	6	52 barrels potatoes	8	13	0
Deduct what he pays				Oatmeal	1	15	0
neighbour to assist him				Turf	0	10	0
and family in planting				Milk, Butter, etc. called			
and digging potatoes	1	0	0	"kitchen" at 6d per wk	1	6	0
	4	12	6	Tobacco	0	10	0
Labourer's Wages	12	0	0	Soap and candles	0	5	0
				Rent of cabin	2	0	0
				Clothes	1	13	6
Total	£16	12	6	Total	£16	12	6

BUDGET FOR THE FIRST CLASS OF LABOURER OCCASIONALLY EMPLOYED

INCOME				EXPENDITURE			
Sundry gains as above	5	12	6	52 barrels potatoes	8	13	0
Labourer's wages	6	15	0	Meal for a few weeks			
				at harvest	0	8	0
				Turf	0	10	0
				Kitchen at 3d a week	0	13	0
				Rent of cabin	1	10	0
				Left for clothes, kitchen			
				etc.	0	13	6
Total	£12	7	6	Total	£12	7	6

BUDGET FOR SECOND CLASS OF LABOURER OCCASIONALLY EMPLOYED

INCOME				EXPENDITURE			
Sundry gains as above	5	12	6	52 barrels potatoes	8	13	0
Labourer's wages	5	5	10	Rent of cabin	1	10	0
				Left for fuel, kitchen			
				clothes	0	15	4
Total	£10	18	4	Total	£10	18	4

BUDGET FOR THIRD CLASS OF LABOURER OCCASIONALLY EMPLOYED

INCOME				EXPENDITURE			
Sundry gains as above	5	12	6	52 barrels potatoes	8	13	0
Labourer's wages	3	6	4	Left for rent of cabin,			
				fuel, kitchen, clothes	0	5	10
Total	£8	18	10	Total	£8	18	10

Source: *Poor Inquiry, First Report,* Appendix D, pp 100-1.

2. Barony of Portnahinch, Queen's County

BUDGET OF LABOURER CONSTANTLY EMPLOYED

INCOME	£	s	d	EXPENDITURE	£	s	d
Profit on pig	1	10	0	Rent 1 rood conacre potato land, tilled and manured by farmer	2	10	0
Profit on fowls in eggs and chickens	0	10	0	20 barrels eating potatoes to supplement those grown by family for themselves and pig	4	0	0
Earnings by wife and children by field-work, gleaning, manufacture	0	10	0	Rent of cabin	2	0	0
Labourer's wages	9	10	0	Turf	0	12	6
				Kitchen	0	17	4
				Clothes	1	5	2
				Tobacco, soap, candles	0	15	0
Total	£12	0	0	Total	£12	0	0

BUDGET OF FIRST CLASS LABOURER OCCASIONALLY EMPLOYED

INCOME	£	s	d	EXPENDITURE	£	s	d
Profit on pig	1	10	0	Rent 1 rood conacre as above	2	10	0
Profit on fowls in eggs and chickens	0	10	0	20 barrels eating potatoes as above	4	0	0
Earnings by wife and children as above	0	10	0	Rent of cabin	1	15	0
Labourer's wages	8	1	4	Turf	0	10	0
				Kitchen	0	12	6
				Left for clothes, etc.	1	3	10
Total	£10	11	4	Total	£10	11	4

BUDGET OF SECOND CLASS LABOURER OCCASIONALLY EMPLOYED

INCOME	£	s	d	EXPENDITURE	£	s	d
Profit on pig	1	10	0	Rent 1 rood conacre as above	2	10	0
Profit on fowls	0	10	0	16 barrels eating potatoes as above	3	4	0
Earnings by wife and children as above	0	10	0	Rent of cabin	1	10	0
Labourer's wages	5	19	8	Left for turf, kitchen, clothes, tobacco, etc.	1	5	8
Total	£8	9	8	Total	£8	9	8

BUDGET OF THIRD CLASS LABOURER OCCASIONALLY EMPLOYED

INCOME				EXPENDITURE			
Profit on pig	1	10	0	Rent 1 rood as above	2	10	0
Profit on fowls	0	10	0	100 barrels potatoes as above	2	0	0
Earnings by wife and children as above	0	10	0	Rent of cabin	1	10	0
Labourer's wages	4	6	4	Left for everything else	0	16	4
Total	£6	16	4	Total	£6	16	4

Appendix D, p. 105

3. Barony of Talbotstown Upper, County Wicklow (16)

SUNDRY GAINS

Produce of 1/2 acre conacre potato ground, 25 barrels eating potatoes at 4s a barrel	5	0	0
7 1/2 barrels small potatoes used for pig and seed, profit on pig	1	10	0
Total	£6	10	0
Deduct rent of 1 1/2 roods potato ground tilled and manured by farmer at £2 15s a rood (ie. £11 an acre)	4	2	6
(the remaining half rood was rent free, manured by the pig)			
Total profit from potato ground, the work on it being by the labourer and his family	2	7	6
Profit from fowls in eggs and chickens	0	10	0
Earnings by wife and children by field work, manufacture, gleaning etc.	0	10	0
Total	£3	7	6

BUDGET OF LABOURER CONSTANTLY EMPLOYED

INCOME				EXPENDITURE			
Sundry gains as above	3	7	6	40 barrels at 4s a barrel	8	0	0
Labourer's wages	9	17	1	Rent of cabin	2	0	0
				Turf	0	10	0
				Kitchen, 4d a week	0	17	4
				Clothes	1	8	0
				Tobacco, soap, candles	0	10	1
Total	£13	5	5	Total	£13	5	5

BUDGET OF FIRST CLASS OF LABOURER
OCCASIONALLY EMPLOYED

INCOME				EXPENDITURE			
Sundry gains as above	3	7	6	37 barrels potatoes	7	8	0
Labourer's wages	7	14	0	Rent	1	15	0
				Kitchen, 3d a week	0	13	6
				Left for turf, clothes, soap, tobacco, etc.	1	5	0
Total	£11	1	6	Total	£11	1	6

BUDGET OF SECOND CLASS OF LABOURER
OCCASIONALLY EMPLOYED

INCOME				EXPENDITURE			
Sundry gains as above	3	7	6	34 barrels potatoes	6	16	0
Labourer's wages	5	11	6	Rent	1	10	0
				Left for kitchen, turf, clothes, soap, tobacco.	0	13	2
Total	£8	19	2	Total	£8	19	2

BUDGET OF THIRD CLASS OF LABOURER
OCCASIONALLY EMPLOYED

INCOME				EXPENDITURE			
Sundry gains as above	3	7	6	26 barrels potatoes	5	4	0
Labourer's wages	3	17	0	Rent	1	5	0
				Left for everything else	0	15	6
Total	£7	4	6	Total	£7	4	6

Appendix D, p. 107.

4. Barony of Dundalk Upper, County Louth (17)
SUNDRY GAINS

Produce of half acre potato ground, 30 barrels eating potatoes at 3s 6d per barrel	5	5	0
Also 10 barrels small potatoes, used for pig and seed; Profit on pig	1	10	0
	£6	15	0
Deduct rent 1 1/2 rood potato ground, tilled and manured by farmer at £2 rood, £3. Other 1/2 rood half price, manured by pig	3	10	0
	3	5	0
Total profit on potato ground, the work on it being done by the labourer and his family when they would otherwise be unemployed	3	5	0
Net produce of fowls in eggs and chickens	0	10	0
Earnings of wife and children by field work, manufacturing, gleaning etc.	0	10	0
Total	£4	5	0

BUDGET OF LABOURERS CONSTANTLY EMPLOYED

INCOME				EXPENDITURE			
Sundry gains as above	4	5	0	52 barrels potatoes	9	2	0
Labourer's wages	9	15	0	Milk, butter etc., called "kitchen" 6d a week	1	6	0
				Turf for fuel	0	10	0
				Rent of cabin	2	0	0
				Left for clothes, tobacco, soap, candles etc.	1	2	0
Total	£14	0	0	Total	£14	0	0

Appendix D. p. 99.

5. Barony of Moyfenragh Lower, Co. Meath (18)
SUNDRY GAINS

Produce of 3 roods conacre potato ground, 45 barrels eating potatoes at 3s 4d per barrel	7	10	0
Also 15 barrels small potatoes, used for pig and seed; Profit on pig	1	10	0
Total	£9	0	0
Deduct rent 2 1/2 roods potato ground at £7 acre, tilled and manured by farmer. Other 1/2 rood rent free, manured by pig	4	7	6
	4	12	6
Total profit on potato ground, the work on it being done by labourer and family when they would otherwise be unemployed	4	12	6
Net produce of fowls in eggs and chickens	0	10	0
Earnings of wife and children by field work, manufacturing, gleaning, etc.	0	10	0
Total	£5	12	6

BUDGET OF LABOURERS CONSTANTLY EMPLOYED

INCOME				EXPENDITURE			
Sundry gains as above	5	12	6	52 barrels potatoes	8	13	0
Deduct for what labourer has to pay neighbour to help with potato digging and planting	1	0	0	Oatmeal	1	10	0
				Turf for fuel	0	10	0
				Kitchen	1	6	0
	4	12	6	Soap and candles	0	5	0
				Tobacco	0	10	0
Labourer's wages	11	10	0	Rent of cabin	1	15	0
				Clothes etc.	1	13	6
Total	£16	2	6	Total	£16	2	6

BUDGET OF LABOURERS OCCASIONALLY EMPLOYED

INCOME				EXPENDITURE			
Sundry gains	5	12	6	52 barrels potatoes	8	13	0
Labourer's wages	7	10	0	Meal for men, a few weeks at harvest and potato digging	0	13	0
				Turf	0	10	0
				Kitchen	0	13	0
				Rent of cabin	1	10	0
				Clothes etc.	1	3	6
Total	£13	2	6	Total	£13	2	6

Appendix D, pp 102-3

At first glance the budgets suggest that the woman's only contribution was the small amount entered as occasional earnings. The general thrust of the evidence in this section is also to the effect that her contribution to household earned income was at best trifling. These comments by witnesses were usually made in reference to the reduced earnings by women in domestic industry, and contrasted with the remembered golden days when women's spinning had regularly paid the rent and determined the family's standard of living, they were accurate enough, but they obscured the reality that women were earning in other ways.

It is not until one turns to baronial examinations into the "employment of women and children"[7] that the inclusion here of pigs and poultry provides explicit evidence that women in labouring families were generally recognised as the rearers of both, each of which made a substantial contribution to the family budget. The main reason why these are not immediately recognisable as women's contribution arises from the patriarchal paradigm already mentioned and the resulting ambiguity of language.

In almost every budget pigs and poultry are listed under labourer's income without attribution to the wife. The only exception is the barony of Clonisk in Laois (see below). In the recorded *words* of witnesses both pigs and poultry are at times spoken of as being kept or reared by the labourer's wife and others as being kept or reared by the labourer. Within the terms of reference of a patriarchal paradigm, or of the common law, this may not have been as contradictory as it seems at first sight, but it did make it more difficult to clearly identify women's income-earning activity.

Once the items contributed by women are identified the significance of their contribution can be examined more closely. The first point to be made is that the budgets pass the criteria for reliability. They were constructed on the consensus reached at the baronial examinations and supplemented by personal enquiries made by the assistant commissioners.

They establish that the wife in a labouring family contributed earned income to the family budget on a regular basis. These earnings are accepted as the pattern, and not as occasional or exceptional. They are a constant and unchanging component of every budget irrespective of the employment status of her husband. The value of sundry gains remains the same while his earnings are the variable factor.

Not only were her earnings a regular part of the budget but they represent a substantial percentage of total household income. Their value can be calculated by adding the profit from pigs and poultry and the occasional earnings of women and children. Since, in virtually every examination into the earnings of women and children, it was agreed that *young* children could earn nothing, allocating the whole to the wife cannot greatly overestimate her total earnings. Any small overestimation that might arise should be more than compensated for by the exclusion of the value of her contribution to the potato crop.

Assessed in this way, the woman's contribution to family income in these baronies ranges from fifteen per cent to twenty-five per cent when her husband was constantly employed to over thirty-five percent when he had very irregular employment. The budgets for yearly expenditure for these baronies show that her contribution more than equalled the rent of cabin and conacre in every case. It bridged the gap between relative comfort and distress, and was an important factor in the family's standard of living and in the difference between surviving and failing to survive by independent labour. If Kells is taken as an example the loss of the wife's total contribution of £2.10s would have eliminated much of the relative comfort enjoyed by the family of the constantly employed labourer. It would have reduced the income of the second class occasionally employed to the level of the third class and that of the third to below that of the fourth. The expenditure budgets demonstrate the seriousness of such a drop.

While none of the other baronial examinations produced a series of graded budgets, some did produce detailed typical budgets and, at others, a partial budget was drawn up or can be constructed from the report.

Barony of Kilconnel, County Galway[8]

Here the estimates were based on a family of husband, wife and three or four young children, renting a cabin and 1 acre for £2. With a family of this size they would also need 2 roods conacre at £3.15 rent, giving a fixed outlay of £5.15.

EARNINGS	£	s	d
Profit on pig and fowl	0	15	0
200 days labour @ 6d a day	5	0	0
Oats grown on 1/2 land after potato crop	2	10	0
Total	£8	5	0

This left £2.10 for clothes, milk, kitchen and all other expenses and it was noted that few labourers could in fact grow grain on more than 6 or 7 perches.

Barony of Dromahair, Co. Leitrim[9]

The parish priest of Innismagrath presented the following average budget:

EARNINGS	£	s	d	EXPENDITURE	£	s	d
To wages, 2 days a wk.	3	10	0	Rent of conacre	4	0	0
Profit on pig, at highest	1	0	0	Salt	0	1	0
Sale of eggs and fowl	0	5	0	Herrings and other			
Sale of flax and yarn	0	13	0	"kitchen"	0	5	0
	£5	8	0	Skimmed milk	0	10	0
If near a town and allowed to sell turf, would make about					£4	16	0
	1	0	0	Balance/contingencies	0	12	0
Total	£6	8	0	Total	£5	8	0

8 Barony of Mohill, Co. Leitrim.[10]

After "much conflicting testimony on the subject" the estimate by Francis O'Beirne, a farmer "whose circumstances afforded him much knowledge of the class" was adopted

EARNINGS	£	s	d	EXPENDITURE	£	s	d
Labour, averaged 4 days a week @ 6d per day	5	4	0	To rent of a cabin	1	0	0
Profit on pig	1	10	0	Rent 1/2 acre conacre	4	0	0
Fowls, if permitted to keep them	0	5	0	To fixed dues to clergy	0	2	0
Earnings of his wife and children by spinning 1d per day at most	0	16	4	To "kitchen" consisting chiefly of buttermilk, etc.	1	14	8
				Total	£6	16	8
				Balance on clothes, tobacco, meal in summer etc.	0	18	8
Total	£7	15	4	Total	£7	15	4

9 Barony of Carbery, Co. Sligo[11]

It "was found extremely difficult to obtain an average account of income applying to any large proportion of the labouring classes." Eventually it was agreed to use the personal budget put forward by George Waters, a "middle-aged man, having a family of a wife and four children," as an example of someone who got "a fair share of employment during the year." His budget for the last twelve months was

EARNINGS	£	s	d	EXPENDITURE	£	s	d
To breaking stones @ 1d per barrel	2	5	0	Rent cabin and 1 rood	1	15	0
To labour in fields, chiefly in spring and harvest	1	0	0	Rent 1 rood conacre, manured and ploughed	1	15	0
Profit on pig	0	13	0	Bog	0	10	0
Profit on poultry	0	2	6	Grass for cow, May to May	1	10	0
Sale of 2 barrels surplus potatoes	1	0	0	Priest at Christmas	0	1	0
Sale of turf	0	10	0	Baptism of his child and churching of his wife	0	2	6
Sale of 2cwt. butter	1	10	0	Candles, soap, tobacco, kitchen	0	19	0
Value of wife's spinning	0	6	0	Total	£6	12	6
Total	£7	6	6	(He owes the priest 1s for Easter dues)			

This budget is the only one to include women's earnings by the sale of butter. Few labouring families could afford to keep a cow in the 1830s but the budget shows how profitable it could be.

10 Barony of Gowran, County Kilkenny[12]

EARNINGS OF COTTIER	£	s	d
Cottier's earnings at 6d a day, c. 260 days	6	10	0
Occasional earnings of wife and grown-up children	0	10	0
Profit on pig at most	2	0	0
Total	£9	0	0

EARNINGS OF OCCASIONAL LABOURER	£	s	d
Man's earnings at 7d a day, 180 days	5	5	0
Earnings of wife and children, who have more leisure and opportunity than country cottier family	1	0	0
But no garden and so fewer pigs on worse terms	0	15	0
Total	£7	0	0

It was noted that only the cottier family could afford to buy soap, candles, tobacco or kitchen.

12 Barony of Clonisk, King's County[13]

EARNINGS	£	s	d
Earnings of labourer permanently employed	7	10	0
Earnings of wife by eggs and fowls	0	15	0
Earnings of wife by pig	1	10	0
Total	£9	15	0

13 Barony of Corcomroe, Co. Clare[14]

It was agreed that an "ordinary labourer" constantly employed might work for 240 days per year, and this table was produced

INCOME	£	s	d
240 days wages	8	0	0
Profit from eggs	0	5	0
Profit from pig	1	10	0
Total	£9	15	0

14 Barony of Iveragh, Co. Kerry[15]

INCOME	£	s	d
Wages from 200 days work	5	0	0
Profit from eggs	0	10	0
Profit from pig	1	0	0
Total	£6	10	0

15 Barony of Trugenackmy, Co. Kerry[16]

INCOME	£	s	d
Wages if constantly employed	6	13	4
Profit from pig	1	10	0
Profit from eggs	0	15	0
Total	£8	18	0

16 Barony of Conello Lower, Co. Limerick[17]

INCOME	£	s	d
Wages from 200 days work at 6d and food	5	0	0
Profit from pigs	1	15	0
Total	£6	15	0

17 Barony of Coshlea, Co. Limerick[18]

INCOME	£	s	d
Wages from 200 days work at 7d per day	7	0	0
Profit from pig	2	0	0
Total	£9	0	0

18 Barony of Middlethird, Co. Tipperary[19]

INCOME	£	s	d
Wages from 250 days work at 8d ("full average")	8	6	8
Profit from pigs	3	0	0
Profit from eggs		"a little"	
Total	£11	6	8
			plus

19 Barony of Decies without Drum, Co. Waterford[20]

INCOME	£	s	d
Wages for 220 days @ 6d and food	5	0	0
Profit from pig	2	0	0
Profit from eggs and fowl	0	10	0
Total	£8	0	0

20 Barony of Middlethird, Co. Waterford[21]

INCOME	£	s	d
Wages from 200 days work (no diet)	7	10	0
Profit from pig	2	0	0
Profit from eggs and fowl		10	0
Total	£10	0	0
Wages for 250 days, with breakfast and dinner	6	5	0
Profit from pig	2	0	0
Profit from eggs	0	10	0
Total	£8	15	0

The report from the Ulster counties gives no actual or estimated "typical" budgets agreed by all present at the baronial examination. However, any precise information that does emerge fits the general pattern of the budgets compiled in other parts of the country. In Iveagh Upper, County Down,[22] a budget of sorts emerged in a roundabout way which, incidentally, illustrates the difficulty in making any assessment of women's contribution in cases where no agreed average budget was produced. The assistant commissioners reported that all present agreed with the statement by one witness that a woman with four children "could not do more than keep the home and family clean; she could not make as much as would buy soap to wash the children's clothes". The commissioners then drew up a typical yearly expenditure account based on what witnesses said a labouring family would spend on different items during the year. This considerably exceeded the figures agreed as the average earnings of a typical labourer. When the discrepancy was pointed out the labourers present explained that the difference was made up by "a pig, by some little spinning, and sometimes the husband went over at harvest time to England or Scotland, and earned as much as released the potatoes."

In the barony of Lecale, Co. Down,[23] it was reported that the labourers saw their only certain source of income as the man's labour, valued at labour £10. 8. 0. per annum. In addition they might get £1. 1.10. from a pig and 10s from the woman's labour.

The pattern of women's contribution in these budgets is strikingly similar to that in the graded budgets. The more detailed the budget the greater is the similarity. It is significant that every detailed budget includes earnings by the woman from pigs, poultry, spinning and occasional labour, indicating how widespread and similar the pattern of her contribution was. A pig or pigs figured in every budget, detailed or not, and in the two County Down baronies. Poultry appeared in all except three budgets, and these three, Gowran, Conello and Coshlea were among the less detailed.

In every case where a budget of any kind was produced, or where some sort of agreed budget can be extracted from the report, income earned by the wife was recorded and this ranged in value from 16 per cent to 37 per cent of total family earned income, with the more detailed budgets giving percentages in the 18 to 30 range.

In considering the budgets as evidence for women's contribution to the household economy of labouring families it has to be kept in mind that none of the budgets, even the most detailed, include *all* economic contributions. The unpaid work of women in the bearing and rearing of children, the care of home and the preparation of food is excluded, as it still is in most official calculations of gross national product, and in assessing the relative contributions of husbands and wives in relation to ownership rights relating to the family home and other property.

Clearly women's work in these unpaid and unevaluated areas made a real economic contribution. Reproduction and childcare was of direct economic significance to labouring parents. In the evidence given at the poor inquiry a frequently advanced explanation for the alleged early age of marriage among labourers was the expectation of producing children who would provide support for the parents' old age. Children can be seen as the only available form of pension investment for retirement. This is not to argue that the only reason labouring parents wanted children was their future economic potential, but that this does appear to have been a consideration for some people.

Women's work, in what would today be described as "housework" in the sense of cleaning and washing house and furnishings, was probably not very time or labour consuming, since the material possessions of most labouring families were very limited. But, whatever about housekeeping in this sense, women did expend much time and labour in transforming the family potato crop into a meal for the family table. One witness said of this area of women's work:

> When they have dug the potatoes from the pits, they still have to collect fuel, and to wash them and boil them; in fact, between setting potatoes, digging potatoes, washing potatoes and boiling potatoes, they have hardly time to attend to anything else. They can never be clean or diligent at other matters until the nature of their food be changed.[24]

The labour involved in transforming the raw potatoes in the family pit to the steaming pot of potatoes for the family meal was as essential to family survival as the labour involved in growing them or in earning the means to purchase them. It may be noted that in some budgets the market value of the potatoes grown and consumed by the family is included in income.

What the budgets allow us to calculate is the extent of these women's contribution using the terms of reference of the dominant patriarchal paradigm for what was seen as having economic value. Even within these limited terms of reference the economic contribution of women was significant. They made a substantial and quantifiable contribution to household income in addition to their contribution in the home and in child rearing. This direct contribution is remarkably similar in content in all parts of the country covered.

It appears that, as their earning opportunities in domestic industry shrank, women in cottier-labouring families turned to new possibilities with considerable success. The rising number of pigs and poultry in rural Ireland was a response to the need of these families to increase their income.[25] Nearly one-third of the pigs raised in County Cork in 1841 were raised on holdings of less than one acre.[26] The development of steam navigation had opened the British market to "many of the lesser articles of farming produce, formerly almost without a market, such as eggs, poultry, honey, etc."[27]

Women's Begging as Family Survival Strategy

There were various stages in a family's slide from independent labour, to the need for some outside assistance, to the final stage when women took to the road as public beggars. Relatives or neighbours might offer help. Private application might be made to them, or requests for work which were a disguised form of begging, or such strategies as happening to be in the vicinity at meal times could be adopted. Next came the stage where the wife, with or without the children, begged more openly in her own neighbourhood or at a distance. The final stage was reached when the entire family, or part of it, left their home for a period of weeks or months. In this last scenario the basic division of labour was that the wife supported herself and the children, and her husband saved to re-establish the family at home. He might remain at home to take what employment became available, or he might travel on his own to other parts of the country or to England or Scotland. He might also accompany his family "on the road", taking any employment he could get on the way, and being supported by his wife's begging as necessary. The detailed budgets of income and expenditure graphically demonstrate how reduction in family income pushed a family down a sliding scale of deprivation which eventually reached starvation levels unless neighbours helped or the woman begged.

In the report from the Moyfenragh examination the assistant commissioners explained that the labourers' answers to questions as to how they survived were "vague and contradictory." When their children were young and numerous it was often "next to impossible to discover how they live", but it was evident that both neighbours' help and begging by the wives and children were resorted to, and that the former was "very prevalent."[28] At Portnahinch the assistant commissioners calculated that the amount of potatoes available to the families of the constantly employed and of the first class of occasionally employed labourers was "amply sufficient." That available to the second class of the occasionally employed would suffice "with strict economy." The third class "undergo great privation and distress during the time when potatoes are scarce and dear, unless, as is very generally the case among that class, their wives and children become beggars for the time, or the kindness of their charitable neighbours relieves their wants."²⁹ The situation in Talbotstown was still more dire. Here the family of the constantly employed labourer had "ample" potatoes and that of the first class of the occasionally employed "sufficient with strict economy." The families of the second class suffered "more or less privation and distress" when potatoes were scarce and dear, and with the third class the "most dreadful misery prevails from the almost total want of employment, unless, as is very generally the case in or near Baltinglass, their wives and children 'take to the road,' or, in other words, become beggars for the time..."³⁰

In the town of Ballina, where all witnesses agreed that unemployment among labourers was particularly high, a number of labourers described their own experience. Pat McNamara told how, in ten years as a landless labourer in Ballina with a conacre potato plot, in "no one year has my earnings kept me up, but my wife has begged to support me and the children." It was a story of day-to-day survival. Sometimes she begged, sometimes a friend helped, sometimes he got an occasional day's employment.

> When we had no other means of living, she was able to keep the family up by her begging solely. Two and a half stone of potatoes each day would be scarce enough for my family; my wife would gather one stone or one and a half stone by begging, in summer; very seldom she has begged in winter, but when she has she has gathered two or three stone.

William Hanley, father of six children under sixteen, explained that his wife "is out now begging, striving to gather a prog for myself and the children."³¹

In Roscrea, County Tipperary, women's begging was an integral part of the family economy. The rent was generally paid from the labourer's wages or partly in labour. The profit from the pig paid for clothes. "What remains of both wages and profit is set apart to buy potatoes, and if it be not enough, the wife must make up the difference by begging."³²

In the parish of Templemichael and Ballymacormac in

County Longford work for labourers was scarce both in winter and summer. Survival was easier in winter, even for the family of a town labourer who had no stock or potatoes themselves since they had no conacre. However, in winter the small farmers had plenty of potatoes and the town labourers' wives took salt herrings to the country and exchanged them with the farmers for "two or three times their value in potatoes." In the summer when potatoes were scarce and distress was rife, the labourer's wife might reveal their plight to a better-off neighbour to seek help, or children might loiter around farm houses in the hope of being fed. Families also resorted to purchasing meal and potatoes on credit, or might pawn clothes or sell their pig. The final option was for the wife and children to beg while the husband went away to seek work.[33]

In County Antrim, where begging appears to have been less prevalent than in many other parts of the country, reports from about half the parishes said that the wives of unemployed labourers begged while half said they did not.

At Naas, County Kildare, it was said that when the Connaught labourers came to cut the harvest they accepted lower wages, thus putting the locals out of work with the inevitable result that the latter's "wives and children are of course obliged to beg for their support."[34]

At Burrishoole, County Mayo, it was reported that when

> stocks of potatoes failed, the general rule is, that the wives and families beg in a remote part of the country. Strangers, similarly circumstanced, come into this parish; so that at certain seasons of the year there is nearly an exchange of paupers between parishes. The men generally remain at home and never beg, at least publicly.[35]

The summer months were the season of the year which saw the greatest family exodus. This was the period between the exhaustion of one year's potato crop and the readiness of the next. In many parts of the country it was also a season when employment was particularly scarce.

At the parochial examinations in all parts of the country

witnesses agreed that the vast majority of the seasonal yearly invasion of strolling beggars in their locality was comprised of able-bodied women accompanied by young children. Some of these women were identified as widows but the majority were the "wives of labourers." Estimates of the proportion of all strolling beggars these women represented ranged from two-thirds to nine-tenths. So widespread was this pattern that one of the commissioners, G. E. Cornewall Lewis, pointed to a problem that would arise if vagrants were prosecuted.

> It is...observed, that the main body of vagrants in Ireland are the wives and children of able-bodied labourers, who beg in the summer when the stock of potatoes is exhausted; the husbands themselves rarely beg. Now, if the wife is apprehended and convicted for vagrancy, what will be done with the husband and children?[36]

Women's potential contribution through begging was taken into account in decisions to marry. In Ballina one labourer, claiming to speak for all present, explained that a poor man would marry early without any dowry with his bride. The couple married

> without any fear of being worse off than before; for when he has no work, if he is ashamed to beg himself, the wife and children will beg and support him; or, if he chooses to take a fling out of the country to some other part of Ireland, or to the English harvest, they will support themselves by begging till he comes back.[37]

For the Poor Law commissioners begging, and particularly begging combined with vagrancy, was an undesirable mode of relief because it did not operate on the principle of distinguishing between the "deserving" and the "undeserving" poor, and for this reason they believed it contributed to the further spread of begging.

> The great cause of the extensive mendicancy which drains and impoverishes the small farmers of Ireland is their want of system and good judgment in bestowing relief. It is

given by them without discrimination, without regard to the character, nay, without even knowledge of the circumstances of the applicant.[38]

From the point of view of the cottier-labourer population begging and vagrancy had the aspect more of a vast informal system of mutual insurance against unemployment. Indeed, the commissioners themselves recognised that women's begging played this role in the household economy of these families. In their first report they noted that one of the major problems facing them in their task was to guage the extent of Irish poverty. This they found to include the vast majority of the population, a majority which was "constantly fluctuating between mendicancy and independent labour."[39] In their third report they noted that the "wives and children of many are occasionally obliged to beg: they do so reluctantly, and with shame, and in general go to a distance from home that they may not be known."[40]

For the labouring family begging was a strategy for family survival when all efforts to do so by independent labour had failed. The evidence of the inquiry shows that it was an effective strategy. The constant report is that when independent labour failed families fell into serious distress unless they turned to begging. It is the families who refused to beg in such circumstances who were in real misery. The contrast led the assistant commissioners at Killaloe to comment that it was "strange that the labourers do not envy the condition of the beggars."[41] Begging as a family survival strategy was women's work and with it women took over the main, and sometimes the sole, breadwinner role in the family.

Conclusion

Since only a limited amount of the information collected in the poor inquiry has been considered here it would be premature to attempt an overall assessment of what it tells about the status and role of women in Irish society. However, the information used for this paper does raise questions and suggest pointers.

In good times and bad labourers' wives shared the provider-breadwinner role with their husbands. If the location of status and power within families was determined by the economic contribution of their different members then the evidence of the poor inquiry suggests that men and women in labouring families should have enjoyed relatively equal status and power.

Contemporary commentators, usually observers from outside Ireland, did not believe that this was the case. They tended to see women in labouring families as a generally downtrodden group, overburdened with work, oppressed by their husbands and living in affectionless marriages.[42] At least one of the poor inquiry commissioners formed similar views. J. E. Bicheno argued that

> extreme poverty has a tendency to degrade the woman lower than the man, as may be inferred from her being worse clothed, and from her being the first to suffer privations; the very reverse of what happens in a better condition of life. She is made the drudge and the slave. The man's pride will not suffer him to ask alms, but he sends forth his wife and children as beggars. In an improving district, shoes and stockings are first seen on the man. The woman's position before marriage being one of entire dependence, the same necessity of courting her affections does not exist as in countries where women can obtain the means of subsistence.[43]

George Nicholls, who presented his own separate report, observed that women's "duties appear to be much more laborious than those of the same class in England. Their dress, too, is very inferior, and so likewise seems their general position in society."[44] Bicheno's view that, while a woman in Ireland, "does not take full status as a wife, she takes higher as a mother," supports this view to some extent while also qualifying it.

On the other hand, folklore sources indicate that marriage in Ireland conferred status as a "full member of the community" on both men and women,[45] and that a wife was seen to have an "absolute right as an independent money-earner, coupled with the right to dispose of the money earned as she wished."[46]

The categories of the destitute in Irish society, listed above, indicate that the politics of gender, that is, the social, political and economic consequences for individuals which resulted from their being born male or female, were a factor in determining a person's status on the scale from rich to poor. For example, the reasons why illegitimate children and their mothers were found among the regularly destitute did not lie in any biological determinism. These reasons included a value-system that attached a label, either "legitimate" or "illegitimate", to every new-born infant, as well as a distribution of resources that placed the "illegitimate" child and its mother, but not its father, in serious danger of destitution.

In the case of labourers' wives the paradigm of male-female relationships in the minds of the organisers of the poor inquiry obscured to the point of near invisibility the fact that these women were active breadwinners. From this it does not necessarily follow that labouring men or women did or did not share the same view of these relationships. However, if the commentators correctly interpreted what they observed, it suggests that a patriarchal paradigm did influence relationships between labouring men and women. If it did, it is likely to have distorted the operation of a direct causal relationship between economic contribution and status and power.

The role of begging in the household economy has implications regarding roles in labouring families. Apart from the question why the report does not give explicit recognition to the contribution of women's begging, there is the further question why able-bodied men rarely or never begged. Witnesses explained it on some logical grounds, such as that women earned more at begging than men, and that there was generally more work available for men. But perhaps the most frequently recurring explanation, and one on which there was universal consensus, was that men were more ashamed to beg than women. Men were said to have more feelings of "independence." They were reluctant to see their wives and children begging either but "let" them when things got very bad. It appears that what men were ashamed of was not begging in principle—they did not after all refuse to live on its proceeds—but to be seen begging themselves. The issue seems to have been a somewhat vulnerable masculine identity based on the need to be seen *not* to be doing something. By contrast women could be seen as having more robust self-identity and to have been the realists who did what had to be done.

Begging combined with vagrancy raises questions about authority and autonomy. Here was an accepted pattern of family economy whereby women left their husbands, took their children with them and travelled to distant parts of the country where they were not known, and successfully earned enough to provide food, shelter and other necessities for themselves and their children for a period of weeks or months.[47] This is not a scenario which suggests that husbands exercised strict control over their wives' behaviour, sexual or otherwise, or over their freedom of movement. It strongly suggests that these women, whether or not they were oppressed by their husbands and by Irish society generally, as some observers believed, were also resourceful, independent and self-sufficient.

These issues and others await further research. However, the evidence from the poor inquiry considered here indicates that the politics of power, status, autonomy and decision-making in labouring families will not be fully and satisfactorily explained in terms of a single model, whether that of an oppressor-oppressed relationship between men and women, or of a one-to-one relationship between economic contribution on the one hand and power and status on the other.

The gender relationships specific to a particular group, time and place appear to develop from the interaction between the political, social and economic structures of the national and local society, the location within these of the group in question, and the currently prevailing paradigm of male-female relationships. As feminist historiography develops the evidence increasingly indicates that the obverse of this is also true, and that historical research into the structures of a society or the experience and contribution of individuals and groups requires the use of gender analysis in conjunction and interaction with other analytic approaches, such as, for example, those based on class, colour, race, religion, and many more.[48]

Notes

1 *Reports of his Majesty's Commissioners for Inquiring into the Condition of the Poorer Classes in Ireland*, (Hereafter *Poor Inquiry*) First report, H. C. 1835 (369) xxxii, pt. v.
2 See Anne V. O'Connor, "The revolution in girls' secondary education in Ireland, 1860-1910" in Mary Cullen (ed.), *Girls Don't Do Honours: Irish Women in Education in the 19th and 20th Centuries* (Dublin, 1987), pp 31-54; Eibhlin Breathnach, Charting new waters; women's experience and higher education 1879-1904", in *ibid.*, pp 55-78.
3 *Poor Inquiry*, supplement to appendix D, H. C. 1836 (36), xxxi, p. 1. Joel Mokyr notes the "rampant" confusion but uses the estimates by controlling for error. Idem, *Why Ireland Starved* (London, 1985), p. 25.
4 *Poor Inquiry*, p. viii.
5 *Ibid.*, pp ix-x.
6 Sir William Blackstone, *Commentaries on the Laws of England* (London, 1826), ii, p. 432.
7 *Poor Inquiry*, appendix D, pp 84-92.
8 *Ibid.*, p. 92.
9 *Ibid.*
10 *Ibid.*, p. 94.
11 *Ibid.*, p. 95.
12 *Ibid.*, p. 97.
13 *Ibid.*, p. 98.
14 *Ibid.*, p. 108.
15 *Ibid.*
16 *Ibid.*, p. 109.
17 *Ibid.*

18 *Ibid.*
19 *Ibid.*
20 *Ibid.*, p. 110.
21 *Ibid.*, p. 111
22 *Ibid.*, p. 112.
23 *Ibid.*
24 *Ibid.*, p. 86.
25 L. M. Cullen, *Life in Ireland* (London, 1968), p. 121.
26 James S. Donnelly Jr. *The Land and the People of Nineteenth Century Cork* (London, 1975), p. 43.
27 *Report of the Select Committee on the State of the Poor in Ireland* H. C. 1830 (589) vii, p. 5.
28 *Poor Inquiry*, appendix D, p. 102.
29 *Ibid.*
30 *Ibid.*, p. 106.
31 *Ibid.*, appendix A, pp. 367-9
32 *Ibid.*, p. 454.
33 *Ibid.*, pp. 405-6.
34 *Ibid.*
35 *Ibid.*, p. 371.
36 *Ibid.*, Remarks on the third report by George Cornewall Lewis Esq., H. C. 1837 (91) 1i, p. 18.
37 *Ibid.*
38 *Poor Inquiry*, Third Report, H. C. 1836 (43) xxx, p. 4.
39 *Poor Inquiry*, First Report, p. vi.
40 *Poor Inquiry*, Third Report, p. 4.
41 *Ibid.*
42 S. J. Connolly, "Marriage in pre-Famine Ireland" in Art Cosgrove (ed.), *Marriage in Ireland* (Dublin, 1985), p. 89.
43 *Poor Inquiry*, H. C. 1836 (42) xxxiv, p. 19.
44 *Ibid.*, H. C. 1837 (69) ii, p. 28.
45 Caoimhin O Danachair, "Marriage in Irish folk tradition," in Cosgrove, *op. cit.*, pp 99-100.
46 *Ibid.*, p. 46.
47 Potatoes were the usual currency of begging. They were the cheapest and most readily available items to the donor and they could be used to purchase lodgings and other necessities by barter or money exchange.
48 For the most recent review article see Gisela Bock, "Women's history and gender history; aspects of an international debate," *Gender and History*, no. 1, vol. 1 (Spring 1989), pp 7-30.

Workhouses and Irish Female Paupers 1840-70

Dympna McLoughlin

Background to the Poor Law

The Poor Law Act of 1838 was the basis from which 130, later to be increased to 163, workhouses and Poor Law districts were set up throughout Ireland. Instead of being grafted onto existing social structures or prevailing forms of landscape organization the Irish Poor Law was implemented through new administrative units called Poor Law districts.[1] These districts were forged through the merging of several townlands, and each district had its own workhouse. [2]

Workhouses were deliberately grim buildings and were a physical manifestation on the landscape of the prevailing social doctrine with respect to the destitute poor. They were set up primarily as institutions of containment. Their secondary concern was the diminution of pauperism rather than the alleviation of distress.[3] With the establishment of a regular steamship service linking Ireland and Britain in 1815, Irish labourers were no longer contained in their own island but could effortlessly expand their horizons and seasonal job opportunities to include England, Scotland and Wales. In times of greatest need for manual labour such as the rural seasonal agricultural cycle or in the industrial realm where skilled and unskilled labour was needed in building up the infrastructure to facilitate the growing momentum of the Industrial Revolution, Irish labourers duly obliged. While many of these labourers remained seasonal, adapting their travels to correspond with the work rhythms of the home and host areas, there were others who responded to the labour crises in Ireland by moving permanently with their families to Great Britain. Many of these labourers were unable to maintain their families on a seasonal wage. Others, through illness or misfortune, were unable to secure employment. These labourers, men and women, remained on as destitute in Britain. It was the increasing visibility of these Irish poor on the English scene and their perceived threat to both wages and social order which provided the principal impetus for the 1838 Poor Law Act and the initiation of the workhouse system of relief.

In an age of laissez-faire individualism, poverty was not seen to have a social cause, but was an outward manifestation of the failure of individuals to secure work and support themselves as a result of their own particular vices such as idleness, sloth or laziness. However, when individuals were destitute through illness or misfortune they were perceived in a new light as the "deserving poor." It was for this category of people that the workhouse was intended. The Poor Law administrators wanted only a minimal mode of relief made available to these "deserving poor" otherwise there was a fear that paupers would readily give up work preferring to be supported by the state. Thus ran the theory behind the framing of the Poor Law. However, its implementation and functioning reveals something quite different. Despite claims of centralization and uniform national working the fact is that each Poor Law district responded to the needs of its own micro-regional economy. A lively exposition of this chasm is gained through the study of the women who utilized the workhouse in the period 1840-70. The aim of this paper is to reveal the way pauper women used this theoretically rigid institution to suit their own particular needs (needs that changed according to the weather and season, the employment market, their health and age, the number of children they had and their own life cycle), and in the process to give some insight into the nature of nineteenth century female pauper life.

Workhouses were capable of accommodating up to three thousand inmates in times of crisis such as the famine and its aftermath. From the mid 1860s through to the the 1870s, the numbers declined to their pre-1845 level of under a thousand inmates and never again reached famine proportions. As Table 1 illustrates, able-bodied females constituted the largest category of workhouse inmates. Adult able-bodied females tended to outnumber their male counterparts by a ratio of 3:1. The proportion of aged and infirm males and females tended to be comparable though infirm females were slightly over-represented. The number of females is most exaggerated in the Cork Union for 1860 where the categories of able-bodied and aged/infirm females constituted over half of the total workhouse population.

Table 1 Categories of Workhouse Inmates in New Ross (1853), Cork (1860) and Kenmare (1850) Unions.

	Able-bodied		Aged/infirm		Youth	Children	Children	Infants
	M	F	M	F	(9-15)	(5-9yrs)	(2-5yrs)	
New Ross	185	559	145	153	252	253	80	89	92
Cork	170	562	299	575	163	104	99	103	133
Kenmare	329	848	145	149	539	524	128	33	129

Source: Minute Books of New Ross, Cork and Kenmare Unions.

The large number of pauper women resident within the workhouse undermines the common assumption that all women functioned within a framework of stable domesticity. Further evidence of the fact that these women were not tied to a single abode was their high rate of geographical mobility. Indeed, some of them gained notoriety among workhouses hundred of miles apart. Despite the rigidity of workhouse admission procedures, which were by law strictly limited to paupers within certain territorial confines, the lives and horizons of pauper women were not by any means bounded by parochial or workhouse boundaries. A common concern voiced in the workhouse minutes[4] reveals the exasperation of the functionaries at the defiance shown by these women to the Poor Law administrative boundaries. Many meetings were held to decide the chargeability of female paupers who seemed to be rooted in no fixed place. The absence of a rooted domestic existence is evident in the frequent, angry and frantic tirades of workhouse functionaries against foundlings, infanticide and the temporary abandonment of children. Finally, the inappropriateness of utilizing a concept of domesticity is manifest throughout this study in that pauper women rarely, if ever, were dependant on their husbands, fathers or sons for their security, protection and daily sustenance.

Notions about the ignorance and vulnerability of these pauper women must likewise be questioned. It may be argued that these concepts are aspects of a nineteenth century middle class ideology of "sentimentality and romanticism" that presented all women as idealized creatures and the passive recipients of masculine attention, affection and security.[5] This social ideology did not percolate to the female pauper culture, despite sporadic attempts by middle and upper class reformist women to train workhouse girls into codes of "proper" behaviour. Workhouse women may have been ignorant in the sense that they did not have a basic education or the three Rs, and were lacking in the social graces and coy codes of feminine public conduct. However, they were certainly not ignorant about the lay of the land, the availability of work, the economic opportunities in England, the movement of their men or the location and availability of medical attention when ill. Furthermore, when the Boards of Guardians put forward proposals to assist female paupers to emigrate, those who wished to emigrate flocked to the workhouse with amazing rapidity. For example, in the Enniscorthy workhouse eighty-two women were assisted to emigrate to North America in the period from April to September 1857. The following year the Guardians noticed that

> many females wanted admittance to the house, and it appeared were drawn to the house upon a flying report that

the board were about to send out a number of emigrants to America. They were able-bodied and evidently not in a destitute state.[6]

These enterprising women were disappointed to learn that the "board had no intention of sending out emigrants this season."[7]

Pauper women were not vulnerable in the sense of being timid individuals seeking only to be placed under the protection of a husband or father. Many of them, after leaving or being left by their men, lived for long years on their own, often bringing up large families unaided. Yet there was a certain vulnerability about these pauper women though it was not the artificial vulnerability of timid, weak and helpless women written about in romantic journals of the time. Rather it was their vulnerability to unscrupulous men in positions of power—to masters who overworked them until they were ill and then got rid of them, to workhouse functionaries who abused them physically and sexually and Boards of Guardians who were deaf to their complaints of cruelty and abuse. They were vulnerable also in that, whilst burdened with the lethargy of pregnancy and the weakness of childbirth and nursing, the fathers of their children were not obliged to pay anything towards their maintenance.

The reasons why women entered the workhouse were many. It is suggested here that there was a major disparity between the stated reasons for entry and the actual ones. According to the Poor Law Act, relief was only to be given to individuals who were unable to support themselves or their families. Not surprisingly then many female inmates stated themselves incapacitated through injury or sickness, or rendered destitute and friendless on the death of a parent or relative. None mentioned the fact that they wished to participate in one of the proposed workhouse emigration schemes or that they needed shelter and sustenance on their travels from one part of the country to another. Most times they entered the workhouse along with their children not when destitute, but when the subsistence nature of the family economy was in crisis, such as the "hungry month" of May, before the potatoes were ready for eating, or during particularly bad winter weather when they could no longer travel, sell or beg.

A regular feature of the workhouse minute books was the admission of single women who had left the workhouse to go into situations and returned pregnant. The willingness of these women to name the father of their child caused but the occasional man to leave town, such as the father of Julia Doyle's child named as John Deveraux of Dromgard in Enniscorthy in 1857.[8] Deveraux was unusual in fearing the repercussions of his actions. For the most part, the naming of the father was a formality as the majority of these men were the pauper women's employers against whom no prosecution charge would stick, or else they were servants, often already married. Sarah Ryan left the workhouse at eleven years of age to work for a Mr Patrick Ryan of Ballinakillin, county Wexford. Ten years later she and her child sought re-admission to the workhouse naming Tom Ryan, the brother of her employer, as the father.[9] Similarly, Nicholas Hamilton, who worked as a groom for Mr Ashton in Enniscorthy took no responsibility for Jane Timmons and their child, with the result that she too sought the workhouse as her only available refuge.[10]

Not all these single pregnant women sought out the workhouse as a first option. Some stayed there if their families or friends were unable to maintain them. After having her child, twenty-three year old Mary Breen took to begging but the inclemency of the winter weather made it impossible for her to procure sustenance by this method. She then had no option in the short term but to apply to the workhouse for admittance.[11]

Other common types of admission were older women, still with young children, who were no longer physically able to do manual work because of injury or feebleness. Such was the case of Margaret Mc Donnell and her daughter who, having been formerly employed in cutting turnips, could no longer do this work but "who would work in Bownell's Mill if the prospect came up."[12] Similarly forty year old Sally

Collins and her child could no longer work as she had cut her hand. It was discovered later that she was also pregnant. Meanwhile Bridget Murphy, aged sixteen, could not work because of a scalded foot.[13] Mary Murphy, who previously had earned her living "by selling a handfull of herrings from the sea-side up to Balagh and very much around Glenbyran," was also incapacitated and entered the workhouse.[14] Many of the older women were admitted after taking ill on the road while going about their travelling as was Anne Murphy, aged seventy-two, admitted to the Enniscorthy Union, and Peggy Foley, aged fifty.[15] Some of these women in their fifties were admitted into the workhouse because they could no longer get work. Mary Armstrong searched for work for six months before giving up and applying to the workhouse.[16] Occasionally women in their early forties sought the workhouse on becoming incapacitated through a pregnancy. Thus the previously mentioned Sally Collins and her twelve year old child entered the workhouse, the clerk duly noting that her children had different fathers.[17]

Sometimes women entered the workhouse proclaiming themselves deserted by their men, often many years after the actual event. Johanna Bolger's husband was transported to Australia leaving her to care for two children aged ten and twelve. She survived well without him for nearly eleven years (albeit admitting the father of the youngest child was a servant boy where she worked) and then entered the workhouse proclaiming herself deserted.[18] Although she was not strictly deserted, sixteen year old Mary Mc Call's husband could not provide for her, incarcerated as he was in Wexford jail. She too sought workhouse relief.[19] Shortly after Mary Donnelly's marriage her husband deserted her, and she would not return home as her mother, who lived on a few acres, proclaimed herself unable to support her.[20] Other young women who could no longer depend on their families for relief included twenty year old Catherine Byrne whose father was a labourer with many children and was no longer able to support an adult daughter.[21] Her situation was just one of many in which a labourer's wage was not sufficient to maintain a large dependent family, and certainly not to take care of an able-bodied adult.

Some parents were glad to be rid of their grown children and declared themselves unable to keep them. Mary Sinnot, aged fourteen and of "weak mind", was unable to earn her living while living with her mother in Liverpool.[22] Her mother duly despatched her back to Ireland, much to the considerable chagrin of the Board of Guardians of the Enniscorthy Union. Likewise, Mary Anne Wilson, aged seventeen, was also returned to the workhouse. All the Board of Guardians' efforts in ridding themselves of the girl had been in vain and now, once again, they had the additional expense of her maintenance.[23] Incidents such as these drew the workhouse Guardians towards the advantages of assisted emigration of female paupers to America and Australia. At least they were guaranteed not to come back.

The Mobility of Pauper Women

One of the associated features of pauperism was an immense geographical mobility. In defiance of the various Poor Law administrative boundaries, paupers wandered the length and breadth of the country entering the nearest workhouse in times of need. As an attempt to curb the geographical mobility among a subsistence stratum of society the Poor Law failed utterly. Efforts to contain the poor within areas of their birth, in some futile effort to put an order on the seeming chaos and flux of pauper life, never succeeded. Because of the subsistence nature of their lives, as beggars, travellers and wandering hucksters, paupers needed access to a large and intimately known geographical area. Their frequent and temporary need for the institution of the workhouse was incorporated into their travelling life. Neither was this travelling the domain of only one sex; both men and women participated equally depending on their own circumstances.

Much time and effort at the meetings of the Poor Law Guardians went into deciding the chargeability of inmates. The greater the number chargeable to one area the greater the expense to the rate payers of that particular region. In many instances the chargeability of an inmate was so complex and difficult that they were charged to a category called the "union-at-large." This category was formulated to classify paupers who seemed to be without a place of origin. It would be a grave error to perceive this category as a miscellaneous rag-bag of undifferentiated pauperism. This would be to ignore the commitment to order, exact numbers, and precise detail which characterised the new scientific methods of record keeping of the nineteenth century. Rather, the charging of inmates to the Union at large was a last resort, the irksome and unhappy culmination of a lengthy and often expensive process of deciding a pauper's place of primary residence. The Poor Law Guardians came slowly to realise that the two—paupers and place of primary residence—seldom went together and this requirement for the admission of inmates was, strictly speaking, unworkable and largely ignored. Thus the number of paupers in the Union at large category was always at a considerable level.[24]

Again it is worth pointing out that the administration of the workhouses was not carried out uniformly throughout the land but varied according to the vicissitudes of local economies. The administrative practices of some Unions actually promoted mobility among paupers. In 1848 the Master of the Armagh Union reported that 160 itinerant paupers had been accommodated with supper, a bed and breakfast during the week. A year later in the same Union the Guardians were unhappy with the practice of admitting up to 15 paupers nightly realizing that

> this is in fact a premium to tramps and an encouragement to that very act which is punishable by statute. Any person wandering abroad in search of alms, or going from one union to another in search of poor law relief is liable to be admitted to gaol as a vagrant. No able bodied person of that class should be received in a state of health and only in extreme cases where there are young children.[25]

Similarly, in the Coleraine Union, the practice of keeping

paupers from Saturday to Monday as vagrant lodgers was discontinued.[26]

Another practice encouraging mobility and promoted by the more benevolent of workhouse functionaries was the giving of documents to paupers going to another part of the country, wherein they recommended the Masters of the several workhouses, at which they might apply, to afford them food and shelter for one night.[27] The workhouses which carried out these practices were probably more in touch with the reality of pauper life than those Unions who tried, always unsuccessfully, to adhere rigidly to the letter of the law.

The issue of the proper chargeability of the children of single mothers took up a considerable amount of time at the Board of Guardians' meetings as the movements of pauper mothers were considerable and complex. For example, Bridget Doyle who was aged twenty-two, single, and pregnant, sought admission to the workhouse in Enniscorthy for her approaching confinement. Accounting for her movements over three years she stated that she

> came from Ferns where she lived one month, was in the care of Mr Rudd for two months, was in Mr Rowson's in the townland of Forties for three months and Samuel Rowson is the father of the child; was at P Murphy's in Lower Ferns for nine months, at Knocaduff, Ballydaggin twelve months and for six months previously in the same district with Mr Edward Doyle; and lived for six months with Mr Sullivan in the diocese of Rossard.[28]

Bridget Doyle's longest stay with any one employer was nine months and her considerable geographical mobility was a cause of alarm. However, one redeeming feature of Bridget's workhouse application was the fact that she had been in continuous employment with named employers rather than taking to the travelling life as a hawker or beggar.

Another case which caused grave concern to the Guardians of the same Union was that of Eliza Connor, mainly because of her frequent flittings in and out of the workhouse, but also because she could not make up her mind whether to have her child registered as a Protestant or Catholic. The details of Eliza's entry and exits from the workhouse are extracted from the Enniscorthy Union Minutes and presented here as they give a good indication of the fluidity of the workhouse and furthermore support the argument that workhouses did not function as institutions of absolute containment.[29] Alas, the precise details of where Eliza spent her time when not in the workhouse were not included in the original Minutes.

> Admitted 8th June 1849, discharged 22nd June 1849.
> Admitted 19th November 1850, discharged 11th February 1851.
> Admitted 19th June 1851, discharged 8th July 1851.
> Admitted 8th July 1852, discharged 12th July 1852.
> Admitted 13th January 1853, 8 months pregnant and her child was born on the 12th February and she left the workhouse on 15th March 1853.
> Admitted 24th March 1853, discharged 2nd August 1853.
> Admitted 3rd November 1853, discharged 6th February 1854.
> Admitted 6th March 1854, discharged 11th June 1854.
> Admitted 7th September 1854, discharged 26th July 1855.
> Admitted 13th December 1855.

There does not seem to be any pattern or seasonal uniformity in her entries to the workhouse. She sought relief both in winter and summer and her longest stay within the house was in the eight-month period June to December 1855, whilst her shortest stay was the four days from the 8th to the 12th July 1852. It is evident that Eliza Connor's stays within the workhouse became longer and more frequent after her child was born.

Deserted Wives and Independent Women

The particular norms and values of middle class society can be evidenced in the mixture of effort and bluster by which the Poor Law Guardians sought out the parents of "orphan" children and the husbands of "deserted" wives. These rulings were part of a middle class ideology of the family where the husband was the provider and the woman and the children his dependants. Many of the Poor Law Guardians accepted this ideology uncritically. From this ideology came the various rules and regulations of the Poor Law Act compelling men to support their wives or risk prosecution and for pauper women to remain at all times with their young.

Pauper women did not depend on their men in the same way as middle class women did. Many of them could look after themselves, becoming dependant only in the latter stages of pregnancy or when burdened down with a number of small children. They did not retire from active life on marriage or on commencing motherhood and many of them experienced these two life phenomena in reverse order. Marriage for pauper women was without a "settling down" aspect. A possible motivation in getting married was not the legitimacy it gave to the children of such unions but that it gave pauper men and women a certain respectability in middle class eyes enabling them to become the virtuous and thus the "deserving" poor. It also gave them a social norm to deviate from, to proclaim themselves widowed or deserted and thus entitled to workhouse relief. However, much more research is needed on the idea of marriage and pauper life. The nature and duration of this marital attachment defied the contemporary middle class notion of that institution. Finally the absence of a marital contract was no obstacle to single women forming long term attachments to men or married women forming alternative alliances. What these attachments brought to the fore was the risk of pregnancy. With a constant partner, a greater number of pregnancies were likely to occur. Knowledge of contraceptive methods coupled with the significant infant mortality of the period may be factors in accounting for the fact that few of the pauper women in the workhouse are listed as having more than four children. Again this is a difficult area, considering the many ploys paupers had in keeping a true account of their domestic situations away from the Poor Law Administrators and the many inaccuracies contributed by the functionaries themselves in their own record keeping.

Women presenting themselves as deserted were a

considerable source of aggravation to the Poor Law Commissioners. All cases of deserted women were scrupulously noted and prosecution proceedings issued against their husbands. The prosecution of these men despite the time, cost and effort involved was deemed essential, otherwise the workhouse would "be overrun with such cases and the Union improperly charged for their support."[30] Some Unions advertised rewards ranging from ten shillings to one pound for information leading to the apprehension of "persons guilty of desertion."[31] Not all women were anxious to have their husbands prosecuted for desertion and those women who refused to swear evidence against their husbands in a court of law were dismissed from he workhouse. It could be suggested that this temporary desertion of wife and children was part of a subsistence family survival strategy. In Londonderry in 1843 warrants were sent to Glasgow for John Bryson of the city of Derry and John Gallagher of Ruskey, Co. Donegal.[32] More than likely these men were partaking in the longstanding practice of seasonal migration from that area.

Those men prosecuted for desertion usually had to be transported back across the Irish Channel. Thus it cost £5-00-06 to bring one deserter back from Liverpool to Limerick in 1852[33] and £6-09-07 to bring yet another offender from Scotland to Ballymena.[34] No Poor Law Union could afford to invest so much time and money in bringing back deserting husbands so one or two successful prosecutions were felt to be sufficient in acting as a deterrent. The successful carrying of a prosecution charge meant that the offender was imprisoned.

The women who did issue information against their husbands might be presumed to be truly deserted in that their husbands had no intention of returning to them. The trades of these men were not always specified in the Minutes. However, the largest occupational category given for men was soldiers.[35] These men generally entered British regiments under the pretence of being unmarried. The Paymaster General of the various regiments must have received a significant amount of correspondence from the clerks of Irish Poor Law Unions with respect to desertion cases.[36] Once the men acknowledged their wives and children, a portion of their military pay was transferred for their dependants' support.

Women, although deserted, often had precise information on their husband's whereabouts. An awareness of the exact location and situation of a husband none too anxious to return and take his wife out of the workhouse is evidenced by the complaint of Eliza Wright to the Dublin South Board of Guardians in 1855. She claimed that her husband was a whipmaker in London and earning good wages and "requested the intervention of the Guardians in her favour."[37]

For many cases, however, it can be argued that an agreement was reached between husband and wife that he in some instances, she in others, would seek work unhampered, whilst the other would tide themselves over the lean period by a short residence within the workhouse. Thus the reluctance of women to give evidence against their men. In cases where the workhouse functionaries discovered the husbands of "deserted" wives working outside the workhouse the wives were immediately discharged. The situation in Limerick workhouse in 1846 was not unusual. The husbands of Bridget McMahony, Jane O'Shaugnessy, Mary Murphy, Margaret McGrath, Anne Hartnell, Mary Barry and Betty Kennedy were discovered to be working locally and they were all instantly discharged. Neither was it unusual for men to be discharged from the workhouse if they had a wife or children working outside. In the same Limerick workhouse in 1845, Michael Coghlan was discharged when it was noted that "his wife and children are outside and in employment."[38] Orders were also issued for the removal of a man named Sullivan on discovery that "he had a wife outside in comfortable circumstances."[39]

If pauper women worked independently of their men they travelled independently of them also, as will be evident with respect to emigration. In some instances a woman might only travel as far as Dublin whilst her husband and family remained in the workhouse.[40] In other instances, all links with husband and children were severed and the women travelled to England or America to start a new life there.[41] The desertion of a spouse was not always by men. Women too, left their men but obviously never cited this reason in their application for workhouse relief.

Many of these pauper women were decision makers in their own right and their consent could not automatically be presumed to schemes agreeable to their men or indeed to the workhouse authorities. In the Limerick Union in 1852 Thomas Hackett applied to the Poor Law Guardians for permission to be assisted to emigrate to North America along with his two children.[42] He then told the Guardians that his wife was outside and in service and that she appeared unwilling to emigrate. The Poor Law Guardians were loath to sanction the emigration of Hackett and his two children without his wife, stating that

> Commissioners will not consent to a separation which may be regarded as permanent between the man and his wife, whereby she may become hereafter a burden on the rates of the union.[43]

However, Hackett's wife, for whatever reason, did eventually consent to go and the whole family duly emigrated. Examples of pauper women evaluating their circumstances and making a decision favourable to their own interest are numerous. In certain cases where the decision of a pauper inmate was at odds with that preferred by the workhouse functionaries, then it was the woman who suffered. The aged Mary McMahon, an inmate in the Cork Union in 1855, was offered a situation minding a child, which she refused to accept saying she "would rather stay where she was."[44] The old woman was then ordered to be discharged from the workhouse, a fate she probably preferred to the drudgery of minding someone else's child for what was an uncertain pittance in most cases.

The Nature of the Links between Women and Children
The Deserted
The temporary abandonment—desertion—of children is not indicative of callousness on the behalf of pauper women. Rather it was essential if these women were to survive themselves. Women burdened with children were unable to enter situations unless they could leave them with their husband, friends or relatives or, failing all these, the workhouse. This separation from their children was only for the length of time it took women to gather enough means to provide for their children. As an alternative to desertion some women applied to the Poor Law Guardians for permission to leave their children in the Union whilst they took up outside employment. If the request was refused, which it automatically should have been if the Poor Law Act was strictly enforced, then the destitute parent would have had no option but to enter the workhouse also. The Poor Law Guardians would then have been left with a dependent family, remaining on in the Union without any hope of ever leaving. Furthermore, if it were known in pauper circles that certain Unions rigidly adhered to the letter of the Poor Law, then a "real" desertion of children was the only option open to women who needed to earn an independent livelihood. On the other hand, certain Unions, whilst seeming to strictly adhere to the Poor Law, took in pauper children, knowing their parents were labouring outside, and conveniently labelled them as "deserted" or "orphaned."

However, many petitions from women seeking work, and leaving children in the workhouse, were accepted by Poor Law Guardians. Husbands were also allowed to leave their families behind as they searched for employment. Thus, Henry Shanahan was granted a fortnight's leave and Michael Fagan a month, before being obliged to come back and remove their families from the workhouses.[45] The Limerick Union in particular was very favourable to this practice, so much so that when Daniel Mc Garry, in 1843, had the means to take his two daughters out of the workhouse, he was allowed to leave the sickly one behind until she was well and thus able to contribute something towards her own upkeep.[46]

If the biological bonds between parents and their offspring seem loose and uncaring, there were instances also when paupers fought to have their children with them at all times. The Cork Board of Guardians reported the difficulty of getting women with more than one child "to permit the sick children to be sent to hospital unless they were allowed to take the healthy children with them also."[47] It seems also that the medical officer had a lot of difficulty in dealing with such situations.

In the Killarney workhouse in 1869 the Guardians dismissed the mother of an "illegitimate child" from the workhouse on the grounds that she refused to give up possession of the child to the putative father. He had, under decree of court, paid for its support in the workhouse and had expressed a desire to relieve himself of the liability of further payments by taking the child out. The Board, on a re-assessment of the situation, re-admitted the mother stating that

> it appears repugnant to common humanity to separate a child from its mother for the purpose of placing it in charge of a person who has been reluctantly compelled to burden himself with the cost of its support.[48]

Even if the Board of Guardians overstated the case with respect to the natural attachment of mother and child, the fact remains that the mother did put herself at great risk in refusing to give up her child. To be outside the workhouse when times were bad meant the opportunities available to her to procure a sustenance were very limited.

It would be inaccurate to present the cases of uncaring desertion on one hand and a militant reluctance to be separated from one's children on the other as two very different ways of dealing with dependant children. Rather, to a greater or lesser extent they both are evidence of the flexibility, tenacity and durability of the parent-child bond and, furthermore, take cognizance of the individuality of each "family" unit.

In understanding these arrangements, it is essential to get rid of twentieth century notions about the rigidity of the family unit or the too simplistic assertion that abandoned or temporarily deserted children were from "broken homes." The point has already been made that, for the pauper household, dependent or sick children were a burden that many families had to find alternative strategies to cope with. For pauper women to be a long time in one place, and taking care of a sick and helpless dependant meant the severing of their subsistence lifeline—geographical mobility. There were many strategies utilized by paupers in dealing with his dependency— the temporary abandonment of children was an obvious one, the short term desertion of one's spouse was another, and the placing of the sick, the feeble or the very young in the workhouse was yet a final option.

After spending some years in the workhouse registered as "deserted," these children were usually reclaimed by their parents when the latters' circumstances had improved. Furthermore, children reclaimed out of the workhouse were usually over ten years of age and thus were able to survive the hazards of either a Channel or an Atlantic crossing. At this age they were also old enough to be able to make a contribution to the household economy (whatever way it was structured). Parents who had gone to America did not risk their remittances in sending for very young—dependent—children. Children would have had considerable difficulty in making such crossings alone and would have been unable to fend for themselves while their parent(s) worked and travelled.

Leaving children behind in the workhouse was part of a planned emigration strategy. Once the parents had accumulated a portion of their children's passage, they knew the Poor Law Guardians would pay the remainder and thus rid themselves permanently of the cost of maintenance. One example is Margaret Smith Dodd who wrote to the Poor Law Guardians stating that a child of hers, Michael Sullivan, was an inmate and that

> She is extremely desirous of having him sent to her in America, that owing to the severity of last winter in America, she is not in a position to pay the entire expense of his emigration but can pay thirty shillings, and beg the guardians to pay the remainder thus getting rid of the burden of the child's maintenance besides conferring a great favour on his afflicted mother.[49]

However, some women were so anxious to have their children emigrate to them that they paid the full cost of their passage without any help from the Poor Law Guardians. One Mary Knight was sent to Canada in an assisted emigration scheme from the South Dublin Union, in 1854. Two years later, this "young orphan girl" sent for her child, Richard McDonnell,[50] whom she had had no option but to leave behind at the time of her emigration. Had she acknowledged her relationship to him at the time, she would have lost her place on the emigration list, in that she presented herself as an orphan. In the South Dublin Union in particular, numerous other cases existed of parents sending remittances for the full passage fare of their children. The women who sent for their children and sometimes even their mothers, sisters or relations were, for the most part, sent out in the female "orphan" emigration schemes. For example, Patrick Hanly received a remittance in 1849 from his sister, "one of the female orphans emigrated from the Limerick Union."[51] This case was just one of many. The Guardians were aware that women were very dutiful emigrants and that each one sent out at the expense of the Union was almost guaranteed to initiate a whole chain of emigration.

However, the Poor Law Guardians did not unequivocally support the emigration of single female paupers. When Hannah Moynihan applied for assistance to enable her and her daughter Mary Ann to emigrate to New York where she had some relatives "who promised her assistance in procuring a livelihood for herself and her children," the Guardians were loath to aid her emigration.[52] Perhaps it was because on her second request for assistance, she included another daughter Margaret, aged eleven. The Guardians then realized that she had yet another three children whom she proposed to leave behind her in the workhouse. They concluded

> It would be a bad precedent to allow her to leave any of her children behind her in the country and moreover it is very improbable that she would succeed in maintaining herself and her two young daughters whom she proposes to take with her.[53]

Hannah Moynihan's most insurmountable barrier was not the fact that she had five children, but that the Poor Law Guardians had knowledge of that fact. The knowledge of her domestic situation meant that she was effectively confined by the expectations the Poor Law Guardians had of the resoucefulness and ability of single women.

The Orphaned

One must approach the category of orphan in the workhouse Minutes with a considerable degree of scepticism. To be an orphan, or indeed to be sent as such in one of the government emigration schemes to Australia or North America, did not necessarily imply as a logical corollary that these young women were without parents or relatives. It would appear that many of these workhouse "orphans" had parents, sometimes living in the immediate vicinity of the workhouse and sometimes as far away as America. Other children were brought to the workhouse by their uncles, aunts or grandparents who could no longer afford their maintenance. Some of these children were only "temporary orphans" and their parents reclaimed them in time through the sending of remittances from North America or else by simply acknowledging them. By the same token, however, the desertion of children was an ever constant feature in the workhouse Minutes. Some foundling children spent all of their childhood within the confines of the workhouse and the experience of such a childhood militated against an independent adult existence. Female foundling children in particular were notorious for flitting in and out of the workhouse in their adult years. The Poor Law Guardians sought to permanently curb this practice by including these in the assisted emigration schemes.

The circumstances which led one or both parents to desert their children reveal much about the nature of the nineteenth century pauper family.[54] Very high rates of desertion or temporary abandonment, coupled with significant rates of infanticide, suggest very different views of children from those which exist for all socio-economic groups in the twentieth century. On the surface, these abandonments and desertions may seem indicative of callous and uncaring parenthood but, on delving into the issue further, the relationship of mothers with their children is the key to understanding the functioning (survival) of the nineteenth century pauper family.

The penalty for being caught abandoning a child varied enormously. Mary Cahill of Enniscorthy got one month's imprisonment with hard labour in 1853,[55] whilst in 1857 Catherine Kelly was warned that if she attempted to abandon her child again she would be subject to transportation for life.[56] Prosecutions, the circumstances of which were not elucidated, were the norm.[57] The Poor Law Guardians considered it worth their while to undergo the expense of prosecution procedures as a warning to other inmates.[58] Significantly enough, most of these prosecutions were against mothers.[59] However, there were also prosecutions against fathers: in Kilrush in 1854, Thomas White was prosecuted for absconding from the workhouse leaving his child behind,[60] as was George Byrne for deserting his two children Eliza, aged twelve, and Catherine, aged eight, in the Limerick Union in 1843,[61] while in Tralee Thomas Hartnett was charged with deserting his fourteen year old son, Michael.[62] There would seem to have been little point in prosecuting a destitute pauper, but the trouble and expense of such proceedings may have been undertaken in order to emphasize the concept of culpability and also to serve as a warning.

The ways in which pauper children were deserted varied considerably. Only a small number were left on doorsteps, in fields or outside the workhouse gate. The main mode of desertion, especially when the child was beyond the infant stage or where there was more than one child, was for the parent(s) to enter the workhouse with the child or children and then abscond, leaving them behind.[63] There were also more elaborate desertion procedures as Mary Grimes recounted to the Enniscorthy Poor Law Guardians in 1858. She sought admission for a three-year old child, stating that

> (its) mother gave me five shillings to wash some clothes and care for it until she returned. It is now six weeks since this occurred and she did not come back according to her promise and it appears that she deserted the child altogether.[64]

A similar case also occurred in which a pauper was caught abandoning a child on the workhouse steps.[65] She claimed the child was not hers but that she was merely minding it. These cases in which women stated that they were looking after a child for someone else were not always true, as in the case of the O'Sheas of Limerick. They submitted a new-born female child as deserted and, shortly afterwards, were before the county board of magistrates for conspiring to defraud Guardians by placing their female child in the workhouse.[66]

By law, deserted infants were entitled to a wet nurse, but even then few young infants survived. The infant mortality rate was so high in the Cork Union that the Board ruled in 1851 that

> the admission of foundlings at age three years be rescinded, that in consequence of a large proportion of deaths of foundlings as now received into the house that they not be received before age five.[67]

In Kilrush in 1854, the medical officer also reported on the high mortality rates among the orphan and foundling children, stating that the Guardians needed

> strict attention to the person in charge of that most helpless class (infants) that they need constant supervision and should be daily washed and prevented from unnecessary exposure to cold and have warm clothes.[68]

Pauper women within the workhouse were well recompensed for their efforts in looking after these deserted children, receiving extra allowances of such items as tea and sugar, though they had no real interest in their charges. The Master of the Cork Union issued a pint of porter to each of the paupers nursing deserted children.[69] His later suggestions to them to go without their liquid sustenance resulted in their threatening to give up the children and, as a consequence, the daily porter rations continued.

Either because of the high mortality rate or the refusal of female inmates to nurse and care for children, the practice came about of advertising and paying for wetnurses outside the workhouse. The acceptance of a workhouse child to nurse was recompensed at the rate of about six pounds per annum and was a source of additional income for childrearing women, some of them taking out up to two children at any one time.[70] These woman were supervised by a relieving officer of the workhouse who reported back on the children's state of health and wellbeing to the Poor Law Guardians. The relieving officer of the Ennis Union was able to report that the child Mary Jane Rowlan, who had been put out to nurse, "is strong and healthy and appears to have been well cared for."[71] These children were supported by the Union out of the poor rates up to the time of their fifth year when they were either sent back to the workhouse or their nurses took them as their own. The latter happy fate befell thirteen foundlings in the Londonderry Union in 1843, but their lot was more the exception than the rule.[72] The majority of foundling children at nurse either died or did not sustain the interest of the Poor Law Guardians as there are very few instances of the workhouse clerk reporting in the Minute Books of their progress.

As with the cases where wives were deserted by their husbands, the clerk applied great diligence in seeking out information about the parents of deserted children and "orphans." In the Coleraine Union in 1848 there were 218 deserted children on the workhouse register and the Poor Law Commissioners recommended the Guardians

> to adopt rigorous measures for the punishment of parents of deserted children in order that the workhouse may not become a vast boarding school to the great disencouragement of the religious and moral condition of the poor.[73]

As a result, assiduous enquiries were made and rewards were given for information on deserting parents. In the Ballymony Union, the Guardians were urged to issue handbills offering a reward and containing a description of the offender and four relieving officers were put to the task of hunting out these invisible parents.[74] An alternative strategy to curb rates of desertion was adopted by the Naas Union in 1852. They sought to put an end to the practice of offering assistance to workhouse inmates to join their parents in England and America "as it operates injuriously as a premium to desertion."[75] Their objection was only verbal and, like all other Unions, they were only too glad to rid themselves, at a cheap rate, of the dependent children and young adults who were otherwise likely to remain a permanent burden on the poor rates.

In the Ennistymon Union in 1851 a most rigorous campaign was carried out to discharge children whose parents were outside and at work. Over fifty children, on the workhouse register as orphans, were later found to have parents living and working outside the Union. The clerk bitterly wrote that the parents ought to be prosecuted for desertion.[76] Although he was conscious of the time and expense involved in bringing fifty cases before the court, he believed the riddance of these children from the workhouse a fair reward for his endeavour. The presence of parents or at least kin outside was implicit in the Christmas proceedings of the Cork Union in 1850 when the master

> requested(ed) the Board to instruct him as to whether he shall discharge from the workhouse a large number of children under age fifteen. These children appear on the register as "orphan" or "deserted" but they allege that they have friends with whom they wish to spend Christmas.[77]

The Board of Guardians agreed to allow the children to be taken out by persons claiming to have nursed them or by their relatives, but by no persons claiming to be their parents. There can be no doubt that some Unions were aware that the parents of "deserted" children were outside but, because of considerable strain in the household economy, were unable to take them out. Because of the temporary nature of this abandonment, most Unions turned a blind eye to the practice.

Women with unwanted newborns had a final option open to them—infanticide or the concealment of its birth. The concealment of a birth was difficult within the institution of the workhouse where the close confinement of many women soon made the condition evident. Moreover, on finding a dead infant, the workhouse was one of the first places the police went to find the putative mother. In 1854, the police enquired of the Master of the Rathdrum workhouse as to whether any woman had left the house lately near her confinement.[78] The Master could find no such woman on his books but he did find a woman named Mary Troy who left his house with a twenty-seven day old male child. Further proceedings were undertaken and the clothes found on the dead child were identified by two female pauper inmates who stated that they had given the mother a cap and shirt on her departure from the workhouse. Prosecution charges were then brought against Mary Troy. However, if the workhouse women did not want their new-born infants, there were also less dramatic ways of ensuring that they did not survive. Deliberate neglect could lead them to succumb to death from "natural causes."[79]

Conclusion

This article argues firstly for a scepticism towards traditional views of the workhouse as functioning uniformly throughout the island and monitored closely by central commissioners. An elucidation of some aspects of the lives of pauper women reveals both the flexibility of the institution and the resourcefulness of its female pauper inmates. Secondly, the portrayal of pauper women begs for a re-evalution of the traditional concept of the family, a belief in the maternal instinct, of women as dependents and men as wage earners. This accepted view does not explain why women emigrated alone leaving young children behind in the workhouse, It fails also to reveal different concepts of childhood where pauper children were not seen as dependants to be protected but often as unwelcome burdens on the subsistence nature of the family unit, and in particular as an obstacle to the mobility of the mother. The modern idea of childhood also gets in the way of understanding why the minding of foundling children was the least desirable of all occupations. Women outside the workhouse had to be paid an attractive wage to act as wetnurses. Pauper women within the workhouse had to be cajoled with a daily jug of porter to undertake the task, a task which was lower in prestige than washing the dead or cleaning the workhouse toilets.

The most lasting impression of these pauper women is of resourceful, if at times, vulnerable individuals. Whilst these women were often exploited by employers and workhouse functionaries and made into victims, they also presented themselves as deserted and destitute while in fact they were not, in order to gain entry into the workhouse. Whilst they were vulnerable, they also used these vulnerabilities to achieve a desired end, entry to the workhouse or participation in an emigration scheme. These women cannot be easily presented as either victims or as independent individuals. The life experiences of such a complex group cannot be so tidily summarised. The only real conclusion that can be drawn with respect to these women is that even in the most trying of situations and pressing of circumstances they were resourceful and came up with survival strategies; be it the short term stay in a work house, the temporary abandonment of children, or agreed seasonal "desertion" of a spouse. A further point of note is that within the limited range of options open to them, these women made the choices affecting their own lives. Their relationship to their men was of association and mutual benefit. These women could and did look after themselves.

Notes

1. The existing social structures in this case would be the continuation of parish charity financed by philanthropic individuals and supplemented by occasional alms-giving on behalf of individual parishioners. The prevailing form of landscape organization was the townland, the parish and the county. However, the townland was considered too small a unit from which to administer this new relief system and the county was too large so an intermediary unit, the Poor Law district, was forged. For more detail on the nineteenth century Irish landholding pattern see Patrick J. Duffy, Population and landholding in County Monaghan, (Unpublished PhD dissertation, University College Dublin, 1976).
2. There was no uniformity with respect to the size of the Poor Law districts. An indication of the immense variation between districts is that of Glenties Union in 1854 which covered 257,434 acres and the Dublin South Union for the same period which covered only 40,768 acres. I am indebted to Paul Ferguson for this information.
3. Testimony to this concern with reducing the number of paupers in a Malthusian age were the later workhouse emigration schemes which were designed to relieve the workhouse of the "deadweight" of fecund female paupers. It is estimated that up to 50,000 pauper women were sent out of Ireland in these schemes. For further detail see Dympna Mc Loughlin, Shovelling out paupers, female emigration from Irish workhouses, 1840-70. (Unpublished PhD dissertation, Syracuse University, New York, 1988).

4 The workhouse Minute Books of 32 Poor Law Unions are the primary source material on which this study is based. Each workhouse had a Minute Book in which the weekly proceedings of the institution were inserted. They included such details as the number, age and sex of the paupers in the workhouse and the general business of the house such as the food consumed, the number of punishments during the week, as well as notices on proposed emigration schemes. Some unions had the added attraction of surviving rough Minute Books in which greater detail of the more unsavoury aspects of workhouse life were entered—entries which were not transcribed into the "good" Minute Books which had the greater likelihood of coming under the scrutiny of the Poor Law Commissioners. (In the notes the dates in which particular entries were made in the Minute Books are given. In some few instances no dates were inserted so the page number of the entry is presented instead).

5 This, in fact, was what is commonly termed the "cult of domesticity" which originated in new England during the period 1820-50. It was an ideal disseminated by literary writers for middle class American women. This cult of domesticity stressed conjugal family intimacy, the home as a refuge from the world wherein men, as economic wage earners, would be cared for by their women before their daily embarkation into the competitive marketplace of industrial capitalism. Increasingly, the better off American women were removed from economic production which was no longer carried on in the household unit, and they became more leisured. As a corollary to that leisure, middle class women for the most part became totally dependent on their fathers/husbands/sons for public status and economic support. Thus, the cult of domesticity emerged to reconcile women to their marginal productive—as distinct from reproductive—position under industrial capitalism. Women were urged to spend their lifetimes in the cultivation of the virtues of piety, purity, submissiveness and domesticity. For further details on the cult of domesticity, see the following: Gerda Lerner, "New approaches to the study of women in American history," *Journal of Social History,* 3, (1969-70). Barbara Welter, "The cult of true womanhood, 1820-60," *American Quarterly,* vol xviii, (1966). Kathryn Kish Sklar, *Catherine Beecher: A Study in American Domesticity* (New York, 1973). Ann Douglas, *The Feminization of American Culture* (New York, 1977). Nancy F. Cott, *The*

Bonds of Womanhood: Women's Sphere in New England (Yale University Press, 1977). Ann Firor Scott, "Women's perspective on the patriarchy in the 1850s," *The Journal of American History,* vol ii, no 1, (June 1974).

6 Minutes of the Board of Guardians, Enniscorthy Union, 16 June, 1858.
7 *Ibid.*
8 *Ibid.*, 12 December, 1857.
9 *Ibid.*, 26 December, 1857.
10 *Ibid.*, 9 January, 1857.
11 *Ibid.*, 3 April, 1858.
12 *Ibid.*, 3 December, 1857.
13 *Ibid.*, 16 January, 1858.
14 *Ibid.*, 11 June, 1858.
15 *Ibid.*, 12 January, 1858.
16 *Ibid.*, 11 June 1858.
17 *Ibid.*, 13 March, 1858.
18 *Ibid.*, 16 January 1858.
19 *Ibid.*, 20 January, 1858.
20 *Ibid.*, 30 January, 1858.
21 *Ibid.*, 26th December 1857.
22 *Ibid.*, 30 January, 1858.
23 *Ibid.*, 3 April, 1857.
24 *Ibid.*, 13 March, 1858.
25 Minutes Armagh Union, 12 February, 1850.
26 Minutes Coleraine Union, 12 June, 1848.
27 Minutes Mount Bellow Union, 30 May, 1849.
28 Minutes Enniscorthy Union, 30 April, 1859.
29 *Ibid.*, 5 January, 1856.
30 Minutes Galway Union, 25 February, 1854.
31 Minutes Ballymoney Union, 24 June, 1848.
32 Minutes Londonderry Union, 4 November, 1843.
33 Minutes Limerick Union, 4 September, 1853.
34 Minutes Ballymena Union, 19 August, 1849.
35 Minutes Kenmare Union, 4 September, 1852. Minutes Limerick Union, 28 June, 1845.
36 Minutes Dingle Union, 25 October, 1852. Minutes Tralee Union, 5 February, 1853. Minutes Limerick Union, 6 September, 1845.
37 Minutes Dublin South Union, 20 August, 1856.
38 Minutes Limerick Union, 8 September, 1845.

39 *Ibid.*, 1842, p 925.
40 Minutes Rathdrum Union, 20 October, 1849.
41 *Ibid.*, 8 April, 1854.
42 Minutes Limerick Union, 24 September, 1852.
43 *Ibid.*, 24 September, 1952.
44 Minutes Cork Union, 16 February, 1856.
45 Minutes Limerick Union, 1843 p 1246
46 *Ibid.*, 1843 p.1296.
47 Minutes Cork Union, 17 March, 1860.
48 Minutes Killarney Union, 21 May, 1867.
49 *Ibid.*, 6 May, 1868.
50 Minutes Dublin South Union, 24 January, 1857.
51 Minutes Limerick Union, 1849, p 338.
52 Minutes Killarney Union, June 15, 1867.
53 *Ibid.*, 15 July, 1867.
54 There is a whole literature on the changing nature of the family 1500-1800. France and Britain form the main case studies. There is no comparable work on Ireland to date.
55 Minutes Enniscorthy Union, 7 January, 1853.
56 *Ibid.*, 30 May, 1857.
57 *Ibid.*, 16 February, 1853.
58 Minutes Kilrush Union, 23 September, 1845.
59 Minutes Rathdrum Union, 17 June, 1854. *Ibid.*, 12 October, 1861. *Ibid.*, 28 December, 1861. Minutes Naas Union, 29 September, 1862. Minutes Enniscorthy Union, 12 February, 1853. Minutes Londonderry Union, 4 January, 1845. Minutes Kilrush Union, 23 September, 1854. Minutes Ennistymon Union, 25 October, 1851. Minutes Clifden Union, 31 January, 1852. Minutes Cork Union, 26 October, 1850.
60 Minutes Kilrush Union, 4 November, 1854.
61 Minutes Limerick Union, 20 September, 1843.
62 Minutes Tralee Union, 31 May, 1856.
63 Minutes Naas Union, 10 October, 1863.
Bridget Flaherty and her three children were admitted. She absconded immediately afterwards, leaving the three children behind.
64 Minutes Enniscorthy Union, 13 August, 1859.
65 *Ibid.*, 11 June, 1853.
66 Minutes Limerick Union, 28 January, 1854.
67 Minutes Cork Union, 7 May, 1851.
68 Minutes Kilrush Union, 14 January, 1854.

69 Minutes Cork Union, 11 June, 1859.
70 Minutes Glin Union, 1870, p 135.
71 Minutes Ennis Union, 3 January, 1863.
72 Minutes Londonderry Union, 4 November, 1843.
73 Minutes Coleraine Union, 17 November, 1849.
74 Minutes Ballymoney Union, 11 August, 1849.
75 Minutes Naas Union, 14 August, 1852.
76 Minutes Ennistymon Union, 9 August, 1851.
77 Minutes Cork Union, 14 December, 1850.
78 Minutes Rathdrum Union, 3 June, 1854.
79 The area of nineteenth century pauper fertility, more particularly the concealment of a true birth rate through the practice of infanticide, is the subject of my current research.

Life For Domestic Servants in Dublin, 1880-1920

Mona Hearn

Domestic service was the major employment for women in Ireland in the nineteenth century; in 1881 48 per cent of employed women were in the domestic class. Between 1881 and 1911, years for which comparable statistics are available, there was a steady decrease in the number of indoor servants in each successive census, 39,000 less in 1891 than ten years previously, 35,500 less in 1901 and 40,000 fewer in 1911. In that year domestic service was surpassed by manufacturing industry, but it was still the second largest employer of women, with 125,783 female indoor servants.[1] The numerical significance of domestic service is reflected in the fact that a separate occupational class in the census was devoted to it.

In this article, sources of domestic servants, their duties, rates of pay, board and lodgings and working conditions are examined. The fact that domestic servants were especially vulnerable to exploitation by their employers—due to their sex, age, isolated and subordinate position and the fact that they were not protected by a trade union—is discussed. It is argued, however, that in spite of these seemingly formidable disadvantages, servants were not without power and were often able to use the system to their own advantage.

Sources of Domestic Servants

Domestic service was, in the period under review, an inevitable part of life for many thousands of girls. The expected pattern of existence for middle and upper class girls was life in father's home followed by life in their husband's home; for working class girls it was life in father's home followed by employer's home and finally husband's home.[2] Girls went into domestic service because it was very often the only thing for them to do. It appealed to parents, especially as a career for daughters, because it offered board and lodgings as well as money wages. Domestic service was also acceptable to the ideology of the time which considered the home, albeit someone else's home, the natural place for a girl or woman; the work was what any woman would do in her own home; also, it was considered the obvious destiny for those without families of their own—those from orphanages, industrial schools and reformatories.

Taking up a "situation" as it was called for an indoor servant was a more fundamental step than taking up a position in most other industries. It involved a complete break with home, friends and a familiar way of life; it entailed living in a dependent and subordinate position in the home of people who were not only strangers, but who were also of a different social class with different habits, values and lifestyle. The employer's household embraced the servant's whole life. Total loyalty to master and mistress was expected. Apart from some limited free time, the servant was always available to see to the wants and comfort of her employer. The total control of servant by master, which was in fact reinforced by legislation, meant that the domestic servant had little discretion over the day-to-day conduct of her life.

The vast majority of Irish servants were children of small farmers, estate workers, the semi-skilled and the unskilled. The lack of alternative employment in Ireland was a crucial factor in limiting career choice for these girls; in fact the usual choice facing them was domestic service or emigration.[3] Those who emigrated very often entered service in their adoptive country.[4] A government committee which reported on the cost of living of the working classes in Ireland in 1908, drawing on the 1901 census, stated: "the number of domestic servants to which attention is called in this and other reports is a characteristic of Irish life which has come into prominence since the decay of Irish industry."[5] This report also pointed out the absence of any industry employing women in large numbers: "the greatest number of women are engaged in occupations found in every town and regarded as the special sphere of women, viz. domestic service and the making of articles of clothing."[6] The ratio of servants was high in towns and cities in which there were only traditional occupations available to women; Dublin had 50 servants for every 1000 of the population. Cork had 49 per 1000[7] and Belfast, where there were manufacturing jobs for women, only 22.[8]

Domestic service was the cause of considerable migration especially of young girls.[9] Of the servants working in Dublin houses in 1911, 28 per cent were born in Dublin city or county—half were born in the city—21 per cent were from the adjoining counties of Meath, Wicklow and Kildare, and 21 per cent were from the rest of Leinster. Thirty per cent came from further afield, 22 per cent from the other three provinces, 7 per cent from Britain, and 1 per cent from abroad. While the number of servants working near home was small, the majority of servants had not come from too far afield. In 1911, working even in the next county could mean infrequent visits home. When the birthplaces of these servants was compared with that of the general population in Dublin city and county the difference was striking. While only 28 per cent of the servants were born in Dublin city and county, 70 per cent of the general population of the city and 65 per cent of the population of Dublin county were born in Dublin city and county.[10] Mary Daly mentioned this contribution of service to migration in *Dublin the Deposed Capital* when she pointed out that servants tended to come from rural areas and added significantly to the number of migrants in the Dublin suburbs.[11] The main reason why most domestic servants worked a distance from their birthplace was the unavailability of work at home and the great demand for servants in cities and large towns.

Because service was usually the only choice available it became the traditional haven for women from rural Ireland

and from many towns and cities. This in its turn added its own momentum, so that positions as servants were sought automatically without consideration of alternatives which might, in some cases, particularly towards the end of the period, have in fact existed, in factories, shops or offices. Many women entered service immediately on leaving school, sometimes the day after. There was obviously no discussion about their career: it was accepted that they would go into service.[12] A nun in a school in Kells in 1913 recommended one of her pupils as a kitchen maid to a doctor in Merrion Square. The girl went to Dublin for the interview; it was not only her first visit to Dublin, it was also her first journey by train.[13]

Wages of domestic servants compared very favourably with wages in other industries.[14] (see below). The servant had very few expenses and could save, or send money home to help relations.[15] In addition to wages, domestic servants had free board and lodgings and many appreciated this advantage.[16] Other reasons which might have attracted people to domestic service were a desire to improve their social position—working in a "good place" in Merrion or Fitzwilliam Square for instance, was considered desirable—and the fact that service provided a relatively simple way for girls to enter urban life. Certainly the attractions of town or city life and the desire to escape from the poverty and hardship of subsistence farming and crowded tenements would have played a part. Parents welcomed the control and security which they felt service offered their daughters.[17] Being part of a household where one's "comings and goings were matters of interest and moment in some household" was considered preferable to living on one's own in rented accommodation.[18]

Workhouses, industrial schools and reformatories also provided servants. From the point of view of an industry employing 125,783 women in 1911, this was not an important source as it provided less than 400 new recruits each year.[19] Domestic service was, however, of paramount importance to these institutions as the occupation most likely to employ girls when they reached sixteen years of age. Indeed girls were more likely to get formal training for domestic service there than anywhere else with the exception of a couple of schools in the country which catered specifically for domestic servants like the Killarney School of Housewifery and the Domestic Training Institute for Protestant Girls in Charlemont St., Dublin.[20] The inspector of reformatories and industrial schools in his report in 1880 said: "farmers, even with large farms, complain that industrial school children receive a training and instruction in trades which their sons and daughters cannot hope to obtain."[21] In the case of their daughters the main "trade" in question was, of course, domestic service. Workhouses were an important source of servants for middle and lower middle class people and for farmers who lived in the neighbourhood. The author Frank O'Connor's mother, who spent her early years in the Good Shepherd Orphanage in Cork, got a number of jobs when people from the Sunday's Well area called looking for servants. The orphanage placed many young girls in that way.[22]

Servants' Duties

The majority of servants were young single women working in houses where only one servant was employed. They were usually called general servants and were responsible, with the help of the housewife, for all the work of the house. The general servant was the only one for whom Mrs Beeton had any sympathy, describing her life as "solitary," and her work as "never done." She had to do all the work which in larger establishments was undertaken by a number of servants. "Her mistress's commands are the measure of the maid-of-all-work's duties."[23] The hard household work required at that time was blamed for much of the tension in middle class homes: "...the amount of daily menial labour involved in keeping the middle class home was overwhelming, and physically exhausting for only two women, especially a home that had the care of at least three children which was the norm by the end of the century."[24] Many Irish homes had more than three children; for example, Mr and Mrs John Kenny, who lived at 3 Triery's Terrace, St. Patrick's Road, Drumcondra, in 1911, had four young children aged from 6 years to 3 weeks, and one 17 year old girl to mind them and tend to the household chores.

Houses at this time were often poorly planned and were usually devoid of labour-saving appliances and there was indeed a vast "amount of daily menial labour" involved for the general servant. Chores included: lighting and tending the coal range in the kitchen, fires in the living rooms and perhaps the bedrooms; carrying hot water for shaving and bathing to the bedrooms and emptying slops; trimming and lighting the oil lamps; cleaning the steel knives with bathbrick. Quite elaborate meals were prepared and cooked on the temperamental coal range and served in the dining room which was often on the floor above the kitchen; dishes were washed in a dark scullery with water heated on the range and washing soda to help remove the grease. In addition, the servant had to mind the children. Flagged and tiled floors and passages, common in those days, were frequently scrubbed, and the granite steps leading to many Dublin houses scrubbed regularly. Every room was cleaned thoroughly once a week and lighter chores, for example cleaning the silver or brass or ironing the clothes, were done in the afternoons. Some general servants also did the weekly wash while in other households a char woman was hired.

In two-servant houses the most common servant employed was a cook; the second servant, whose function it was to look after the cleaning of the house, was usually called a general servant, housemaid, house/parlourmaid or was given no specific title. This was the beginning of specialisation in the service hierarchy. Not all two-servant houses had a cook; presumably the housewife did the cooking herself or it was done by the general servant. The second servant was often a nursemaid for the children. The usual three servants employed in Dublin houses were a cook, parlourmaid and housemaid. "With three servants—cook, parlourmaid and housemaid—a household is complete in all its functions. All else is only a development of this theme." In larger households the cook had an assistant, a kitchen maid or perhaps a second assistant, a scullery maid; the parlourmaid's duties were taken over by the butler, and the housemaid had the assistance of other housemaids who might be called upper and lower housemaids.[25]

Age and Marital Status of Servants

Domestic service was an occupation for young people and the old family retainer was probably a rarer phenomenon than her appearance in literature suggests. In 1911 47 per cent of indoor female servants in Ireland were under 25 years of age and only 18 per cent were over 45.[26]

Table 1: Percentages of female indoor servants in different age groups in 1911 compared with the general female population in square brackets.

Age group					Total
15-19	20-24	25-44	45-64	65 & over	
24 (13)	23 (12)	35 (38)	12 (22)	6 (15)	100

Source: Cen. Ire. 1911

The age structure of servants in the three censuses from 1881 to 1901 also show that servants were predominantly young.[27] In the Dublin houses in 1911, 62 per cent of servants were under 30 years of age and 80 per cent were under 40.[28] The large number of servants under thirty was, no doubt, due to the fact that virtually all female servants left service on marriage. Also, employers preferred to engage young servants. This was reflected in advertisements for servants and from evidence given by former servants. Advertisements in the *Freeman's Journal* on Tuesday the 22 January, 1889 sought: "Respectable girl, general servant, £1 per quarter, Girl about 16 mind children and housework £4, Smart girl as general servant £6, Smart tidy little girl about 13 to mind children 13/- a quarter." While employers were offering higher wages in the *Irish Times* on Thursday 1 July 1909, they looked for young servants: "Young General Foxrock, good plain cook, small washing, small family, £14, Smart Young General—plain cook, no washing, early riser, £12-£14, 80 Leinster Rd." Young servants could be paid less, were presumed to be more amenable to new routines and surroundings, to be stronger and have more energy and far removed from the problems that an ageing servant could create for an employer.

Ireland, however, had more old servants than England. This was pointed out by a report in 1899 by the labour department of the Board of Trade, Miss C. E. Collet's *Report on the Money Wages of Indoor Domestic Servants*. According to the census of 1891, Ireland had 21 per cent of female servants aged 45 and over whereas the figure for England was only 9 per cent. Miss Collet concluded that the unfit and infirm were not eliminated to the same extent in Ireland as in England.[29]

The majority of servants were single, they either married comparatively late and left service, or they did not marry at all.[30] That employers preferred unmarried servants is clear from newspaper advertisements which often either stipulated that an applicant must be single or asked for a declaration of marital status. In Dublin in 1911 92 per cent of female servants were single, 6 per cent were widowed and only 2 per cent were married.[31] When the marital status of female servants is compared to that of women in the general population it is clear that at any age female servants were less likely to be married than their peers. Approximately half of the female population between the ages of 25 and 34 were married, compared with only 3 per cent of servants.[32]

Conditions of service and the attitude of employers did not facilitate the meeting of the sexes in circumstances conducive to courtship and marriage. Servants worked long hours and had very little freedom; they therefore had limited opportunities to meet each other.[33] This was especially true of those working in one or two-servant households, which included the majority of servants. These girls tended to marry milkmen, breadmen, butchers, roundsmen, or small shopkeepers, probably the only men they met regularly. Marriage was looked on by many servants as a way of escaping from service.[34]

The process of acquiring a spouse was actively discouraged by many masters and mistresses. The disparaging term "follower" was used to describe a servant's boyfriend; it was the subject of jokes and cartoons. A "no followers" rule pertained in many households.[35] It was even mentioned by some employers when advertising for servants.[36] This rule isolated servants further from their own social class. The low status of their occupation also made it harder for them to acquire an eligible young man. A number of former servants said that they pretended to boyfriends that they worked in factories.[37] One woman who used to go to dances with two other servants said that one of them who was "very grand" always told the men she had an office job; she used to arrange to meet them in places like Grafton St.[38]

Wages of Domestic Servants

The wages of domestic servants were very difficult to ascertain for a number of reasons. Domestic service was neglected by Royal Commissions on wages. The difficulties of obtaining information on such a large and widely diffused work force were of course formidable. Money wages were only one aspect of servants' remuneration. Board and lodgings formed a considerable part of the real wages of servants. When comparing servants' wages to those of workers in other industries, an estimate must be made of the actual expenditure on food and lodgings by women of the same social class.[39] Also, servants often got an allowance of tea, sugar and beer; they received presents, tips and other perquisites.

Information on wages was obtained from wage books, reminiscences of former servants and mistresses, and from rates of pay quoted in newspapers. The disadvantages of newspapers as a source are that they refer to starting salaries, and, as many servants got rises, they are not representative of those already in service; however, changes in the starting rates of pay reflect changes in the latter. Secondly, they probably do not reflect the lowest paid adequately as these servants were not usually recruited in this way. Miss Collet's report, even though the number of Irish servants surveyed was only 359, showed that wages in Ireland were lower than in Great Britain.[40] This report also showed that the average wages of servants varied with the number of servants in the household.

Table 2: Average Wages of Female Domestic Servants classified according to Number of Servants in Household.

Households employing	Dublin	Belfast	Cork and Limerick	Total Ireland
	£	£	£	£
One servant	10.8	12.6	9.5	11.3
Two servants	13.5	13.9	11.1	13.3
Three servants	15.3	16.7	13.9	15.5
Four servants	16.6	17.1	14.7	15.9
Over four servants	19.8	19.7	17.4	18.7

Source: Collet, *Report,* pp 10-18.

There were great variations in wages from one household to another and from one servant to another. This is stressed by many writers.[41] The wage was affected by the income level of the employer, the age and experience of the servant, the number of staff employed, the location, supply and demand. It will be seen from Table 2 that wages were highest in Belfast where there was more alternative employment and that rates were higher in Dublin than in Cork or Limerick. Servants in capital cities earned higher wages than those working in other parts of the country as there was greater demand for servants in these cities and more wealthy employers. The wage paid was finally a personal one—that agreed between employer and servant.

In spite of these difficulties a certain consistency is discernible in wage rates quoted in newspapers, those recorded in Miss Collet's report and wage books, and earnings mentioned by former servants and mistresses. Wages for general servants given in the *Irish Times* and the *Freeman's Journal* were very different, the former being consistently higher than the latter and showing that readers were usually seeking older, more experienced servants. This reflected the different readership of the two papers. The *Irish Times* was the paper of the upper classes—the prosperous professional and landowning classes and those aspiring to join their ranks. On the other hand, the *Freeman's Journal* was read by the lower classes who were mainly Catholic.

Table 3: Average wages of servants in Ireland 1880—1920 from advertisements in the *Irish Times* and *Freeman's Journal*.[42] (Wage span in brackets)

Dates	General Servant		Cook	
	I.T.	F.J.	"ordinary"	"superior"
1880-9	8. 3 (6 - 10)	5. 6 (3 - 8)	13. 8	30
1890-9	9 (8 - 14)	7. 6 (4 - 12)	14. 2	30 - 35
1900-9	12. 5 (10 - 18)	9 (5 - 15)	18	30 - 40
1910 - 20	14. 3 (12 - 22)	14. 8 (9 - 20)	18. 7	30 - 40

There were two clearly discernible rates of pay for cooks, a rate of from £14 - £19 for what was described as an "ordinary cook," and a rate of from £30 - £40 for a "superior cook."[43] Cooks were the second most common type of servant employed in one to three servant households.[44] In many of these houses cooks had duties other than cooking; their wages and indeed their job were more akin to those of a superior general servant. The higher rate was paid to cooks who had purely culinary duties; advertisements for cooks offering wages of £30 often mentioned whether or not a kitchenmaid was kept, showing that a larger staff was employed and that there was a degree of specialisation.[45]

The next most common position sought or advertised was that of children's maid or nurse. Employers using the *Freeman's Journal* and the provincial papers often looked for a "a smart little girl to mind the children," or "a young girl to look after children and help with housework." The wages offered in these cases were usually low, as little as 52/- a year; £4 a year was usual in the 1880s and 1890s and not unknown much later.[46] On the other hand employers seeking children's nurses in the *Irish Times* offered between £12 - £16 in the 1880s and £14 - £20 between 1910 - 20, again reflecting the different social classes of the readers of the two papers. Housemaids, parlourmaids and house/parlourmaids were paid between £8 - £14 in the 1880s, rising to between £12 - £28 in the 1910 - 20 period.[47]

The lowest rates offered for general servants, £4 - £8 in the 1880s, were also offered in the 1890s and into the twentieth century though their number had greatly decreased. Between 1910 - 1920 there were some advertisements for a general servant at £8 - £9 and an agency offered to supply general servants from £8 - £20 a year.[48] Low rates of pay were usually offered for "young," "young country," "to train" or "never-out-before-girls." Many young girls were recruited as general servants from orphanages, and by word of mouth through relatives, shop-keepers and roundsmen. The wages given to them right up to the 1920s were low, from £4 - £8 a year.[49] Wages given to children from the workhouses in 1879 were usually about £2 per year.[50] Domestic servants on farms in Ireland were paid as little as 32/- a year in the 1870s,[51] and 50/- in 1896;[52] about 1906 - 1910 they were paid £8 - £12.[53] Registry offices also advertised in the newspapers. On 1 July 1909, in the *Irish Times*, Kennedy's Agency, 68 Sackville St. sought two footmen, a butler at £50, a general man and a number of servants who were required for Great Britain. Not surprisingly, newspapers advertised their own agencies. *The Freeman's Journal,* on the 19 January 1891, carried a more striking advertisement:

Important to Servants

Good Cooks, Housemaids, Nurses and General Servants will find it to their advantage to call at the Freeman Registry Office 96A Grafton St. The new Matron in this office finds it difficult to supply with servants the numerous demands made of her by Lady Patrons, and will be glad to hear from useful and reliable servants of all classes. An immediate personal call is desirable.

Registry offices received fees from employers and servants. Sometimes a fee of perhaps 2/6 was paid to put one's name on the books and an additional set fee or a proportion of the first month's wage was paid when the client was "suited." Sometimes a higher fee, perhaps 5/-, was paid by the mistress and servant and this covered the placement charge. If a situation or servant was not obtained the fee was forfeited.[54]

A large proportion of a servant's total remuneration was in the form of board and lodgings. The value of this should be calculated on the cost of living for women of the same social class as servants. The findings of a Board of Trade inquiry into Expenditure of wage-earning women and girls in England in 1911 is useful for that purpose.[55] Many of these girls were living at home and for that reason their expenses were often less than those of a girl living independently. At that time most girls working in shops, factories or offices lived at home. The girls included in the inquiry earned between 12/6 and 30/- a week. Girls at the lower end of the scale, those earning 12/6 to 14/10, had a mere subsistence standard of living and expenditure was equal to, or a few pence below, income.[56] One girl, described as a camera maker and optical worker, earned 13/11 a week and spent 13/9. She lived alone in a top back room for which she paid 3/- per week rent; her food cost 5/7, fuel and light 8d, sick club 7d, washing 11d, bath 2d, dress 2/5, miscellaneous 4d, holidays and fares nothing.[57] With the exception of dress, all the other expenses would be included in the board and lodgings of servants.

In 1911, 12/6 a week or £32 a year, seemed to have been the minimum wage for a girl if she lived an independent life in England—the camera maker's expenditure on food was higher than that of others in the survey. Even if a girl in Ireland rented a room for 1/6 a week[58] and spent less on dress and food, at least 8/- a week, or £21 a year, was necessary to live independently. If a girl at home contributed 5/- a week towards household costs, 1/- for rent and 4/- for food, this would seem to be the minimum. Thus frugal living cost for a member of the lower social classes was £13 a year if living at home and £21 a year if living independently. However, £13 a year was higher than the wages paid to the majority of young general servants—many earned £8 - £10 throughout the whole period 1880 - 1920. So even when the cost of board and lodgings is calculated on cost to the servant, money wages were at the most half the total remuneration of the servant and were probably much less than half, because most servants were not living at subsistence level but, as far as food and accommodation were concerned, had a middle class standard of living.

In addition to money wages, servants frequently obtained presents, tips and other perquisites. The practice of giving servants Christmas presents was widespread.[59] The gifts were usually money, dress lengths or other items of uniform, cardigans, shawls or nightshirts, pipe and tobacco, books, bibles or stationery boxes. The amount of money given usually varied from 5/- to 10/- depending on seniority; occasionally as much as £1 was given. Most presents were practical which was probably appropriate at a time when people found it hard to supply themselves with the necessities of life. Servants also received tips for performing particular services or from guests staying in their employers' homes. Tips of 2/6 and 3/- were given by members of the Vere O'Brien family to maids in the homes of their friends between 1880 and 1886.[60] This was quite high when it is considered that a housemaid at that time might have earned 5/- to 8/- per week. Another source of income was perquisites which were often considered the right of servants holding special positions; tradesmen were only too willing to give discounts on orders placed by cooks or housekeepers.

The cook considered she had a right to sell dripping, rabbit skins and used tea leaves; these "rights" could be, and often were abused.[61] It is impossible to put a money value on these other sources of income, but their prevalence has to be remembered as an added bonus for service.

Wages of servants compared very favourably to wages in other industries competing for their services. Shop assistants and domestic servants had much in common. It was usual for the former also to live in, either over the shop or in rented rooms. They were subjected to the discipline of the employer for practically twenty-four hours a day, six days a week. Often accommodation was crowded and food poor. Assistants were expected to behave with respect to their employers, to dress well, the women usually wearing special outfits.[62] Shop assistants worked for long hours. Dermot Keogh, discussing the conditions of drapers' assistants in Ireland in 1906, were said: "there was no half holidays, neither was there a uniform closing hour, a practice which often forced employees to work over 80 hours a week with only Sunday off."[63] *The Draper's Assistant* in September 1912 recorded that a draper was prosecuted for allowing one of his young female staff members to work 97.5 hours in the week. It was estimated that women assistants earned from £10 to £25 a year with board and lodgings; these figures were based on information supplied by the secretary of the National Union of Shop Assistants for the period prior to 1894.[64] Keogh notes that in Ireland in 1906 a draper's assistant was paid between £40 and £50 a year.[65] This rate was paid after a seven year apprenticeship and was probably the top rate for men. Women earned considerably less, and women working in small shops where appearance and speech were not considered important, even less. Working conditions in factories were much inferior, from the point of view of the environment and the type of work, to those in the average middle class home. Wages were low and workers had to pay all living expenses from their wages. In 1894 the average female wage in the box trade was 5/3 weekly and in match-making it was much lower.[66] Contemporary observers considered that service had many advantages over the far less remunerative and less propitious conditions of the factory worker.[67] Unfortunately working in a shop or even in a factory had a higher status than working in domestic service. A correspondent to *The Irish Homestead* in 1902 said that a young woman who, in the old times, would naturally have become a servant "now has ambitions to stand behind a counter, or to perform upon that entertaining musical instrument, the typewriter."[68]

Working Conditions

Working conditions were of paramount importance in an occupation which encompassed the whole life of a servant. It is very difficult to generalise about conditions in domestic service. There were vast differences between working as one of a staff of six or seven in Merrion Square, or working as a general servant in the homes of the lower middle classes. Great differences could also exist between conditions in households of a similar kind. This is clear from reminiscences of servants and writings of employers.[69] Sir John Ross, the last Lord Chancellor of Ireland, said of the mansions in Merrion Square and Fitzwilliam Square "the accommodation for servants is miserable."[70] Servants working in some of these houses were quite content with their sleeping quarters.[71]

One of the difficulties of assessing the standard of accommodation and food provided is that masters and servants judged them from very different perspectives. Sir John Ross was unusual; generally employers and commentators drawn from the same social class, stressed repeatedly that accommodation and food was infinitely better than servants were used to in their own homes. Servants, on the other hand, tended to compare their bedrooms and food to conditions enjoyed by employers and their families. There was no such thing as a set standard for food and accommodation which should be provided by employers and expected by servants. An attempt was made in 1911 to set standards when Mr Bottomly, M.P., introduced to parliament the Domestic Servants' Bill "to regulate the hours of work, meal times and accommodation of Domestic Servants, and to provide for the periodical inspection of their kitchens and sleeping quarters." It was rejected on the second reading.[72]

Servants usually slept in the attic or top floor bedrooms which they may have shared with one, or sometimes, two others. These rooms were generally sparsely furnished.[73] Many former servants were content with the accommodation provided for them; the majority had a single room though some shared with another servant. These rooms were plainly furnished with an iron bed, chest of drawers, wardrobe and perhaps a wash-hand basin.[74] Servants in small houses rarely had a sitting room, the kitchen was used by the servants, and, could be "quite equal the house-place of the cottages of their own mothers."[75]

Some servants undoubtedly had very poor sleeping accommodation. A writer in the *Irish Homestead* in 1905 drew attention to the number of times she had to speak about accommodation offered to domestic servants: "the cupboards and black holes in which so many Irish domestics are expected to sleep are a disgrace to civilisation."[76] In the same year *The Lancet* was extremely critical of the unhealthy living conditions of many domestic servants.[77] A 92 year old former servant remembered sleeping in the bathroom—in a house in which she worked in 1902. One of the residents took a bath at 7 a.m. so she had to rise before that and she could not retire until midnight when everyone was finished in the bathroom.[78] Obviously living accommodation varied greatly: "in the best households, a servant would have a room fit for a daughter of the family. In the worst, servants had no room of their own."[79] Servants were probably, as employers maintained, at least as well housed as they would have been in their own homes, but that in the nineteenth and early twentieth centuries was not necessarily justification for complacency.

Food supplied to servants varied very much, depending mainly, it would seem, on the generosity of the employer. On the whole the literature on domestic service indicates that food supplied to servants was good.[80] A woman who worked as a kitchen maid in Merrion Sq. in 1913 and ordered the food for staff, described it as "the best of food."[81] A lady's maid who worked in a "big" house said that the servant's food depended on the cook who was often too lazy and careless to cook the food properly for the servants.[82] Most former servants stated that the food in service was good or very good, and in many cases the same as that eaten by the family. It was in households which really could not afford servants that shortage of food was usually experienced.

The working hours of domestic servants are difficult to assess. If the time spent in an employer's home is considered as working hours—and many servants would have said that they were on duty from 6.30 a.m. until they retired at 10 or 11 p.m.—then the number is formidable indeed and well in excess of the working hours in any other occupation. Of course many people contended that servants were not working all the time, they went for messages and, depending on the type and organisation of the household, had free time in the afternoon or evening.[83] Servants did not work at a steady pace throughout the day, there were busy times and times when there was little or nothing to do; they could also, to an extent, work at their own pace. Most servants, however, when in their employer's house, were considered available, if required, for any chore that might arise. Servants' leisure varied greatly but the usual was a half day every week starting after lunch and a half day every second Sunday with a fortnight's holiday in the year.[84] Servants' free time was not inviolable. Half-days only began when all the work after lunch was done and everything prepared for the evening meal; as a result "half-days" of only two and three hours were recorded. Servants mentioned having to wash up after dinner or supper when they returned from their evening out. It must be remembered that at this time holidays and leisure were restricted for the majority of the population; amusements and entertainments were few and reserved for special and rare occasions. Thus the lot of domestic servants was not any worse than that of most people. However they had, perhaps, a greater need than most for leisure away from the work place where they spent so much of their time.

Employer Power: Servant Power

Domestic servants were particularly vulnerable to exploitation by their employers. Being predominantly female—in the 1911 census, 93 per cent of servants were woman and only 7 per cent men[85]—they were more easily intimidated. They were usually young and the vast majority were untrained when they entered service. Moreover, most worked in one or two-servant households and lacked the support which membership of a larger work force would supply. Servants spent twenty-four hours a day in their work place and were generally in constant daily contact with their mistresses. All these factors gave employers an unusual amount of control over servants.

Servants never achieved the collective power which membership of an effective trade union could have supplied. Attempts to organise them in trade unions in Ireland met with very little success; this was also the experience in England, France and the United States. The fact that servants worked alone or with one other undoubtedly made unionisation very difficult. Other reasons for the failure were the close relationship between employers and servants, the constant movement of servants from one situation to another, the fact that unmarried women looked on service as only a temporary occupation and the fears of servants of losing their places and being deprived of references.[86] Servants were afforded very little protection by the law while the employer had extensive rights to protect himself against his servant.[87]

The master was obliged to supply food and lodgings but not medical attention or medicine for his servants. He could dismiss a servant without the customary one month's notice for "a good and valid reason." Obviously "good and valid reason" could be interpreted in many ways. Reasons for dismissal without notice were: wilful disobedience to a lawful and reasonable order, theft, drunkenness, habitual or on one occasion only, insolence—if sufficiently gross, violent conduct, immorality, negligence, if habitual or of a "gross character," illness, but only if permanent or prolonged. A servant had to obey lawful orders, exercise care in the performance of his duties and "abstain from doing that which he ought not to do." A master was under no legal obligation to give his servant a character.[88] This was very serious as a reference was absolutely essential when a servant was seeking work. Many efforts were made in the early twentieth century to compel employers to give references to their servants but without success.[89]

Domestic servants, however, benefited from general legislation—the provision of old age pensions in 1908, sickness benefits in 1911, and the Workman's Compensation Act of 1906. The National Insurance Act of 1911, which was designed to give workers free medical treatment and cash benefits while ill, met with strong opposition from both employers and servants—though principally from the former—in Ireland and England. A threepenny weekly contribution was required from mistress and servant. The Women's Freedom League urged that the act should be resisted because women were not consulted and it was passed by an assembly which did not include representatives of women. The *Irish Citizen* published articles from the W.F.L. and letters from the public on the subject.[90] In spite of protests, and furious letters to the papers claiming that the measure would divide society, the act came into operation in July 1912.[91]

Employers could and did exploit the unequal situation. The very low money wages paid to some servants—as little as £4 a year up to the 1920s—is testimony to this. Food was rationed by some mistresses and food supplies kept in a locked cupboard; sleeping accommodation could be very poor.[92] Some servants had no half-day.[93] Others had no holidays.[94] Servants were sometimes physically assaulted by their employers. Special legislation to safeguard young people under eighteen years of age was brought in in England in 1851 as a result of a couple of cases of extreme cruelty against servants.⁹⁵ Sexual exploitation of servants by masters and sons of the house was not uncommon. Former servants had experience of masters who made sexual overtures to them or to other servants.⁹⁶ Employers sometimes hired servants who had illegitimate children. One servant worked in a household where the cook's illegitimate daughter was housemaid. She was known as the cook's "sister." She had been given the position by the employers, who had full knowledge of the circumstances, when, at the age of sixteen, she had to leave the orphanage.⁹⁷

The ability to change jobs was the only real power servants had when work conditions were unfavourable. It was one which was used frequently. The majority of writers agreed that servants did not remain long in their situations.⁹⁸ Miss Collet's report showed that 54 per cent of servants surveyed had been in their situations less than two years.⁹⁹ Advertisements by servants seeking jobs indicated that they considered two years in one household a long time. The fact that various awards for loyalty and long service were initiated in a number of countries shows that high turnover was a universal problem; it is significant that one year's service was considered worthy of award.¹⁰⁰

The threat to change jobs was also, it seems, an effective weapon. Servants who demanded rises, with or without threats of departure, usually had them granted. As shown, wages and conditions of work in service compared, on the whole, very favourably with those in other industries. This is a surprising achievement for an employment which was not unionised. Evidence from former servants indicated that when they moved from one situation to another they invariably got higher wages. This can be attributed to their experience but it also highlights that each servant had a base line which she was not willing to go below. One servant, who was a cook in a guesthouse in Kensington and earning £40 a year in 1926, returned to Ireland in 1927 and got a situation as cook in a private house in Shankill at £48 a year. Her employers were Americans which may help to explain what was an exceptional wage for that position in Ireland at the time, but it also shows the reluctance of servants to, as they would see it, worsen their position by accepting a lower wage.[101] This element of personal negotiation was also seen in the fact that former servants always got conditions—free time and holidays—which were at least as good as those in their previous situation.

An interesting fact is that domestic service did not appear to be free of practices usually associated with membership of trade unions. In 1918 the Ministry of Reconstruction in England set up a Women's Advisory Committee on the Domestic Service Problem. A sub-committee of this group stated that it would not be possible to allow the servant greater leisure unless "she is prepared to accept as part of her conditions of service far greater interchange of duties with her fellow workers than has hitherto normally been the custom."[102] Advertisements for servants also showed that inflexibility existed. Employers evidently found it necessary to mention certain chores specifically, such as: washing, minding children, sewing, waiting at table, helping in the dairy or with fowl. This meant that mistresses found it difficult, either by persuasion or threat, to get servants to undertake tasks which were not seen by the servants as part of their "proper" duties.

The capacity of servants to control, to a certain extent, their own destiny, shows a work force which was far from powerless. The power came from the ability to disrupt the household by withdrawing their labour permanently. However, servants could disturb the peace of the home without leaving. This power derived from the close personal relationship which existed between mistress and maid especially in small households. Servants were exposed to the moods and humours of the mistress but the opposite was also true. This close association very often led to the growth of mutual respect and perhaps affection; even when there was lack of empathy between the two, the mistress was very much aware of the satisfaction or dissatisfaction of the servant with her "position." Apart from treating the girl well because she knew and liked her—after all a maid was not an anonymous pair of hands in a factory—it was in the interest of the mistress and her family to have a happy and contented servant in the home. Servants were of the utmost importance to the employing-class in the nineteenth and early twentieth centuries, their domestic well-being depended on servants, and while they sometimes used their positions in society to block or try to block legislation favourable to servants, on an individual basis, this dependence favoured domestic servants.

Study of the Employment of Domestic Servants in Dublin Houses in 1911

This study was based on a sample of approximately 850 Dublin households in 1911. The rateable valuation of houses was used as the criterion of the social and economic status of the occupier. Samples of houses with rateable valuations of £10 - £19, £20 - £39, and £40 or over were chosen. It was considered very unlikely that any household with a rateable valuation of less than £10 would have a servant and this was borne out by the pilot study and also by the small number of households in the lowest group selected, £10 - £19, in which servants were employed.

It was decided to select 250 houses with a rateable valuation of £20 - £39, 250 with one of £40 or over (it was found that there was approximately equal representation of these R. V. groupings in Dublin city and the urban county districts) and 300 houses with a rateable valuation of £10 - £19. This group was over-represented deliberately as a pilot study had shown that the number in this category employing servants was small. An effort was made to have a fairly wide geographical coverage of Dublin city and the urban districts. The houses were selected randomly from Thom's *Directory* for 1911. Half of the houses were from the suburbs, Blackrock, Kingstown, Killiney, Pembroke, Rathmines and Rathgar where there was a high concentration of servants— one for every ten people. In Dublin city in 1911, there was one for every 25 of the population. A sample of 53 prominent citizens was selected from Thom's *Directory* by choosing people who held important positions in the church and the government, administration and defence of the country, as well as some of the leading lawyers, doctors, educators and most important businessmen. This ensured that some households with larger staffs would be included in the study. In all, 860 employers and 1,038 servants—970 women and 68 men—were involved in the study.

Information on the households selected was obtained from the enumerators' returns for the 1911 census. These gave data on the sex, age, religion, occupation, literacy, marital status and place of birth of the head of household and the other members and their relationship to the head. The enumerators' returns offered a unique opportunity to study household composition in Dublin and to relate servants and their known characteristics to the status, occupation and religious affiliation of employers and the possible needs of their households.

Notes

1 *Census of Ireland, General Reports,* 1881, 1891, 1901 and 1911.
2 Leonore Davidoff Lockwood, "Domestic service and the working class cycle," *Society for the Study of Labour History,* bulletin no. 26 (Spring 1973), p. 10.
3 A Donegal woman who wrote to the author said of the 1920s that whole families of girls from small farms went into service. Boys and girls, she added, were are their "wit's ends" for any kind of work (from Fohan, Co. Donegal on 26 February 1980).
4 "Irish-born servants comprised 44 per cent of all servants in 1880 in New York City and the then independent borough of Brooklyn, 34 per cent in Philadelphia, and 19 per cent in Chicago. In Boston, Cambridge, Fall River, Hartford, Jersey City, New Haven, Providence and Troy, Irish-born servants exceeded 40 per cent of all servants." David M. Katzman, *Seven Days a Week: Women and Domestic Service in Industrialising America* (Oxford, 1978), p. 66. Robert E. Kennedy showed that 81 per cent of Irish female emigrants in employment in six American states were domestic servants. See idem., *The Irish: Emigration, Marriage and Fertility* (London, 1973), p. 71.
5 *Cost of Living of the Working Classes. Report of an Enquiry by the Board of Trade into Working Class Rents, Housing and Retail Prices,* H. C. 1908 [Cd 3864], cvii, p. xxxvii.
6 *Ibid.,* p. xxxix/359
7 *Ibid.,* pp 359, 372
8 *Ibid.,* p. 366.
9 Derek Hudson, *Munby—Man of Two Worlds: the Life and Diaries of Arthur J. Munby, 1828-1910* (London, 1972), p. 47.
10 *Census of Ireland,* 1911.
11 Mary E. Daly, *Dublin the Deposed Capital: A Social and Economic History* 1860-1914 (Cork, 1984), pp 138, 142.
12 From former servants to the author at St Patrick's Tce., Monkstown on October 15 1980; at Tara, Co. Meath on 12 April 1980. A study done in Buffalo in 1859 by Lawrence Glasco said that the propensity of Irish girls to work in service was so high that "virtually every Irish girl during adolescence spent several years as a live-in domestic." Quoted in Katzman, *op. cit.,* p. 80.
13 From a former servant to the author, at Farrell Street, Kells, on 1 March 1980.
14 "Except amongst the lowest class of domestic workers, wages

(with which must be estimated cost of maintenance), have for many years been higher than those of workers in comparable occupations, such as clerks, shop assistants and factory employees, and they continue to rise." Ministry of Reconstruction, *Report of the Woman's Advisory Committee on the Domestic Service Problem*, H. C. 1919 [Cmd 67]. xxix, p. 29.

15 Rowntree, in his study of York, states that it was well known that Irish and Welsh children not living at home and working as domestic servants sent considerable sums home to their parents. Seebohm Rowntree, *Poverty: A Study of Town Life* (London, 1902), p. 112.

16 A former servant said that she gave up her job as a shop assistant and became a servant for this reason (from former servant at Leighton Road, Crumlin to author on March 23 1980). See also Frank Dawes, *Not in Front of the Servants* (London, 1973), p. 111; Theresa M. McBride, *The Domestic Revolution* (London, 1976), p. 49; Katzman, *op. cit.*, p. 4.

17 Lockwood, *art. cit.*, p. 10. Katzman, *op. cit.*, p. 151.

18 Brighid, "Domestic service as a profession for women," *The Irish Homestead*, viii, no. 6, (February 1902), p. 113.

19 *Annual Reports of the Inspector of Industrial and Reformatory Schools (Ireland)*, 1879-1919. *Twenty-Eighth Report of the Inspector Appointed to Visit Reformatory and Industrial Schools*, H. C., 1890, [C6168], xxxviii, pt. 1, p. 473, stated that 386 girls left industrial schools and 13 left reformatories for "employment in service." The *Forty-Eighth Report of the Inspector Appointed to Visit Reformatory and Industrial Schools*, H. C. 1910, [Cd 5318], lviii, p. 1, recorded 419 leaving industrial schools and 9 leaving reformatories for "employment or service."

20 The Killarney School of Housewifery was founded in the nineteenth century by Lady Kenmare to train servants. In 1906 the Domestic Training Institute for Protestant Girls opened in Charlemont Street, Dublin.

21 *Eighteenth Report of the Inspector Appointed to Visit Reformatory and Industrial Schools*, (Ireland) H. C. 1880, [C2692], xxxvii, p. 26/398.

22 Frank O'Connor, *An Only Child* (London, 1961), pp 49, 60.

23 Isabelle Beeton, *The Book of Household Management* (London, 1892), p. 1180.

24 Patricia Branca, *Silent Sisterhood: Middle Class Women in the Victorian Home* (London, 1975), p. 56.

25 Charles Booth, *Life and Labour in London* (London, 1903), p. 218.
26 *Census of Ireland*, 1911.
27 *Census of Ireland*, 1881, 1891 and 1901.
28 Percentage of female servants in different age groups in Dublin houses in 1911.

Age group	15-29	30-39	40-49	50-59	60+	Total
Number	599	178	98	50	45	970
%	61.8	18.4	10.1	5.1	4.6	100

29 Miss C. E. Collet, *Report on the Money Wages of Indoor Domestic Servants*, H. C. 1899, [C9364], xcii, p. 9/17, (hereafter cited as Collet, *Report*).
30 This is also pointed out by McBride, *op. cit.*, pp. 56, 84, and by L. Davidoff and R. Hawthorn, *A Day in the Life of a Victorian Domestic Servant* (London, 1976), p. 86.
31 Percentage of female servants single, married and widowed in Dublin houses in 1911.

	Single	Married	Widowed	Total
Number	889	18	63	970
%	91.6	1.9	6.5	100

32 Percentage of women, in different age groups, married and widowed, in the general population and in service in Dublin in 1911.

Age Group	General Population	Servants
20-24	13	0
25-34	46	3
35-44	69	20
45-54	75	27
55-64	79	30
65+	80	33

33 This is also stressed by many writers. See McBride, *op. cit.*, pp 56, 90; Katzman, *op. cit.*, p. 269; Davidoff and Hawthorn, *op. cit.*, p. 88.
34 Miss C. E. Collet, *Report on the Statistics of Employment of*

Women and Girls, H. C. 1894, [C7564], lxxi, pt. 11.

35 "This meant that you could not ask anyone in," (former servant at Dublin Central Mission, Marlborough Place to author on 12 March, 1980).

36 *Freeman's Journal*, 5 October 1880.

37 A former employer said that she told her servants to tell boyfriends that they were housekeepers (employer at Eglinton Park, Dublin to author on 18 April 1980).

38 "Kathleen" wrote to author in 1980.

39 This is stressed by W. T. Layton in his article "Changes in the wages of domestic servants during fifty years," *Journal of the Statistical Society of London*, lxxi, (1908), part iii, iv, p. 516.

40 Collet, *Report*, pp 2, 9-10, 17.

41 Pamela Horn, *The Rise and Fall of the Victorian Servant* (Dublin, 1975), p. 124. McBride, *op. cit.*, p. 60.

42 These wage rates were taken from the *Irish Times* (hereafter *IT*), and the *Freeman's Journal* (hereafter *FJ*), in three different years for each decade. Twenty-two issues of the former and twenty-eight of the latter were examined.

43 These were based on wages for cooks (68), taken from the same issues of the *IT* (see fn 42 above). The number of cooks for whom wages were given in the *FJ* was so small, and most employers seemed to require a general servant who would do the cooking, that these were ignored.

44 This was seen from the Dublin study.

45 Molly Keane in *Good Behaviour* (London, 1981), described the cook, Mrs Lennon, as middle-aged, with the family for fifteen years and earning £30 a year. Unfortunately she died and the mistress offered the house/parlourmaid £3 extra to do the cooking. She then had £12 a year (pp 72, 74). This shows the big differences in pay between the specialist cook and other servants.

46 *FJ*, 22 January 1889; 19 January 1892, 16 January 1894.

47 These wage rates were taken from the *IT*, *FJ* and the *Wicklow People*. The wage book of Elizabeth, wife of John Dillon, who lived in North Great George's Street, Dublin, shows that in August 1899 a housemaid was engaged at £16 a year and a house/parlourmaid at £18 a year. A replacement for the latter was paid £20 in 1902. Elizabeth Dillon wages book, 1896, Ms 6,717 Dillon Papers (Trinity College, Dublin).

48 *IT*, 25 January 1910.

49 A general servant, aged fourteen, was paid £3/18 in 1902 (former

servant in Old Folks' Association, Dun Laoghaire to author on 15 October 1980).
50 *Poor Law Union and Lunacy Inquiry Commission* (Ireland), H. C. 1878-1879, [C2239], xxxi, pp 305-32.
51 Ms 462, Folklore Department (University College Dublin), p. 275.
52 *Ibid.*, vol 172, p. 82.
53 *Agricultural Statistics of Ireland*, 1906, p. 158/786. Former farm servant from Emly, Co. Tipperary, to author 16 April 1980. Charles Booth found that lower grade servants in London, especially the younger ones, were paid consistently less than the average servant in middle and upper class houses. The same thing happened in Ireland. Booth, *op. cit.*, pp. 216-7. 223.
54 From former servants to author, one seen at the Old Folks' Association in Dun Laoghaire on 15 October 1980 and the other at the Coast Road, Malahide on May 1 1980. See also, *Minutes of Evidence to Royal Commission on Labour*, H. C. 1893-4, [C6894-IX], xxiv, p. 446.
55 Board of Trade (Labour Department), *Expenditure of Wage Earning Women and Girls*, H. C. 1911, [Cd 5963], lxxxix, pp 2892.
56 *Ibid.*, p. 6/536.
57 *Ibid.*, pp 90-91/620-1.
58 The rent of two rooms in Dublin was 3/- to 4/6 a week in 1912. *Report of an Enquiry by the Board of Trade into Working Class Rents and Retail Prices in 1912*, p. 290/572. A girl could rent a room in the Girls' Friendly Society Lodge in 23 South Frederick Street for 1/9 a week in 1899, *Annual Report of the Girls' Friendly Society for 1899*.
59 Entries for December 1905, 1908 and 1912 in the Account book of Sir Robert Hodson of Hollybrooke House, Kilmacanoge, Co. Wicklow, 1899-1914. Ms 16,436, Hodson Papers (National Library of Ireland). Clonbrock Papers, Ms 19, 567, entry for 12 December 1907 (National Library of Ireland). Entries for 1904, 05, 06, in Ms 6721, Dillon Papers, private accounts 1904-7 (Trinity College Dublin). D. Thompson and M. McGusty (eds.), *The Irish Journals of Elizabeth Smith, 1840-1850* (London, 1980), p. 243.
60 Entries for November 1882 and January 1883 in Ms 5042, vol. 1, Vere O'Brien Papers, personal account books, 1876-86, (Trinity College Dublin).

61 Horn, *op. cit.* pp 60, 128. Frank E. Huggett, *Life Below Stairs* (London, 1977), p. 42.
62 Lady Dilke, A. Amy Butler, Margaret White, *Women's Work* (London, 1894), p. 58. Dermot Keogh, "Michael O'Lehane and the organisation of Linen Drapers' Assistants," in *Saothar* 3, p. 36, describes the insanitary and hazardous conditions in many of these premises in Ireland.
63 Dermot Keogh, A study of the Dublin trade union movement and labour leadership, 1907-1914, (Unpublished M. A. thesis, National University of Ireland, 1974), p. 37.
64 Keogh, *art. cit.*, p. 37.
65 *Ibid.*
66 Dublin Trades Council Minutes, 11 June 1894.
67 Mostyn M. Bird, *Woman at Work* (London, 1911), pp 108-11. Booth, *op. cit.*, p. 224.
68 Brighid, *art. cit.*, p. 113.
69 The *Report of Commission on Vocational Organisation* (Dublin 1943) stressed that conditions largely depended on the employers, p. 416.
70 John Ross, *Pilgrim Script* (London, 1927), p. 79.
71 Former servant at Farrell Street, Kells, to author on 12 March 1980.
72 *Journals of the House of Commons*, vol. 166, 1911, no. 73, Wednesday 17 May 1911; no. 81, 29 May 1911, p. 250; Horn, *op. cit.*, p. 159.
73 *Ibid.*, p. 111; Davidoff and Hawthorn, *op. cit.*, p. 82; Flora Thompson, *Lark Rise to Candleford* (London, 1973), p. 173.
74 A former servant stated that she had white furniture in her room, "it had to be different." (Telephone conversation on 26 March 1980).
75 Booth, *op. cit.*, p. 219. A former servant described the kitchen where the servants played cards as warm and comfortable. (To author at Terryglass, Nenagh on 29 August 1980).
76 L. de K. K., "Household hints on furnishing bedrooms," *The Irish Homestead*, xi, no. 45 (Nov. 1905), p. 833.
77 Anon., "The housing of domestic servants", *The Lancet*, (19 Aug. 1905), p. 546.
78 Former servant interviewed at Old Folks' Association, Dun Laoghaire on 15 October 1980.
79 Katzman, *op. cit.*, p. 108..
80 Booth, *op. cit.*, p. 219. McBride, *op. cit.*, p. 55.

81 Former servant at Farrell Street, Kells to author on 12 March 1980.
82 Former servant at Nutley Park to author on 9 May 1980.
83 McBride, *op. cit.*, p. 68. Horn, *op. cit.*, p. 97.
84 Former servants and employers to author.
85 *Census of Ireland* 1911.
86 Davidoff and Hawthorn, *op. cit.*, p. 84. Horn, *op. cit.*, pp 157-8. Katzman, *op. cit.*, p. 234. Minutes of evidence of the ITGWU to the Commission on Vocational Organisation in 1940, Mss 922-41 (National Library of Ireland), vol. 7, 928. p. 2345, par. 14423.
87 McBride, *op. cit.*, pp 15, 25.
88 *Mrs Beeton's Household Management* (London, 1923 ed.), pp 1518-20.
89 Horn, *op. cit.*, p. 46.
90 "What is being done in England. Hints for Irish Registers," from the Women's Freedom League published in the *Irish Citizen*, 13 July 1912, p. 62. Letter from F. Sheehy Skeffington in the *Irish Citizen*, 6 July 1912, p. 53.
91 Horn, *op. cit.*, p. 163.
92 Booth, *op. cit.*, p. 219.
93 A former servant, an orphan, who worked in the west of Ireland in 1936.
94 "Holidays were never heard of." (Former servant in Fennor, Slane to author on 5 March 1980). An employer explained that she did not give her servants holidays as they generally lived nearby. (Former employer from Oughterard to author, 27 February 1980).
95 Horn, *op. cit.*, pp. 118-20.
96 Former servant at Nutley Park on 9 May 1980; servant from Emly on 16 April 1980.
97 Former servant at Farrell Street, Kells on 12 March 1980.
98 Katzman, *op. cit.*, p. 138. McBride, *op. cit.*, p. 71. Horn, *op. cit.*, p. 24. Branca, *op. cit.*, pp. 56-7. Rose Mary Crawshay, *Domestic Service for Gentlewomen: A Record of Experience and Success* (pamphlet, London, 1896), p. 23.
99 Collet, *Report*, p. 25-33.
100 Katzman, *op. cit.*, p. 249.
101 Former servant at Milltown, Mullingar to author on 10 October 1980.
102 Ministry of Reconstruction, *Report of the Domestic Service Sub-Committee on Organisation and Conditions*, pp 4-10, 23-29.

"The Tune of the Stars and Stripes"— The American Influence on the Irish Suffrage Movement

Cliona Murphy

The American influence on Irish life, history and politics has long been of interest to observers and historians of Irish society. O'Connell, Parnell, Redmond, de Valera and many other nationalist leaders were conscious of the importance of the American connection, financially and otherwise, and were continually cultivating the sympathy of their trans-Atlantic cousins. And, indeed, their efforts were rewarded with contributions to their funds and sporadic attempts by the Americans to pressurise the British to solve the Irish problem. The contact was one between powerless subjects of a British colony and their more influential relatives who, as a formal colony, had pitted themselves against imperial Britain and ultimately won their independence. By the end of the nineteenth century Irish Americans, both recently arrived and those earlier emigrants whose memory of the famine was still vivid, were motivated to maintain the bond not only by a common American/Irish distrust of the British but also by the experience of a common struggle. This important relationship has been documented over the years by American, Irish American and Irish historians.[1] The historiography has been vast, in depth and of diverse quality; however, there is one aspect of this relationship (reflecting the general trend in Irish historiography) which has not received attention.

The Female Connection
The strong emotional ties between Ireland and the United

States were not restricted to contact between men. This connection is reflected in the relationship between Irish and American women also. One area where it is particularly apparent is between the women's suffrage movements in the two countries. Their relationship, evident in the nineteenth century, was specially noticeable and of significance in the twentieth century. Women in both countries were looking for the franchise. They wished to vote and sit in parliament or Congress. There certainly were differences in their situations; the American women were looking for the franchise from their own state and federal governments[2] while the Irish women were looking for the vote from the British government.[3] The Irish women could be enfranchised under a general Women's Suffrage Bill which would apply to women in Britain and Ireland or under a women's suffrage amendment to the Home Rule Bill which was going through parliament 1912-1914.[4] Notwithstanding the differences, the bond was fairly constant and, at times, strong. American contact and support was important for Irish women for the same reasons as it was important for Irish men. Living in a small colony they needed all the aid they could get. This took the form of intellectual, moral and, to some extent, political support. Ironically enough, financial support does not seem to have been forthcoming, or requested, from the American women while on at least two occasions it arrived and was accepted from the British suffragists.[5]

Irish women, too, like the Irish Parliamentary Party were looking for something from the British parliament. They had little chance of success on their own. They did not have the support of their own countrymen nor did they have a native parliament to petition. Their demand was opposed by the British government and a large number of their country's representatives at Westminster. For the Irish suffrage movement to survive and achieve its goal it needed to exploit every possible method of getting the demand heard and implemented. Therefore, strong contacts with the American movement were critically important in a number of ways. Besides being a source of encouragement and support, the contacts helped to counteract the many accusations, more often than not coming from nationalist quarters, that the Irish suffrage movement was merely another branch of the British movement. One nationalist wrote, "The suffrage movement is turning thoughts of the average Irishwoman Englandwards. That is its greatest danger in the present state of this country".[6] On this ground alone Irish politicians felt they could claim that women's suffrage was not an Irish issue and therefore need not be on their political agenda. The Irish women by their many international contacts were openly declaring that this was clearly not the case. Therefore, contacts with the Americans from several points of view was important for the Irish suffrage movement to survive, grow, have significant impact and, curiously enough, establish their independence as a movement.

The Irish Suffrage Movement

Before further examining the strong connections between American and Irish women it is appropriate to say a few words about the origins of the Irish women's suffrage movement. As in other countries, the Quakers were involved in its foundation.[7] A Quaker couple, the Haslams, founded the Irish Women's Suffrage and Local Government Association in 1876. They had been inspired by the British Liberal MP and author of the controversial essay *On the Subjection of Women*, John Stuart Mill, who attempted, and failed, to attach a women's suffrage amendment to the 1867 Reform Bill.[8] Their organisation worked quietly and steadily into the twentieth century and was successful in promoting women's participation in local government. However, by the early 1900's a number of women were becoming impatient with their lack of progress in gaining the national franchise. The gentle petitioning and quiet drawing room meetings used by the IWSLGA irritated the younger, university educated ambitious women. They wanted more than the local franchise for propertied women and were not happy with the minor successes which included being able to sit on Poor Law and School Boards (1896) and having the local government franchise (1898).[9] Therefore, a number of alternative groups were formed. In true Irish style there was a suffrage group to represent every branch of the Irish political spectrum which ranged from nationalist to unionist, from Protestant to Catholic to non-denominational.[10] According to one source in 1912, there were 3,000 members of the suffrage movement spread throughout the cities, towns and country districts of Ireland.[11] Needless to say there were many intra-and inter-group disputes, again following another typical Irish pattern. These disputes usually centred on the relative importance to the movement of nationalism, militancy, trade unionism and debate over what type of relationship to have with the British suffrage movement.[12]

The most important of the new suffrage societies was the Irish Women's Franchise League. It was founded in 1908 by two couples, Frank and Hanna Sheehy Skeffington and James and Margaret Cousins, who were very much a part of the turn of the century cultural and nationalist movement, the Irish Renaissance. They associated with Shaw, Yeats, the Colums, George Birmingham, James Stephens, Countess Markievicz and others. Though many in the IWFL were interested in the national question, their primary concern was attaining the suffrage.[13] Differences of opinion as to the role of the movement and other issues were examined in a newspaper they established in 1912, the *Irish Citizen*. Its aim was to reflect the views of all suffragist groups in Ireland but it, nevertheless, was clearly a mouthpiece for the Irish Women's Franchise League.[14] It was to survive, first as a weekly and later as a monthly, until 1920.

From the beginning of the suffrage movement in Ireland there was a consciousness among Irish women that they were not alone and were part of an international movement. Louie Bennett, the Irish suffragist and trade unionist, expressed the hope that "every Irish suffrage society will work to keep alive the consciousness that the women's movement is a world wide movement; that we suffragists are working for all women and that we recognise the bond of sisterhood uniting women of every nationality." As a number of comparative studies on suffrage movements have shown, contact between women in different countries was very important in terms of moral support and intellectual stimulation.[15] Reading one another's literature, writing letters and exchanging visits all served to reinforce the suffragists' determination. The Irish women were particularly conscious of the movements in Britain and the United States, but they also had strong contacts with Norwegian, Australian and South African women, among others.[16] They subscribed to foreign suffrage journals such as *Jus Suffragi, The Woman's Outlook, The Vote* and *Votes For Women* and many of the British journals carried a "Notes on Ireland" section.[17]

The American Connection

However, it is their relationship with the American movement which is of particular importance since it mirrored, and arose out of, the already existing strong bond between the American and the Irish people. A number of factors made the Irish American relationship different from the other foreign contacts. It was a reciprocal relationship between a small, powerless, subject country and a large important independent country. The situation in the United States encouraged the Irish women, and gave them hope when they saw individual states were gradually being enfranchised.[18] However, it was not a relationship solely for the purposes of mutual moral and intellectual support alone, it was also a devious way of putting pressure on both Irish and British politicians to include a women's suffrage amendment in the Irish Home Rule Bill. Irish women hoped to use their international contacts, particularly their contacts with the United States, to further their own situation at home.

Suffragists in Ireland were familiar with the major landmarks in the history of the movement for suffrage in the United States. They were conscious of the significance of the Seneca Falls meeting in upstate New York where American women drew up their Declaration in 1848[19] and they studied the writings of Charlotte Perkins Gilman and Alice Paul. They closely followed developments in the United States as individual territories or states got the vote and pointed out to antisuffragists at home that there were no ill-consequences. Children were not being neglected and husbands did not go without their supper, and the sun was still setting in the west.

Not only were Irish women conscious of the movement for suffrage in the United States, Irish men, too, were aware that it was of growing importance and foreshadowed the direction future politics was to take. For example, Daniel O'Connell, at the request of the American women, requested that women should be admitted to the Antislavery Conference of 1840 in London and he was significantly impressed by the women of Seneca Falls.[20] Charles Stewart Parnell, too, was influenced by American women, not least his American mother.[21] In 1877 he presented a petition in parliament signed by the people of Dublin in support of women's suffrage.[22] Neither O'Connell nor Parnell could be described as ardent woman suffragists, but they were aware that this issue was of growing significance and unlike some later Irish politicians, who will be discussed below, they did not actively resist it and were more or less sympathetic. Sir Horace Plunkett, politician, pioneer of the cooperative movement in Ireland, and founder of the Irish Countrywoman's Association, was very much impressed by what he had seen in the United States. He had spent a number of years ranching in Wyoming where the first women in America were enfranchised in 1869. When he returned to Ireland and became an M.P. he wrote about women's suffrage and was among the male supporters of the Irish Women's Franchise League. One of his biographers, Margaret Digby, recounts him "amusing the House [of Commons] with an impromptu speech on women's suffrage, drawn from his Wyoming experience back in 1892".[23] Indeed such positive observations by Plunkett must have had some role in his decision to form the Irish Countrywoman's Association.[24]

The relationship between the Irish and American suffrage movements was not merely one in which Irish women were observing what was going on in the United States. There was interest, too, among the American women in the Irish movement. They communicated with their Irish counterparts and encouraged their efforts. This becomes evident in an examination of the newspaper of the Irish Women's Franchise League, the *Irish Citizen,* which routinely published letters from American women giving advice and encouragement and relating what was happening in the movement in the United States. In January 1914 a letter arrived from Mrs Alice Park "the well known Californian suffragist." She wrote that actions of suffragists in different countries helped the cause in general. "... Every outbreak in England, Scotland and Ireland gives all women everywhere great publicity in newspapers great and small, without any effort on the part of women outside of the British Isles. Publicity is an absolute necessity in pushing a forward movement".[25] Park was right, and suffrage actions in various countries served to put politicians under added pressure in their home countries. The National American Women's Suffrage Association frequently sent messages of encouragement to the *Irish Citizen*. Among American correspondents were suffragists Jane Addams, Alice Paul, a New Jersey Quaker and suffragist, and her lieutenant Lucy Burns, the only prominent American suffragist leader of Irish Catholic ancestry.[26]

The *Irish Citizen* looks to America

The *Irish Citizen*, observing what was going on worldwide as regards women's issues, carried articles as diverse as how women influenced temperance legislation in Finland and how women suffragists in New Zealand were the first to achieve a national franchise in 1893.[27] Many issues contained articles on American women. Not surprisingly, the general conclusion in the pages of the *Citizen* was that women were substantially better off in the United States than they were in Ireland. They lived in a country which was independent, which was rapidly opening up opportunities to women in education and in the professions and where one state after another was granting the franchise to women. The *Citizen* compared this to the bleak situation where Irish women were looking for the vote from a foreign parliament and where the vast majority of their parliamentary representatives were unsympathetic to their cause. One such article was "The Tune of the Stars and Stripes." It recounted the grievance of Irish women concerning their low status in the eyes of the law and reflected a growing movement which demanded the right of Irish women to become lawyers.

> It is now known that, as far as openings for professional women are concerned, America is one of the most advanced. The other day in New York Grace O'Neill, a "frail woman of 26 years acted as a special judge in a divorce suit, and acquitted herself admirably." Should an Irish woman go to America she would be eligible for like responsibilities—remaining at home the same woman will be deemed unworthy of entering the legal profession. Small wonder our sisters are emigrating in ever increasing numbers.[28]

Interest in the American suffragist movement continued to weave its way through a number of issues of the *Irish Citizen*. Articles appeared on "How the Vote was won in Illinois," and "Women displace Southern Pacific."[29] Admiration of the American movement was often contrasted sharply with criticism of the British movement. The author of an article entitled "Women Suffrage in America; an Irish Women's Impression" commented that "the Suffrage campaign is carried on with an amount of intelligence and serious thought which is, regrettably not so obvious in the English movement ...A man speaker the other day declared that American women did not need to be militant because their men are not so thickheaded as Englishmen...."[30] This statement did not just express frustration with British parliamentarians but also with the Pankhurst movement and its intrusive activities in Ireland.

The *Irish Citizen* was not the only source of inspiration. Studies of individual women suffragists and other women activists in various countries have conveyed the great extent to which women have been, and continue to be, influenced and inspired by their reading.[31] Often they find vague thoughts and discontented feelings verbalised for the first time in books by other women—be they fiction, treatises or other forms of literature. This serves various purposes. The reading women realise that their discontent is not unique, there is a sisterhood out there who feel the same way. Because they realise that they are no longer alone women are often motivated to join support groups in order to change their disagreeable situation and, indeed, sometimes to put pen to paper themselves. This was the case, too, with Irish women.[32] Books they read, written by American writers and others, were important in putting them in touch with an international movement. They either bought books through the suffrage societies, or borrowed them from the circulating libraries[33] and they were informed about important books in a special column in the *Irish Citizen* called the "Citizen's Bookshelf." The *Citizen's* book reviews were concerned with the latest additions in suffrage literature as well as relevant previously published books. The suffrage circulating libraries made a wide body of literature available and were important in educating Irish women. From the reviews it can be seen that Irishwomen were exposed to the same literature as their American, British and continental counterparts and that they were up to date with the literature coming out of the United States. Thus, there was a common intellectual understanding among women who were often 5,000 miles apart. Indeed it was not only women who were influenced by this literature; the Irish writer the Rev O'Hannay, who wrote under the alias of George Birmingham, told Frank Sheehy Skeffington "tell your wife from me that I [am] reading a work by a perfect whirlwind of a feminist, a Mrs or Miss (She would probably disdain both titles) Charlotte Gilman Perkins ... there is no doubt that the reading is good for me".[34] Despite his muddling up the American author's name, his enthusiasm for the book is obvious and must have influenced his supportive attitude towards the suffragists in Ireland which were propounded from his pulpit and women's suffrage platforms.[35] Charlotte

Perkins Gilman's book *What Diantha Did* was recommended by the South Anne Street Library to all "who are interested in the domestic side of the feminist movement."[36]

The Americans Visit

Points made in the articles of the *Irish Citizen* about the suffrage situation in the United States and impressions conveyed in books written by American women were reiterated when American suffragists came to visit and tour Ireland. The lecture tour by foreign suffragists was very much part of Irish suffrage life and the Americans were among a host of other lecturers from Britain, Australia, and Norway. The lecturers visited large towns in Ireland which included Belfast, Dublin and Cork. Their venues were usually city or town halls or, as in the case of Mrs Pankhurst, the ice rink in Rathmines, Dublin.[37] The lectures received a lot of advance publicity in the suffragist and general press and were well attended. The audiences did not just include dedicated suffragist but also a number of curious men and women plus a handful of anti-suffragist hecklers who added colour and humour to the meetings. The American women told their audiences about the lives of women in those states where women had received the franchise and about the efforts women were making in other states to get the vote. The impact of these visits was significant and reassured Irish women they were not alone in their struggle. The visits were also important in giving impetus to recruitment drives carried out by the different suffrage movements. Mrs Colby, the chairman of the National American Women's Suffrage Association, came from the United States and it was reported that "Her clever accounts of suffrage work in the United States gave much pleasure."[38] Her tour was nationwide. She was a particular success on her visit to Cork. Six hundred people attended an "At Home" in the City Hall where she told them about the movement in America.[39] In Belfast she explained "How women use the vote in the U.S when they have it."[40]

Another American visitor was Mrs Helen Frazer. The

Irish Women's Suffrage organisation reported that she "spent a month in Ireland ... drew large [numbers of] members to the Federation."[41] In October 1914 the *Irish Citizen* drew attention to the "enthusiastic reception" that had been given to Mrs Alice Park, a woman who frequently corresponded with Irish suffragists.[42] Sympathetic male Americans also came to speak to Irish suffragists. The Rev William Sperry of Fall River, Mass. spoke to the Irish Women's Reform League about the suffrage movement in Massachussetts.[43] He was adding a voice to the growing support among a portion of Irish clergy for women's suffrage.[44] These Americans always gave special hope to the Irish, coming from a country where some women had been enfranchised, where there were many contacts with Ireland and funds were ample.

Irish Suffragists in America

Having Americans come and talk to Irish suffragists was exciting; however, going to the United States to see the situation for themselves was even better. Just as the United States had beckoned many Irish campaigners before him, it was to lure Frank Sheehy Skeffington in 1915 to get publicity for his campaign against the attempt to introduce conscription into Ireland.[45] While there, he avidly watched what was going on in the American suffrage scene. He sent back enthusiastic letters to his wife about the suffragists he encountered. Writing home he reported on the excitement in New York when it was suggested that women stay off their jobs for one day to show their strength on the labour market. He was impressed, too, when the states of New York, Pennsylvania and Massachussetts were to vote on the Women's Suffrage Amendment to the constitution. Undeterred when neither of these events came off he wrote to his wife that he had been to a suffragist parade "the finest I have ever seen ... About 30,000 marched up Fifth Avenue..." He added, "Some 5,000 men were in the march."[46] It is interesting that Sheehy Skeffington should refer to the male participation in the parade since men played an important role in the IWFL.[47]

After his murder, which took place during the Rising of 1916, his wife went on a tour to publicise his death and to try to get the United States to pressurise the British to bring his murderer, Captain Colthurst, to trial.[48] While there she had observations to make on American suffragism. She had an audience with President Wilson and on the whole admired his policy towards women's suffrage in the United States and more than likely agreed with a National American Women's Suffrage Association document which declared that the president should begin setting the world right for democracy by giving women the vote.[49] Back home she wrote

> Since my return to Ireland I have often been asked my view as to President Wilson's personality ... I think the President's attitude towards progress may best be illustrated by his action upon an internal American policy, namely: The Women's Suffrage Federal Amendment. It tends to show that while the President is not the type of lone pioneer who would push ahead against any odds, he is guided by what one may call a policy of enlightened expediency, and there is no statesman in the world today who knows better the exact time to come in on the right side and to press a reform home to a successful issue.[50]

Irish Women's Suffrage and Home Rule: The American Context

Having established that there was significant contact between the two movements, and that the American influence was important in an intellectual and supportive way to Irish women, it needs to be asked, did it have any wider implications outside the suffrage arena? The answer is most certainly. It posed a significant threat to Irish parliamentarians at Westminster who were looking for Home Rule. However, it was a threat which was not to reach its full potential for a number of reasons.

The demand for Home Rule by the Irish at Westminster was closely followed by Americans, both by the Irish Americans who felt a personal interest and other Americans who felt that Ireland should become independent from Britain as they had. Throughout the nineteenth and into the twentieth century the Americans were a constant presence in the background to Anglo-Irish relations. One historian has called it the Anglo-American Irish problem and contends that American interest in the Irish problem created tensions in the relationship between the United States and Britain.[51]

Americans, like many others, drew the analogy between Irish men looking for Home Rule and women looking for the suffrage. Therefore, many found it incomprehensible that men could look for the independence of their nation and at the same time have little or no sympathy for women demanding the vote. Surely the two issues were the same? How could someone support one cause and not the other? Both were steps in the democratic process. However, this was not a logic which appealed to the majority of early twentieth century Irish male minds. For many it was adequate that the husband should represent his wife. For others the vote still represented property. Others were strict adherents to the separate spheres philosophy. There were, of course, numerous flaws in these beliefs. Not all women had husbands to represent them. Not all husbands had property. Indeed, not all males had the vote.[52] Along with all these and other objections, which ranged from biological to philosophic and were voiced in all countries where women's suffrage was being sought, in Ireland there were numerous peculiarities in the political situation which added to the range of these objections.

The vast majority of MPs in the Irish Parliamentary Party were opposed to women's suffrage. Some of them, like John Dillon and John Redmond, made no secret of their antagonism. They, from the vantage point of their comfortable parliamentary seats at Westminster, saw absolutely no reason why women should vote. However, aside from this gender based prejudice, they had other objections also.[53] They wished to concentrate upon one issue—Home Rule, and once that was achieved other issues could be dealt with in their turn. Many believed it should be left up to Irish men, when they got their own parliament in Dublin, to decide whether or not to give Irish women the vote.[54] The Liberal prime minister, Asquith, a resolute anti-suffragist until 1915, was the pilot of the 1912 Home Rule Bill through parliament. The Irish Party, which was in alliance with the Liberal party, did not wish to do anything to upset him. They also felt that any discussion of women's suffrage in parliament would take up unnecessary parliamentary discussion time and delay the passage of the Home Rule Bill.[55] Furthermore, if women were enfranchised, the opposition in Parliament would be entitled to call for a general election since there would then be a new part of the electorate who were not represented in parliament.[56] If there was a general election the Irish, reflecting a common view of the time that women would vote conservatively, feared a Conservative majority and thus the loss of Home Rule.[57]

While all this was on the minds of the Irish MPs, some Americans, at a distance, saw it simply as Irish men looking for independence for their country and excluding women from their demand. They supported the view of the IWFL who argued (taking John Dillon's slogan referring to the Unionist reluctance to leave the United Kingdom) that there should be "Home Rule for all Ireland or No Home Rule."[58] There was no point in getting independent Ireland off to a bad start by only enfranchising the male population. American concern was reflected in the suffragist press, in concerned letters and demonstrations. Letters appeared periodically in suffragist journals reminding Redmond that votes for Irish women was certainly not a mere domestic issue, but caused grave concern across the Atlantic. Mr Moskowitz, of the Down Town New York Ethical Society, wrote to the English suffragist newspaper, *Votes for Women*, expressing the views of a number of Americans.

> We Americans are intensely interested in the prospect of Irish Home Rule. With us State and local autonomy is no longer a conviction; it is a political instinct ... To a believer in democracy, Irish Home Rule is as inevitable as

> votes for women ... there is no logic in answering the democratic demands of the Irish people with an undemocratic Home Rule Bill. For to deprive the women of Ireland of the privilege of active participation in the political life of their country is not only undemocratic but it is unjust to Ireland and its manhood and womanhood.[59]

In the same year the *Irish Citizen* also endeavoured to bring home to Mr Redmond the pressure of Irish-American public opinion.

> On the 4th of May an immense demonstration of Americans, numbering 10,000 at least, took place in New York, and amongst the demands they put forward was one for the extension of the vote to Irish women in the Home Rule Bill. We trust the Irish Party will not be blind to the significance of the action of the American women and we will learn in time the moral danger of a position which claims Home Rule for the Irish men and denies it for the Irish women.[60]

Therefore, it was not in Ireland alone that Redmond was made to feel the disapproval of suffragists. Every time he went to England he was confronted by women who were angry at him not only for denying Irish women the vote, but also for preventing English women being enfranchised since the majority of the Irish Party voted against every women's suffrage bill or amendment that came before Parliament. He was heckled wherever he went, at public meetings, on trains and even at a bridge opening ceremony where he was asked "When do you mean to open a bridge for the women of Ireland?"[61] He was to get no respite when he went further afield. On visits to Australia and the United States, suffragists informed him of funds being contributed to his party and warned they would be stopped unless he adopted a pro-suffragist point of view.[62] During his visit to the United States in September 1910 he was told by Irish American women that they could not provide him with funds unless the Irish Party at Westminster would press forward on Votes for Women. Despite this he still returned to Ireland with

$100,000 in election funds.[63]

When a woman's suffrage amendment to the Irish Home Rule Bill was defeated in November 1914 the English journal *Men's League for Women's Suffrage* admonished:

> While three of the United States were admitting women to citizenship as an incident in the General Election, our House of Commons was occupying itself in refusing the franchise to the women of Ireland ... Listening to these three speeches of the two Redmonds and Mr Law, one realised what is at the centre of the situation. The Irish Party is resolved at all costs that the Home Rule parliament shall not start with women electors. They dread the disruptive effect of the suffrage on the Liberal cabinet, but even more, it seems to me, they dread the experiment of enfranchising their own sisters and wives ... In order to perpetuate the votelessness of their own women, they must also enforce the subjection of our own.[64]

While Irish and American Suffragists hoped to blackmail Redmond into supporting the suffrage for Irish women they never really succeeded in being little more than an annoyance. Redmond was supported in his antipathy towards the women's suffrage by the bulk of his party and indeed the bulk of his Irish/American male supporters who sprang from the same patriarchical Irish Catholic background. Therefore, threats from the women, both Irish and American, had little impact as regards finance. However, protests from the United States concerning the Irish women's suffrage issue cannot have contributed to Redmond's peace of mind.

The United States was to provide the context for another aspect of the activities of the Irish suffrage movement, the growing tension between Irish and British suffragists. The resentment was particularly evident between the IWFL and the English Pankhurst movement, the Women's Social and Political Union. The relationship between the two organisations had been subject to strain. While the Irish women shared a common purpose with the British women, achievement of the franchise, interaction between the two was complicated because of differences over the nationalist issue. Things were further complicated in Ireland by the existence of other suffrage groups who supported the Union, like the Conservative and Unionist Women's Franchise Association and a number of members of the Munster Women's Franchise League. These groups encouraged the WSPU in their belief that the movement in Ireland was merely an extension of their own. The situation became especially tense when English suffragists attempted to set up branches of their suffrage organisations in Ireland in 1913. They did not appear to recognise that it was a different country. The parallel was drawn in Ireland between Anglo-Saxon male imperialism and this new invasion of English women. And, of course, the centuries of animosity which had been part of the relationship between the two countries did not escape the women in the suffrage movements. English suffragists felt, however, that they were justified in coming to Ireland since it was members of the Irish Party who were the main stumbling block to getting any suffrage measure through Parliament.[65]

Members of the vocal IWFL were insistent that they should have separate representation at International women's conferences from their English counterparts. Frank Sheehy Skeffington wrote to the American founder of the Women's Peace Party, Jane Addams, about this matter in October 1915. The Party was formed as a result of the Great War and its aims included a "Concert of Nations" an international police force and an early cessation of hostilities. He stressed that it was of the utmost importance that Irish women have separate representation from the English. Sheehy Skeffington believed that Irish women should be allowed to make a separate case, since not only was their situation different from the English but they belonged to a separate nation.[66]

Some of the disputes between the IWFL and WSPU were placed within an American setting. After the Great War began in 1914, the nature of the suffrage movements in Ireland and Britain changed, with the English suffragists getting more and more involved in the war[67] and the Irish suffragists becoming increasingly involved with the Nationalist issue and at the same time pursuing a pacifist line as regards the war.[68] These elements complicated the whole suffrage question. In effect, they demonstrated that regardless of whatever the women may have desired, it was not possible to divorce their issue from the wider political framework. Indeed, the whole aim of their movements was to increase participation in the greater political process.

In an article written by Hanna Sheehy Skeffington in 1919 about her visit to the United States she spoke of the threat she posed for the British authorities and how they attempted to deal with her.

> The British Agents in the United States are naturally very perturbed at the Irish propaganda on behalf of our small nation. They dislike particularly propaganda of such Irish exiles as myself who had come directly from Ireland and could speak with first hand knowledge. As one of them observed: "My objection to Mrs Sheehy Skeffington is that she has a lot of damaging facts." Accordingly a trap was laid for me. I was invited by a women's society in Toronto to cross the frontier and lecture there on women's suffrage. I realised that Suffrage was being used as bait to get me on hostile ground where I might be interned, and politely refused the invitation.[69]

The antagonism between the Irish suffragists and Mrs Pankhurst and her followers was increased when Pankhurst was selected as what Hanna Sheehy Skeffington called one of Britain's "regular army of lecturers", turned into the United States, "not only to put her case for the war before American audiences, but to vilify, whenever possible, those nations that did not agree with her imperialist ambitions." Sheehy Skeffington commented that Americans were puzzled at the "curious specimens" of British "democracy" who were sent to the States as Britain's representatives.

> It seemed as if Imperialists of the *Morning Post* brand were furnished with credentials. For instance while Mrs

Pankhurst's campaign, Anti-Russian and Anti-Irish, was facilitated by the British government, Mrs Pethick Lawrence, the distinguished Suffragist and Pacifist leader, was refused passports to America where she was invited by American suffragists to help their campaign.[70]

The friendly relationship with the American suffragists was for the main part one of mutual admiration with the American suffragists taking a big interest in what was going on in Ireland both with regard to Home Rule and to women's equality. This was part of a long tradition of American interest in Ireland. However, this relationship also became strained during the war. While in America in 1915 Frank Sheehy Skeffington wrote "Just what is weak about the big suffrage movement here... [is] its timidity."[71] An article which appeared in the *Irish Citizen* during the war implied that American suffragists had put "suffrage on the shelf for the duration of the war."[72] From the hindsight of 1919 Hanna Sheehy Skeffington repeated the points made in that article.

> When America entered the war the same situation was created with regard to the Woman Suffrage Movement as occurred in Great Britain in 1914. Many of the so called Constitutional Suffragists turned their backs on suffrage and preached to their followers the urgent need of winning the war before all else. Their leaders such as Dr Anna Howard Shaw and Mrs Chapman Catt put suffrage on the shelf as did some of their British sisters, and told their followers that to ask for a vote just then, when their country was in a war to make the world safe for democracy was to be unpatriotic, if not pro-German ... A comfortable and decent burial was accordingly arranged for the suffragist corpse, and the interment would have taken place duly but for the militant section known as "The Nationalist Women's Party," headed by Alice Paul, a Quaker, and Lucy Byrne, an Irishwoman.[73]

Such reflections which Sheehy Skeffington made all too clear in the columns of the *Irish Citizen* during the war angered many American women who felt that they certainly had not put the war first. Indignant letters were written to the

Irish Citizen demanding a retraction and a correct portrayal of the situation, arguing that the number of women who continued to support and fight for the suffrage cause had been under-represented by Sheehy Skeffington. It was easier for Irish suffragists to have a more clearcut policy towards the war (not that all of them had). Patriotic support of the war was not so important in the Irish case since to many in Ireland it was a British war. It was not so easy for British and American suffragists whose leaders were insisting the war was necessary to protect a way of life. However, this was but a small blot on the relationship between the Irish and American suffragists.

The relationship between the Irish and American women is clearly an important chapter in the history of the Irish suffrage movement. Contacts with the women from the new world enabled the Irish women to feel they were part of a worldwide movement. Visits from the Americans encouraged interest and attracted new members to the movement in Ireland. Moral support was important before campaign drives when the suffrage issue was coming up in Parliament. Though not fully realized, the American contact provided another channel through which the Irish Party could be put under pressure. The relationship between the Irish and American women reinforced a feeling of sisterhood, and helped the Irish women formulate their own distinct identity. When they finally won the vote in 1918[74] they were, ironically enough, ahead of American women who were enfranchised in 1920. Nevertheless, there was much for Irish society to emulate in America as regards women's status. With the vote, and a few years later independence and a new state, the future looked optimistic. However, darker forces from unsuspected sources were in the wings ready to create new problems for Irish women.

Notes

1 The following are just a sample of what has been written in this area: F. M. Carroll, *American Opinion and the Irish Question 1910-1923* (Dublin, 1978); Leon O'Broin, *Fenian Fever: An Anglo-American Dilemma* (London, 1971); D. H. Akenson, *The United States and Ireland* (Cambridge, Mass., 1973); Lawrence McCaffery, *The Irish Diaspora in America* (Bloomington, 1976); idem., *Irish Nationalism and the American Contribution* (New York, 1976); J. E. Cuddy, *Irish America and National Isolation, 1914-20* (New York, 1976).
2 Aileen S. Kraditor, *The Ideas of the Woman Suffrage Movement, 1890-1920* (New York, 1981); Eleanor Flexner, *Century of Struggle: The Woman's Rights Movement in the United States* (New York, 1968); Albert Kirchmar et al., *The Women's Rights Movement in the United States 1848-1970: A Bibliography and Sourcebook* (New Jersey, 1972); Mari Jo and Paul Buhle (eds.), *The Concise History of Woman Suffrage* (Chicago, 1979). For a contemporary account see Carrie Chapman Catt and Nettie Rogers Shuler, *Woman Suffrage and Politics—The Inner Story of the Suffrage Movement* (Washington, 1969).
3 The Irish Suffrage struggle has been discussed in greater detail in Leah Levenson and Jerry Naderstad, *Hanna Sheehy Skeffington: A Pioneering Irish Feminist* (Syracuse, 1986); Cliona Murphy, *The Women's Suffrage Movement and Irish Society in the Early Twentieth Century* (Brighton, 1989); Rosemary Cullen Owens, *Smashing Times: A History of the Irish Suffrage Movement 1899-1922* (Dublin, 1984); A.D. Sheehy Skeffington and Rosemary Owens, *Votes for Women: Irish Women's Struggle for the Vote* (Dublin, 1975); Margaret Ward, "Suffrage first above all else!: an account of the Irish suffrage movement," *Feminist Review*, no. 10, (1982), pp 21-36; Mary Cullen, "How radical was Irish feminism between 1860 and 1920?," in P. J. Corish (ed.), *Radicals, Rebels and Establishments* (Dublin, 1985), pp 185-201; Ellen Hazelkorn, "The social and political views of Louie Bennett, 1870-1956", *Saothar*, no. 13, (1988), pp 32-44: Beth McKillen, "Irish feminism and national separatism, 1914-1923," *Eire/Ireland*, xviii, no. 3, (1981), pp 72-90 and continued in *ibid.*, xviii, no. 4, (1981), pp 72-90.
4 The relevant Bills were the readings of the Conciliation Bills in

1911 and 1912. In 1913 Dickenson proposed an amendment to the Reform Bill, which, if passed, would have applied to qualified British and Irish women. Snowden proposed an amendment to the Home Rule Bill (1912) to include the suffrage for Irish women as well as Irish men. See Murphy, *op. cit.*, chapter seven. See also David Martin Pugh, *Women's Suffrage in Britain, 1867-1928* (London, 1980); idem., "Politicians and the women's vote, 1914-1918," *History*, vol. 59, no. 197, (1974), pp 358-75.

5 In the annual report of the Irishwomen's Suffrage Federation it was acknowledged that "last year the NUWSS (National Union of Women's Suffrage Societies) gave a donation of £100 to the federation for a special propaganda campaign." Irish Women's Suffrage Federation, second annual report 1912-1913, p. 11.

6 *Catholic Bulletin*, October 1912, p. 791. Murphy, *op. cit.*, pp. 41-6.

7 Dora Mellone, an Irish suffragist, wrote in 1913 that "the Quakers not only have a good record with regards to women's suffrage but are also fondly remembered in Ireland for their role in aiding the Irish peasants through their soup kitchens during the Irish famine." Dora Mellone, *Englishwoman*, October 1913, p. 1.

8 Ruth Borchard, *John Stuart Mill, The Man* (London, 1957).

9 According to Frank Sheehy Skeffington the IWSLGA "failed entirely to awaken popular enthusiasm or sympathy, and the masses of the population never heard of it." *Votes for Women*, 11 November 1910, p. 83.

10 Suffrage groups in Ireland included the following Irish organisations and branches of English ones with the dates of their establishment: Irish Women's Suffrage and Local Government Association (1876); Irish Women's Franchise League (1908); Munster Women's Franchise League (1909); Conservative and Unionist Women's Franchise Association (1909); Irish Women's Suffrage Society (Belfast, 1910); Irish Women's Reform League (1912); Church League for Women's Suffrage (1913) and the Irish Catholic Women's Suffrage Society (1915).

11 *Irish Citizen*, 25 May 1912.

12 Murphy, *op. cit.*, chapter two and passim.

13 *Ibid.*, pp. 41-6.

14 This was particularly the case with regard to militancy. Both the

IWFL and the *Irish Citizen* felt it was justified. This alienated many readers from the *Citizen*. One correspondent to the paper felt "bound to express to you my very strong feelings against militancy for several reasons—in particular because if the *Irish Citizen i*s to become the organ of militancy I individually cannot in any way support it." *Irish Citizen*, 29 June 1912, p. 44.

15 Irish Women's Suffrage Federation, first annual report 1911-1912, p. 6. For American examples see footnote 2 above. For others see Richard Evans, *The Feminists: Women's Emancipation Movements in Europe, America and Australasia 1840-1920* (London, 1977); Les Garner, *Stepping Stones to Women's Liberty: Feminist Ideas in the Women's Suffrage Movement 1900-1920* (London, 1984); Patricia Grimshaw, *Women's Suffrage in New Zealand* (Auckland, 1987); Susan Kingsley Kent, *Sex and Suffrage in Britain, 1860-1914* (Princeton, 1987); Steven House and Anne R. Kenney, *Women's Suffrage and Social Politics in the French Third Republic* (Princeton, 1986); William O'Neill, *The Woman Movement: Feminism in the United States and England* (New York, 1969).

16 This is very evident on browsing through numerous issues of the *Irish Citizen*. Clearly contact with Britain was strongest because of its geographical proximity. However, contacts with, and visits from important suffrage leaders from other countries were frequent. Murphy, *op. cit.*, chapter three.

17 The following journals carried comprehensive coverage on the activities of the Irish suffrage movement: *Votes for Women: The Vote: Men's League for Women's Suffrage; The Anti-Suffragist; Church League for Women's Suffrage.*

18 The following are examples of the gradual enfranchisement of American women. Wyoming had women's suffrage as a territory from 1869. Utah had it as a territory from 1870 and as a state from 1896. California had women's suffrage as a state from 1911. Illinois was the first state to grant the presidential suffrage by legislative enactment. New York granted women's suffrage in 1917. All these states had received women's suffrage by 1920. For more details see Harold M. Hyman (ed.) *One Half the People: The Fight for Woman Struggle* (New York, 1975), pp 166-8.

19 *Women's Rights Convention, Seneca Falls and Rochester* (New York, 1870).

20 Jacqueline Van Voris, "Daniel O'Connell and women's rights,

one letter," *Eire/Ireland*, xvii, no. 3, (1982), pp 35-9.
21 F.S.L. Lyons, *Charles Stuart Parnell* (London, 1977).
22 *Catholic Suffragist*, 15 December 1915, p. 100.
23 Margaret Digby, *Horace Plunkett: An Anglo American Irishman* (Oxford, 1949).
24 *Ibid*.
25 *Irish Citizen*, 10 January 1914, p. 269.
26 Kraditor, *op. cit.*, p. 28.
27 *Irish Citizen*, 2 November 1912, p. 188.
28 *Ibid*., 15 August 1914.
29 *Ibid*., 10 January 1914, p. 266.
30 *Ibid*., 15 August 1914.
31 See for example, R. M. Fox, *Louie Bennett: Her Life and Times* (Dublin, 1957), pp 33-5. For an interpretation on the influence of reading on modern women see Sue Roe, *Women Reading Women's Writing* (Brighton, 1987).
32 Murphy, *op. cit.*, pp 56-7.
33 *Ibid*., pp 57-8.
34 Ms 21, 617 (VII) Sheehy Skeffington Papers (National Library of Ireland).
35 Murphy, *op. cit.*, p. 152.
36 *Irish Citizen*, 19 April 1912, p. 8.
37 *Votes for Women*, 14 October 1910.
38 Irish Women's Suffrage Federation, second annual report 1912-13, p. 5.
39 *Irish Citizen*, 8 November 1913.
40 *Ibid*., November 1913, p. 190, quoted from the *Belfast Telegraph*.
41 Irish Women's Suffrage Federation, second annual report 1912-13, p. 5.
42 *Irish Citizen*, October 1914.
43 *Ibid*. 6 July 1912, p. 56.
44 Women's suffrage supporters among the clergy did not always back the women's demands for feminist reasons. A number believed that women would improve the moral tone of politics. See Murphy, *op. cit.*, pp 151-9.
45 *Ibid*., p. 71.
46 Leah Levenson, *With Wooden Sword* (Dublin, 1983), pp 185-6.
47 Murphy, *op. cit.*, pp 31-2.
48 Levenson, *op. cit.*, pp 222-6.
49 Kraditor, *op. cit.*

50 Hanna Sheehy Skeffington, *Sinn Fein in America* (New York, 1919).
51 Alan J. Ward, *Ireland and Anglo American Relations 1899-1921* (Toronto, 1969). See also Stephen Hartly, *The Irish Question as a Problem in British Foreign Policy 1914-1918* (New York, 1987).
52 Brian Harrison, *Separate Spheres: Opposition to Women's Suffrage 1867-1928* (London, 1978), passim.
53 Murphy, *op. cit.*, chapter seven.
54 Ms 21,639 (1) Sheehy Skeffington Papers (National Library of Ireland).
55 Quoted from the *Irish Times* in *Votes for Women*, 12 April 1912, p. 440.
56 Garner, *op. cit.*, p. 96.
57 This is an argument which exercises much debate. According to Peter G. J. Pulzer "in certain continental European states religion, especially Catholicism, plays an important part in making women more right-wing. In Britain where this factor is less influential, the 'sex-gap' is much smaller." Idem., *Political Representation and Elections in Britain* (London, 1967).
58 *Irish Citizen*, 22 June 1912, p. 36.
59 *Votes for Women*, 7 June 1912, p. 589.
60 *Irish Citizen*, 25 March 1912, p. 2.
61 Report of the executive committee of the Irish Women's Franchise League 1913, p. 6.
62 In 1912 the Women's Political Association of Victoria reminded Redmond that Australian women "have always subscribed liberally to Home Rule funds" and asked that he "pay the debt that Ireland owes to Anna Parnell and the Land League." *Votes for Women*, 13 January 1911, p. 246.
63 Carroll, *op. cit.*
64 *Men's League for Women's Suffrage*, November 1912, p. 153.
65 *Irish Citizen*, 14 September 1912, p. 129; 6 December 1913, p. 230; *Irish Times*, 23 September 1912. Mss 22,664; 24,134 Sheehy Skeffington Papers (National Library of Ireland). Murphy *op. cit.*, pp 74-80.
66 Ms 21,639 Sheehy Skeffington Papers (National Library of Ireland).
67 Arthur Marwick, *Women at War 1914-1918* (London, 1977).
68 Frank Sheehy Skeffington, War and Feminism, republished in Levenson, *op. cit.*, pp 241-59.

69 Sheehy Skeffington, *Sinn Féin*, p. 11.
70 *Ibid.*, p. 14.
71 Levenson, *op. cit.*, p. 187.
72 *Irish Citizen*, 18 March 1917.
73 Hanna Sheehy Skeffington, *British Militarism as I Have Known It* (New York, 1917), p. 23.
74 In 1918 the franchise was granted to women over thirty who were householders, wives of householders, those who held property with a rateable value of £5 or more, and university graduates. Under the Irish Free State Constitution of 1922 all citizens over twenty-one were enfranchised. In 1928 the vote was extended in Britain to all women over twenty-one.

Aspects of Women's Contribution to the Oireachtas Debate in the Irish Free State, 1922 - 1937*

Mary Clancy

A notable feature of the decades leading up to 1922 was the extent to which women became involved in formal political activity.[1] The social, economic and political situation of women following the establishment of the Irish Free State, however, is less well-known. This article will concentrate on one aspect of that experience—the participation of women in the public political debate in the Houses of the Oireachtas (Parliament) from 1922 to 1937.

Introduction

The revolutionary leaders who came to power between 1922 and 1937 were to adopt a position regarding the role of women in the new Irish state which was as remarkable for its consensus as it was for its conservatism.[2] The function which was regularly declared to be appropriate for women was that of service in the private and domestic domain. Not only was this outlook given a ready imprimatur by the emerging political elite, but the attendant hostility to a public role for women was notably vigorous on occasion. In particular, the opposition of Kevin O'Higgins and Eamon de Valera to the public influence of women encouraged legislative measures which sanctioned such attitudes.

For a number of reasons, however, legislation concerning women was at all times controversial. Motivated by a certain sympathy for women's rights in general, and for the situation of educated, middle-class women in particular, regular support for feminist claims was provided by male University Deputies.[3] Secondly, the extra-parliamentary campaigns which were undertaken by women's organisations ensured that public attention was drawn to anti-feminist legislation. Organisations—notably the Irish Women Workers' Union and the Irish Women Citizens and Local Government Association—wrote to the Press, lobbied members of the Oireachtas and circulated leaflets as part of their strategy.[4] Finally, the response of certain women Senators contributed to the controversy which tended to accompany such legislation. As we shall see, this response was not always motivated by feminist considerations nor was it uniformly applied to all of the measures which were introduced. However, what did emerge was a certain liberal feminist concern on the part of some women Senators, specifically with regard to employment and civil rights.

Dáil Deputies

A marked contrast between the contribution in the Dáil and that in the Seanad was to distinguish the participation of the eleven women who entered the Houses of the Oireachtas between 1922 and 1937 (See Table 1). In general, the level of debate among women in the Seanad was marked by a confidence which was superior at all times to that of the women in the Dáil. Deputies, it would appear, participated in public life more for symbolic reasons deriving from family connections than from any motivation arising from their own political ambitions.[5] Their outstanding contribution to the Dáil lay in their solid enduring support for the political parties to which they belonged. Both Deputy Bridget Redmond (Cumann na nGaedheal) and Deputy Mary Reynolds (Cumann na nGaedheal) were elected following the death of husbands who were Dáil Deputies. The brothers of Margaret Collins-O'Driscoll (Cumann na nGaedheal) and Margaret Pearse (Fianna Fáil) were widely revered as symbolic nationalist figureheads by the political parties which they represented.[6] Mary Reynolds and Margaret Pearse who were elected in 1932 and 1933 respectively, did not speak on any issue in this period, while Bridget Redmond occasionally commented on local Waterford questions.[7] Deputy Redmond spoke against the 1937 Constitution, but only at the insistence of women's organisations, and was absent for much of the debate.

While Margaret Collins-O'Driscoll and Helena Concannon (Fianna Fáil) contributed on a more regular (though by no means impressive) basis, neither initiated any legislation in respect of women, or played any significant role during debates on such legislation. Both Deputies, however, endorsed women's responsibilities towards maternal and domestic duties. Collins-O'Driscoll tended to exalt the traditional tasks of Irish womanhood, and, in 1925, regretting the changing times, she recalled that "In the days of my youth it was regarded as a qualification for matrimony that a woman should be able to make her husband's shirts."[8] The promotion of rural domestic economy schools—similar to those of the Catholic Workers League in Belgium—was continually urged by Deputy Helena Concannon. In 1936 the Deputy declared that

> Everybody has his or her own way of solving Ireland's ills. My method would be to make these rural domestic economy schools general, spread them all through the country and make a course of six months compulsory on all Irish girls before they would be allowed to marry.[9]

When the more difficult problems of female sweated labour, infant mortality or infanticide were raised in the Dáil, such issues were ignored by both women.

Given such enthusiasm for the private and domestic life, surprisingly little mention was made of their role as public representatives during Dáil debates. Collins-O'Driscoll reminded the House, in 1925, that she was not elected to the Dáil "on the question of sex" but sought to serve "the interests of the community at large."[10] Regarding her Dáil behaviour as exemplary "by never missing a day's parliament attendance and rarely a division," Helena Concannon felt privileged to represent Eamon de Valera "in a back-bench way."[11] Any advantage accruing to Cumann na nGaedheal and Fianna Fáil from their parliamentary attendance would appear to be sufficient motivation for the women Dáil Deputies between 1922 and 1937. Since questions of equal rights were not supported by the Deputies in question, this could serve as an appropriate reminder that women public representatives are not necessarily progressive merely by virtue of gender, but that factors such as conservative political orientation, religion and class must also be taken into consideration.

Seanad

In contrast to the Dáil emphasis on women's domestic function, the concept of women's rights enjoyed considerable sympathy in the Seanad, despite some variation in the nature of individual contributions. Little part, for instance, was played by Senator Ellen Odette, Countess of Desart, in any debate concerning women. Indeed, it was noted in her obituary, in 1933, that she had "played an energetic part" in opposing women's suffrage, in the belief that "women should not compete against men at work or play."[12] It is possible, however, that once the vote was granted, her role as Senator could be easily accommodated within the sphere of public and charitable activities which she undertook in her capacity as Countess Dowager of Desart. Alice Stopford-Green spoke only on matters of history and culture and did not contribute to any debate concerning women.[13] Senator Eileen Costello insisted that women's rights were a necessary part of equal citizenship, while Senator Kathleen Clarke was motivated by the concept of equality which was promised in the 1916 Proclamation.[14] Although Senator Kathleen Browne spoke regularly and at length (particularly on agriculture), her contribution to debates on women's issues remained brief.[15] She revealed, in the 1930s, that she recruited women into the Blueshirt movement, but little detail was provided as to the extent or numbers involved.

Of all the women elected to the Seanad between 1922 and 1937, Jenny Wyse-Power was to emerge as the most persistent and determined champion of equal rights for women. This Senator, who was among the thirty Government nominees to the Seanad in 1922, was considered to be representative of the nationalist tradition, as one who had been active in the Ladies' Land League, the Gaelic League, Sinn Féin and Cumann na mBan.[16] When dealing with issues such as homeless children, infant mortality, and the poor, her contribution is significant, in that the voice of Jenny Wyse-Power was regularly the only one arguing on behalf of such groups in the Seanad.

Social Legislation

It was within the sphere of social legislation that the response of the women legislators proved the most problematic and varied. Claims that the moral standards of the new state were not as intact as in the past informed the opinion of many, irrespective of gender. In general, social issues were overlooked by the women Deputies, while the intervention of women Senators varied according to the nature of the issue in question. Divorce reform, contraception and prostitution tended to be ignored, whereas the provision of financial assistance for widows, children, and unmarried mothers and the protection of women from sexual assault, were resolutely pursued. In order to explain this uneven response, sources other than parliamentary debates would need to be investigated. However, the accommodation of Catholic opinion by the Irish legislature in matters of social concern—specifically contraception and divorce—must be emphasized. A more socially acceptable interest in the destitute and underprivileged, on the other hand, could explain to some extent the concern for such groups.

As noted already, divorce reform failed to attract much attention. Deputy Margaret Collins-O'Driscoll did not intervene during the attempt, in 1925, by the Cosgrave government to alter Standing Orders in order to prevent the introduction of divorce bills.[17] Support for the government, along with certain personal opposition to divorce, would explain her non-intervention in the brief Dáil debate on divorce.

In the Seanad, Senator Wyse-Power was refused permission to move a resolution which echoed the Dáil motion. The Senator stated, however, that private Bill legislation was not the appropriate method of dealing with divorce. Although Wyse-Power did not elaborate further on what the appropriate course should be, she reminded the House that present arrangements, particularly with regard to matrimonial property, tended to favour the male petitioner.[18]

State Policy regulating birth-control during the 1920s and 1930s derived from the Censorship of Publications Bill, 1928 and the Criminal Law Amendment Bill, 1934. Based on the recommendations of the Evil Literature Committee, 1926, the Censorship Bill aimed to ban birth-control publications as well as "indecent literature."[19] The Government's enthusiastic welcome for the Bill, along with a notable reluctance to discuss the section on contraception, was likewise reflected by Deputy Margaret Collins-O'Driscoll.[20] As the Deputy explained "…no vote I have ever given here, or will ever give, will be given with more satisfaction than the vote I will register in favour of this Bill."[21] The overwhelming Dáil support to ban birth control literature, along with a reluctance to speak publicly on matters of sexual morality, no doubt tended to negate the need for much discussion on the contraception section.

Underlying the Censorship debate, however, was a significant desire to extend control over aspects of women's lives in general. Not least was the disapproval shared by a number of Deputies regarding the reading material enjoyed by girls and women. Deputy Ua Buachalla (Fianna Fáil), was especially eloquent in his denunciation of the "cheap novels", which were read, and circulated by young girls—"filthy novels, novels with attractively coloured covers, with their suggestive, filthy stories."[22] Of more significance was the proposal to ban the reporting of rape and sexual assault cases. This was proposed in Part 3 of the Bill, which aimed to ban the publication of "very unpleasant details" in cases of murder, seduction and indecent assault.[23] This, according to the Minister, seemed primarily designed to protect the identity of "well-known individuals in the community" who may be charged with such crimes. Although Senator John Keane asked the Government not to impose "the fetters of a medieval code" the issue of contraception did not receive much attention either during the Seanad debate.[24] Senator Jenny Wyse-Power concentrated on the machinery of censorship rather than the content of the Bill, which was predictable, given her membership of the Film Censorship Board, but it is somewhat surprising that she did not offer some opinion on the subject of contraception. It is to be noted, however, that extra-parliamentary discussion of the Bill was undertaken by the Irish Women Citizens and Local Government Association.[25]

The implications, on the other hand, of the Criminal Law Amendment Bill, 1934, were to prove contradictory for women.[26] The raising of the age of consent from 16 to 17 in respect of carnal knowledge or attempted carnal knowledge, and from 13 to 15 years in respect of indecent assault was an important reform. This section of the Bill, indeed, was to attract the most attention from women Senators, womens' societies, social workers and clergy. In the case of indecent assault the age of consent had remained at 13 since the nineteenth century, although, as we will see, the proposed age of 15 was not viewed as a satisfactory advance by the afore-mentioned groups. Secondly, the Bill proposed to control prostitution through the imposition of heavier fines and increased powers for the police. In place of the existing maximum penalty of 40/-, soliciting would, in the case of second and subsequent convictions, now be subject to six months' imprisonment. Finally, Section 17 of the Criminal Law Amendment Bill banned the sale or importation of contraceptives.[27] However, this outright banning of contraception, which represented a severe curtailment for women in the sphere of reproductive rights, failed to attract much debate within the House. Given the overall reluctance to discuss matters such as contraception in public debate, the non-intervention of the women Deputies—Concannon, Pearse and Redmond—was not remarkable. However, their lack of interest in the raising of the age of consent would appear to indicate a more general resistance to the discussion of social issues.

In the Seanad, the appointment of a special committee was supported by Senator Wyse-Power who was critical of the absence of women on a similar committee in the Dáil. The Bill was welcomed by the Senator as "an immense improvement and we all welcome it as a measure to which we have been looking for the protection of women and children."[28] The Seanad debate, however, was characterized by much conflict owing to disagreement with the Dáil on a number of issues. The Government's attempt to rush the legislation through the House without amendment was resented. So also was the attempted deletion of all of the recommendations of the Seanad special committee by the Government. Particularly controversial was the Government's attempt to have the age of consent—in the case of indecent assault—retained at 15 instead of 18 as agreed by the Seanad Committee. As explained by Senator Kathleen Browne, the age had been raised to 16 in Britain, in 1922, and to 16 in the North of Ireland, in 1923. This signified for her that "we are giving less protection to our young girls than the governments of Great Britain and Northern Ireland."[29] The Senator urged the Minister to compromise and leave the age at seventeen. The Minister, Mr Ruttledge (Fianna Fáil) replied that he did not know why the Dáil Committee agreed on the age of fifteen "but it was unanimous, in any case."[30] In this instance, however, Government critics (who included Kathleen Browne and Kathleen Clarke) were successful. Following a Seanad division, the Government amendment to have the age of consent lowered from 18 to 15 was defeated by 23 votes to 19.[31]

The section on prostitution was a source of some disagreement also. In place of the Government-inspired section which read "Every common prostitute who is found loitering..." the Seanad special committee sought to include "every person who in a street or public place solicits or importunes any person of the opposite sex for an immoral purpose."[32] The Seanad proposal was significant, however, in that it aimed to penalise men as well as women, representing a clear departure from conventional double standards of sexual morality, which applied different rules to women and men. The Minister, however, felt that the Seanad section was "unworkable" and that it "would create further difficulties" for the police. Mr Ruttledge added that men who solicited women could be dealt with as the law stood "for insulting behaviour and so on."[33] Such a response aptly emphasised the double standard which the Seanad section proposed to correct. While soliciting by males was described by the Minister as "insulting behaviour," soliciting by women would, under the Government Bill, be penalised by a possible six months prison sentence. Although the Government amendment to delete the Seanad section was successful, it was carried by only one vote, with Kathleen Browne and Kathleen Clarke once more opposing the Government.[34]

The conflict which surrounded the section banning contraception was primarily due to Senator Kathleen Clarke's successful deletion of the section in the Seanad special committee. Her reasons, she added, were subsequently misrepresented in the Press since she was "in perfect agreement with the Church and State in the condemnation of the use of these things."[35] Senator Clarke believed, however, that a ban would prove counter-productive as it would both stimulate interest in contraception and tend to drive it underground.

Senator Oliver St John Gogarty, who in earlier debates was strongly critical of contraception, emerged in 1935 as a champion of birth-control, possibly owing to his experience as a medical doctor. As he had done on a number of previous occasions, Senator Gogarty drew attention once more to "the dreadful alternative facing the unfortunate poor" which was that of infanticide.[36] This question of infanticide had been raised in the Dáil by Deputy Rowlette, also a medical doctor, on a number of occasions, but the issue was never discussed by other members of the Oireachtas. It was also suggested by Deputy Rowlette that a ban would not prevent people from manufacturing home-made contraceptives from ordinary "household contents." This was more fully explained by Senator Gogarty:

> As to those people who are supposed to make an immoral use of a little chemistry after all, it is a very easy thing to destroy the male element; any vinegar will do it; you cannot take all the cruet-stands out of the country.[37]

The Government amendment was carried however and Section 17, which banned contraception, and which had been deleted by the Seanad special committee, was once more made part of the Criminal Law Amendment Bill.

On 14 February, 1935, the Dáil rejected the Seanad amendment to raise the age of consent from 15 to 18 in the case of indecent assault, an amendment which was described as "absurd" by the Minister.[38] The Seanad subsequently agreed not to insist upon the amendment. Considering the generally paternalistic attitude displayed towards women within the Dáil, the low age of consent advocated by that House represented, it would appear, a curious anomaly. For despite the strong and repeated recommendations to the contrary from those arguing on behalf of women and children under the age of 18, the Government did not compromise, as suggested, but held resolutely to the lower age limit. It could be suggested that the all-male Dáil committee which considered the provisions of the Bill, unlike the members of the Seanad committee, was not in touch with the prevailing attitudes regarding the age of consent. Alternatively, it could be argued, that, as with prostitution, so also in the case of sexual assault, a double-standard prevailed which held women responsible for sexual morality, and that legislative reforms accordingly reflected such attitudes. In any event, despite the claim in the Seanad—which was shared by social workers and women's societies—that the age of 15 represented an inadequate measure of protection for children and women, the Dáil refused to accommodate such fears. In response to extra-parliamentary dissatisfaction with the Criminal Law Amendment Bill, however, the Joint Committee of Women's Societies and Social Workers was established on 12 March, 1935. This Committee proposed to study social legislation affecting women and children and to suggest necessary reforms. When monitoring the courts, for instance, it was observed that while women generally made no defence, "what struck those who attended was the almost automatic sentence of six months given on the testimony of one policeman to women brought up for soliciting."[39]

Some years earlier, in 1929, the introduction of the Illegitimate Children (Affiliation Orders) Bill, had also attracted the attention of certain women Senators. The principal significance of this measure lay in the autonomy and control it extended to unmarried mothers over the running of their own lives and the lives of their children. It was possible to bring an action for seduction, but as the law stood, the woman's predicament was evaluated in terms of injury to her father or of services lost to an employer. While the Bill did not propose to discontinue such actions, it enabled proceedings to be brought "by the women in her own name for the support of an illegitimate child."[40] The demand for an *in camera* clause, and the publication of the father's name, were the issues which tended to dominate the Oireachtas debate. Indeed, more time was spent discussing the implications of the Bill for men, than in discussing the situation of unmarried mothers and their dependants. The image which was reinforced throughout the debate was that of the falsely charged, blackmailed, innocent man as against the "hardened sinner" who sought endless affiliation orders. In the Seanad, however, Jenny Wyse-Power argued persuasively on behalf of unmarried mothers, denying the danger of blackmail and emphasising their fear of a court appearance. In this she was supported by Senator Kathleen Browne who agreed that women would have difficulty facing a public court.[41] Senator Wyse-Power, indeed, through her work as a Poor Law Guardian had appreciable experience in the area which the Bill sought to reform. Despite the vehement and persistent opposition of the Minister, Mr Fitzgerald-Kenney (Cumann na nGaedheal), the *in camera* amendment was accepted, and the Bill was passed in June, 1930.

Equal Rights (1) Employment

While restraint, therefore, distinguished the performance of elected women in the sphere of reproductive rights and sexual morality, it was in the sphere of equal rights that the women representatives made their most impressive and sustained contributions. In particular, the legislative control and regulation of women's employment was resisted by the women Senators during the 1920s and 1930s. In 1925, the Civil Service Regulation (Amendment) Bill, represented an attempt by the Cumann na nGaedheal Government to statutorily prohibit women from entering certain areas of the Civil Service solely on the grounds of sex. As explained by Mr Blythe, the Minister for Finance, it was sought to amend existing legislation due to the fact that "the Civil Service Commission had not power to confine examinations to members of one particular sex."[42] The introduction of the Bill indicated a pronounced disregard for existing legislation, notably the 1919 Sex Disqualification Act and Article 3 of the 1922 Free State Constitution, both of which sought to safeguard equality of opportunity regardless of sex. It was not a popular Bill, however, and even though it was accepted by the Dáil, it was the subject of much criticism. Yet, this measure, which had serious implications for the position of women in the workforce, was to receive its main support in the Dáil from Deputy Margaret Collins-O'Driscoll. Having been canvassed "by very influential members of my sex to vote against this Bill," the Deputy added that she "failed to see how it infringed upon women's rights under the Constitution."[43] Despite some recognition that it would limit Civil Service positions for women, it would appear that Collins-O'Driscoll's loyalty to Cumann na nGaedheal dictated that her response would be one of support for the

Bill.

In the Seanad, the Civil Service Regulation (Amendment) Bill met with firm opposition from a number of determined speakers. Senator Eileen Costello attacked the Bill as "morally wrong" and "monstrously unfair." For the Senator, the fundamental issue was that "women are still to be subject to the obligations of citizenship, but their privileges are to be curtailed and restricted."[44] Apart from some isolated support for the Bill, the remainder of the second stage was dominated by the contribution of Senator Jenny Wyse-Power who remained convinced that the proposed legislation was not in the interests of women workers. What Senator Wyse-Power particularly resented was that

> If this sex discrimination is to be made by a male Executive Council and by practically a male Dáil I think it is very unjust. No consultation of any kind took place with any representative women on the subject.[45]

The disparity already in evidence with regard to women was ably highlighted by the Senator who demonstrated that women workers occupied the lowest grade in the Civil Service, with a corresponding absence recorded in the upper grades.[46] Drawing from her long experience in nationalist politics, Wyse-Power was quick to emphasize the changing response to women's participation in public affairs. Although expected to take part during periods of crisis, the subsequent dismissal of a female presence angered the Senator. "No men in a fight for freedom," Wyse-Power added, "ever had such loyal co-operation from their women as the men who compose the present Executive Council." Despite the attendant dangers, women messengers, auditors, and inspectors were asked to undertake work, throughout the country, during the War of Independence (1919-21), "and these are the people who tell us that we are physically unfit." She regretted that such a Bill had come "from the men who were associated in the fight (for freedom) with women when sex and money were not considerations."[47] The Senator also found the second part of the Bill—the "appointment of Civil

Servants without examination"—objectionable, and advised that the only thing to do was to reject it. This is indeed what the Seanad did, and the Bill was rejected on its second reading by 20 votes to 9.[48] In a debate which tended to be dominated by critics of the measure, the contribution of Senators Costello and Wyse-Power proved critical in bringing about the Bill's defeat. Seanad hostility to the measure was but one aspect of a wider campaign, which was also supported by the Irish Women Citizens and Local Government Association, and its success must be viewed as an important achievement for equal-rights feminists in the mid-1920s.

The restriction of women's industrial employment was one of the objectives of the Conditions of Employment Bill, 1935. It was agreed by Mr Lemass, (Fianna Fáil), the Minister for Industry and Commerce, and by most Deputies, that certain forms of work were unsuitable for women. It would appear, however, that opposition to women's industrial employment derived from a more fundamental fear that women industrial workers, encouraged by recent mechanisation, would pose a serious threat to male industrial workers. Although Lemass stated his opposition to the replacement of men by the cheap labour of women, he endorsed, however, the payment of lower wages to women in order to maintain existing economic arrangements—particularly in the readymade clothing industry.[49] In the Dáil, Deputies Helena Concannon, Margaret Pearse or Bridget Redmond did not oppose, or speak on, the measure, Although the Bill, according to the Minister, was generally accepted among workers as well as employers, opposition was "still being expressed by representatives of women workers' organisations."[50] The restrictions incorporated in the Conditions of Employment Bill were indeed being vigorously opposed by the Irish Women Workers' Union, who regarded such control as an infringement of the rights of working women. Firm support for the Bill was evident, however, throughout the Oireachtas debate, while the inherent paternalism in the proposed legislation was most notably underlined by Senator Michael Comyn who declared that "Woman's proper and ideal sphere is in the home."[51]

Significantly, however, once more, efforts to restrict women's work and keep them out of certain trades met with strong resistance from the women members of the Seanad. Jenny Wyse-Power again spoke with some bitterness, when she recalled the hopes of young girls who lost their employment following the 1916 Rising. Those girls believed that "when our own men are in power, we shall have equal rights." Such a belief may have been due to their lack of experience, Wyse-Power added, "but it was part of their faith." The Senator was critical also of Labour party support for the section regulating women's employment since it indicated that "there was no standing shoulder to shoulder."[52] Senator Kathleen Clarke also failed to understand Labour's support for this section, wondering what "their dead leader, James Connolly, would say to their attitude on this."[53] She regarded the proposed legislation as "a very dangerous thing" which represented "the thin end of the wedge against women." Indeed, Kathleen Clarke alleged that other provisions in the Bill were included in order to check any potential opposition which the Labour Party and others might have to anti-women legislation. She continued:

> If a woman goes into a particular form of industry, if she goes in at the same rate of pay as the men receive and says that she will accept nothing less, and if the men's trade unions stand behind her on that, I do not see how employers could face what that means. They would have the whole organised trade union movement of men and women in this country against them.[54]

This represented the most radical demand of the debate in either House of the Oireachtas. The timid response of the Labour party and trade union representatives in the Oireachtas determined that Senator Kathleen Clarke's call for equal pay and trade union mobilisation would remain unanswered.[55] In response to the accusation that "the feminists have run riot" over the Conditions of Employment

Bill, Kathleen Clarke stated that, although she was "sympathetic to the feminist movement," her opposition to Section 16 of the Bill was based on nationalist grounds, and specifically on the 1916 Proclamation which granted equal rights to all citizens. An amendment to have the section deleted was moved by Senator Clarke and seconded by Wyse-Power on Committee Stage. This was supported by Senator Kathleen Browne, who did not have particularly strong views on the subject of women industrial workers. Her opposition to Section 16 was based most likely on her observation of hardships faced by women at local level, along with a virulent opposition to any legislation promoted by Fianna Fáil. The amendment to have Section 16 deleted was, however, defeated by 19 votes to 14.[56] The response to legislation which sought to restrict employment solely on the basis of gender, as attempted by Cumann na nGaedheal in 1925, and Fianna Fáil in 1935, was characterised, therefore, by opposition from certain women Senators. Such legislation was not directed at one class. While the Civil Service Regulation Amendment Bill, 1925, affected the employment of educated, middle-class women, the Conditions of Employment Bill, 1935, on the other hand, sought to regulate the employment of working-class women. It is to be noted that by 1937, the Irish Free State was placed on a black-list at Geneva for its conduct in respect of women workers.[57]

Equal Rights (2) Jury Service

It was during the discussion of jury service, however, that the Free State legislature was presented with the first significant opportunity of discussing the public role of women. The right to sit on juries had been granted under the Sex Disqualification Act, 1919. The Minister for Justice, Mr Kevin O'Higgins was to claim, however, that such equality was not demanded by the Irish electorate but "because we were at that time part and parcel of the political system of Great Britain it applied here."[58] Neither Collins-O'Driscoll not any of the women Senators challenged the Juries Bill, 1924 which in a departure from the 1919 position, provided for the exemption of women from jury service on application. As already emphasised, Margaret Collins-O'Driscoll never challenged Cumann na nGaedheal legislation, and it is likely that Senators Costello and Wyse-Power failed to detect any threat to equal rights in such a move. The proposal to exempt women altogether from jury service, as intended in the Juries Bill, 1927, was to prove controversial, on the other hand. The measure faced some resistance in the Dáil, but once more Margaret Collins-O'Driscoll—the sole woman Deputy at this stage—did not take any part in the debate apart from voting with the Government in Dáil divisions.[59]

In the Seanad, one of the most forceful arguments put forward on the second stage was that of Senator Wyse-Power, whose protest was "entirely influenced by the fact that if this Bill becomes law the civic spirit that is developing in women will be arrested."[60] According to the Senator, the civic spirit of women, which in the past "had been repressed and became stunted and did not grow" underwent radical change in recent times. Political events in the past fifty years meant it was the case that "the men who led political movements and carried them in the main to success utilised women in order to achieve their object." Such activity greatly promoted women's civic spirit and some women "encouraged more or less by the way they have been thrust out, as it were, to do work that they never did before, came gradually into public life and have done social work which is generally regarded as successful." The Minister was doing an injustice, she declared, "to what is really a necessary asset to every State, the co-operation of its men and women."[61] For Senator Eileen Costello, the ideal position was that of 1919, when women were granted equality under the Sex Disqualification Act. The Senator believed that many women—internationally, as well as in Ireland—were slow to respond to public duties. Women, she believed, needed to be educated into responsible citizenship, since "they have not realised their power as yet."[62] It must be remembered, however, that in this period those opposed to the terms of the

Anglo-Irish Treaty (1921) abstained from the parliamentary process. However, women's perception of the campaign leading to enfranchisement in 1918, which was largely undertaken by educated, bourgeois women, could account, perhaps, for this slow response to formal political participation which was of concern to the Senator. In the Seanad, however, opposition to the measure was so strong that it succeeded in bringing about a significant change in form, if not substance, of the Bill's provisions. Women were to be included in Part II of the Schedule along with other exempted classes, while it was to be left open to women to have their names entered on the jury lists on application.

The fundamental factor underlying the debate on women jurors, however, was the Minister's prejudices against a public role for women. Of women in public life, O'Higgins asked the Dáil "but are they normal or the exception?"[63] Submitting to the House that they were the exception, the Minister added, "it is the normal and natural function of women to have children..."[64] Jury service was seen to distract women—presented as better fitted to care for young children—from their domestic duties. Such conservative opinions found widespread acceptance within the Oireachtas, where the general tone not only of the Minister, but also of others, was paternalistic, emphasising throughout the burden of obligations. Although the Minister was at all times aware of the opposition by women's organisations to the Juries Bill, he chose to dismiss such "self-appointed spokeswomen" as not representative of "the vast majority of the women in the State."[65] This departure from the rights granted in the Sex Disqualification Act, 1919, and Article 3 of the 1922 Constitution, must be regarded as a serious set-back for Irishwomen, but one which was, significantly, if unavailingly, opposed by feminists both inside and outside the Oireachtas.

1937 Constitution

Controversy surrounded discussion of the place of women also during the debate on the 1937 Constitution. Although only undertaken by a limited number of Deputies, Dáil opposition to the clauses affecting the status of women was persistent and enjoyed some success. Deletion of Articles 40, 41, and 45—as demanded by women's organisations—was never suggested, however, in the Dáil.[66] Modification, on the other hand, of Article 45—which initially sought to enshrine "the inadequate strength of women"—was noteworthy in view of de Valera's insistence on the inclusion of that concept. Critics also determinedly opposed the President's omission of "without distinction of sex" which was contained in Article 3 of the 1922 Constitution. According to de Valera, it was sought to exclude this phrase because it was only a "reminder that at one time there was a distinction made."[67] Kevin O'Higgins had also dismissed this phrase during the 1927 Juries Bill debate, declaring that "A few words in a Constitution do not wipe out the difference between the sexes, either physical or mental or temperamental or emotional..."[68] Opponents, however, viewed its omission as an attempt to destroy "the constitutional bulwark of women's rights', in the event of discriminatory ordinary legislation.[69] Although de Valera remained resolute in his claim that the phrase was superfluous, his subsequent decision to include it (in Article 16), represented an important achievement for critics both inside and outside the Dáil.

With regard to the three women deputies, Margaret Pearse did not speak, Bridget Redmond did so only under pressure, and Helena Concannon spoke in favour of the Constitution. It could be argued that Helena Concannon's performance was the least predictable within the House. Firstly, she was a member of the National University Women Graduates Association, the prestigious organisation which led the campaign against the Constitution.[70] Moreover, their opposition rested not on feminist principles per se, but on rights granted under the 1916 Proclamation, a standpoint which should not have been incompatible with the views of Deputy Concannon. The Deputy chose, however, not to deviate from her position of uncritical support of de Valera, despite the fears that the concepts contained in the 1937 Constitution opened the door to "Fascist legislation of a very objectionable type."[71]

Conclusion

It has been suggested in this Article that most women Dáil Deputies, in the period 1922 to 1937, entered politics in order to strengthen the position of political parties which were associated with male relatives. If this is the case, then their lack of participation in parliamentary debates, and their lack of support for feminist claims, is more easily understood. However, it is equally important to emphasise that similar observations may be applied to male politicians, whose lack of input tends to escape comment in a way that the participation of women Deputies does not. Indeed, it could be argued that performance in Oireachtas debate was linked to a general involvement in extra-parliamentary public life on the part of those elected, rather than to inhibitions traditionally attributed to women, simply on the basis of gender. Most women in the Seanad, for instance, enjoyed a more active public life prior to, and during, their term in the Seanad. As members of organisations to which they were committed, and in the sphere of Local government, Senators Browne, Clarke, Costello and Wyse-Power, in particular, had considerable experience.[72] In a period that saw an acute crisis in Irish nationalism, characterised by civil war and a deep and enduring distrust, it is interesting to note that issues of women's rights united the antagonistic protagonists. Within the Seanad, the erosion of women's rights drew a united response from politically opposed women Senators, while a similar unanimity, also transcending party political differences, was to characterise Oireachtas support for such legislation.

As we have seen, measures regulating contraception, employment and equal rights undertaken by the Cumann na nGaedheal Government in the 1920s, were replicated and strengthened by the Fianna Fáil administration from 1932 onwards. The emphasis on women's domestic function—

shared and reinforced by women Dáil Deputies—was seen not as one aspect of woman's experience, but was declared to be the sole normal function of womanhood in the interests of the State. It was to be the case, therefore, that throughout the 1920s and 1930s, the equality enjoyed by Irish women in 1922, as guaranteed in Article 3 of the Free State Constitution, was steadily eroded under the impact, and consolidation, of such a patriarchal viewpoint. It was also to be the case that women public representatives in Seanad Éireann, along with extra-parliamentary women's organisations, consistently opposed legislation which they believed sought to restrict their role in the Irish Free State.

Notes
(For Mike Taylor, mentor and friend).

* This article is based on my MA thesis, Women's contribution to public political debate (with particular reference to women's issues) in the Irish Free State, 1922 - 1937, (UCG, 1988). I an especially indebted to Barbara Geraghty and Gearóid Ó Tuathaigh for their comments and advice on earlier drafts of this article.

1 See, for example, R. Cullen-Owens, *Smashing Times: A History of the Irish Women's Suffrage Movement 1889 - 1922* (Dublin, 1984); Margaret Ward, *Unmanageable Revolutionaries, Women and Irish Nationalism* (London and Kerry, 1983); Mary Jones, *These Obstreperous Lassies: A History of the Irish Women Workers Union* (Dublin, 1988); Pat Bolger (ed.), *And See Her Beauty Shining There* (Dublin, 1986).

2 In this period, Cumann na nGaedheal was in power from 1922 until 1932 when Fianna Fáil assumed power.

3 Under the Free State Constitution each university was entitled to elect three representatives to the Dáil until the Constitution (Amendment No. 23) Bill, 1934 provided for the deletion of this clause.

4 The Irish Women Workers' Union, which organised unskilled workers, had been established on a single-sex basis by Jim and Delia Larkin in 1911. See Mary Jones, *op. cit.* and for a study of

Louie Bennett, General Secretary of the IWWU from 1917 - 1955, see Ellen Hazelkorn, "The social and political views of Louie Bennett, 1870-1956," in *Saothar* 13, (1988), pp 32-44. The Irish Women's Citizens and Local Government Association was formed in 1923 in order to continue the work of the Women's Suffrage Association. The Association, which was affiliated to the International Alliance of Women, also monitored legislation affecting women and children, and, in 1948, became incorporated with the Irish Housewives Association. With thanks to Hilda Tweedy, founder member of the IHA (1942), for this information.

5 Published sources are inadequate at present, but brief biographical details may be obtained in Vincent Brown (ed.), *Magill Book of Irish Politics* (Dublin, 1981); J. D. Hickey and J. E. Doherty, *A Dictionary of Irish History Since 1800* (Dublin, 1980); *Missing Pieces, Women in Irish History* (Dublin, 1983).

6 See also Ruth Dudley-Edwards, *Patrick Pearse: The Triumph of Failure* (London, 1977).

7 Deputy Reynolds was subsequently to enjoy a long Dáil career from 1937 to 1961.

8 Dáil debates, Vol. 11, 23 April, 1925, pp. 184-9.

9 *Ibid.*, Vol 61, 2 April, 1936, pp 900-3.

10 *Ibid.*, Vol 13, 18 November, 1925, pp 514-5.

11 *Ibid.*, Vol. 53, 5 July, 1934, pp 1498-1502.

12 Obituary, *The Irish Times*, 30 June, 1933.

13 See also R. B. McDowell, *Alice Stopford-Green: A Passionate Historian* (Dublin, 1967); L. O'Broin, *Protestant Nationalists in Revolutionary Ireland* (Dublin, 1985).

14 Eileen Costello was a local government representative, and a member of the Governing Body of UCG from 1923-1934. A supporter of Cumann na nGaedheal, and later the Army Comrades Association, she was primarily concerned with the promotion of the Irish language.
Kathleen Clarke (1879-1972) was the widow of Tom Clarke, who was executed for his part in the 1916 Rising. In 1922 she became an Alderman on Dublin Corporation and in 1939, Kathleen Clarke became the first woman Lord Mayor of Dublin.

15 Kathleen Browne was a tillage farmer from County Wexford, a Peace Commissioner and committee member of the County Council, and Agricultural and Co-Operative Societies.

16 Ladies' Land League (January 1881 - August 1881); the Gaelic League (founded 1893 — the first nationalist organisation to admit

women); Sinn Féin (formed in 1905 by Arthur Griffith and reorganised in 1917); Cumann na mBan (nationalist women's organisation founded in 1914.) See Margaret Ward, *op. cit.*, and Lil Conlon, *Cumann na mBan and the Women of Ireland* (Kilkenny, 1969).

17 The Divorce and Matrimonial Causes Act of 1857, which transferred jurisdiction from parliament to the courts, was never extended to Ireland. It remained necessary, therefore, to submit private bills to parliament—a procedure which restricted divorce to wealthy middle-class and upper-class petitioners. See Dáil debates, Vol. 10 and Vol. 12 and Seanad debates, Vols. 4 and 5, 1925. See also David Fitzpatrick, "Divorce and separation in modern Irish history," in *Past & Present*, No. 114, (February 1987), pp 173-196.

18 Seanad debates, Vol. 5, 11 June, 1925, pp 460-3.

19 Apart from those directly involved with the book industry, those who submitted evidence to the Evil Literature Committee included the Catholic Truth Society of Ireland, the Irish Vigilance Association, the Boys' Brigade and the Irish Christian Brothers.

20 The Minister for Justice, Mr Fitzgerald-Kenney (Cumann na nGaedheal) declared that "we have decided ... that that question shall not be freely and openly discussed." Dáil debates, Vol. 26, 18 October, 1928, pp 594-611.

21 *Ibid.*, Dáil debates, Vol 26, 19 October, 1928, pp 689-690.

22 *Ibid.*, p. 690.

23 *Ibid.*, 18 October, 1928, p. 594.

24 Seanad debates, Vol. 12, 11 April, 1929, pp 55-75. That some dissemination of contraceptive literature took place was indicated by Senator Michael Comyn, a strong supporter of the Bill, who complained about the sale of 3d. almanacs "going into the hands of the poor people, the working people," and on every second page was "a full-page advertisement of contraceptives and the places where contraceptives could be got."

25 Attention was drawn to the IWCLGA campaign by Deputy Craig, an Independent University representative. Dáil Debates, Vol. 26, 18 October, 1929, p. 656. See footnote 4 re. IWCLGA.

26 The impetus behind the Bill's introduction was the Committee of Enquiry into the Criminal Law Amendment Acts, led by Mr William Carrigan, K. C. and composed of: Rev. Fr P. J. Hannon, SJ., Very Rev. Dean Kennedy, Mrs Power (Senator), Miss O'Carroll, Matron of the Coombe Hospital and Mr F. Morrin. The

Carrigan Committee report was never published but its details were reported in the *Irish Press*, 4 March 1932.
27 Dáil debates, Vol. 53, 28 June, 1934, pp 1246-51.
28 The Seanad Special Committee consisted of: Senators Edward Coey-Bigger, S. L. Brown, Kathleen Browne, Kathleen Clarke, James Douglas, Thomas Foran, Patrick Lynch, Colonel Moore and Jenny Wyse-Power.
29 Seanad debates, Vol. 19, 6 February, 1935, p. 1230.
30 *Ibid.*, pp 1233-4.
31 *Ibid.*, pp 1231-6.
32 Seanad debates, Vol. 19, 6 February, 1935, pp 1231-6.
33 *Ibid.*, p. 1241.
34 On this occasion, Jenny Wyse-Power took the government side, possibly influenced by the recommendations of the Carrigan committee.
35 Seanad debates, Vol. 19, 6 February, 1935, pp 1247-8.
36 *Ibid.*, p. 1253.
37 *Ibid.*, p. 1254.
38 Dáil debates, Vol 64, 14 February, 1935, pp 1985-6.
39 Present at the inaugural meeting were: Mary Kettle, Mrs O'Hegarty, Dr French Russell, Lady Chance, Hannah Sheehy-Skeffington, Lady Franks, Mrs Reddin, Miss Chevenix and Miss Ffrench-Mullen. Louie Bennett and Maud Gonne joined the Joint Committee at a later date. *Report of Joint Committee of Women's Societies and Social Workers, Fifty Years, (1935-1985)*. (With thanks to Hilda Tweedy, Nora F. Browne and Mabel Kelly, of the Joint Committee, for this information).
40 Dáil debates, Vol 32, 30 October, 1929, pp 519-21.
41 Seanad debates, Vol. 13, 19 March, 1930, pp 693-711.
42 Dáil debates, Vol. 13, 18 November, 1925, p. 503.
43 *Ibid.*, pp 514-5.
44 Seanad debates, Vol. 6, 17 December, 1925, pp 245-6.
45 *Ibid.*, pp 255-7.
46 Wyse-Power observed that while there were 451 men in the Junior Executive posts, there were only 4 women, and she was informed by the Minister that there were no women in the administrative grades.
47 Seanad debates, Vol. 6, 17 December, 1925, pp 258-9.
48 The Bill, which was defeated by 20 votes to 9, was supported by the Countess of Desart. The Civil Service Regulation (Amendment) Bill was held up for twelve months after being thrown out

by the Seanad.
49 See Dáil debates, Vol. 57, 27 June, 1935, pp 1217-23.
50 Seanad debates, Vol. 20, 27 November, 1935, p. 1221.
51 *Ibid.*, p. 1260.
52 *Ibid.*, pp 1247-8.
53 Connolly's support for women's suffrage, and equality, was a notable feature of his socialism—indeed, the equal citizenship as guaranteed in the 1916 Proclamation has generally been accredited to his influence, as well as to the feminism of the period.
54 Seanad debates, Vol. 20, 27 November, 1935, pp 1256-9.
55 At all times, it was emphasized by Ministers, Deputies and Senators, that equal pay legislation would draw down male wages.
56 Seanad debates, Vol. 20, 12 December, 1935, pp 1425-6.
57 This was stated by Dr Mary Hayden (National Council of Women) during the anti-Constitution campaign in 1937. *The Irish Times*, 22 June 1937.
58 Dáil debates, Vol. 18, 15 February, 1927, p. 469.
59 Deputy Magennis was especially critical of the Bill, which he regarded as undemocratic, based, as it was, on grounds of sex. Dáil debates, Vol. 18, 15 February, pp 481-2.
60 Seanad debates, Vol. 8, 30 March, 1927, p. 682.
61 *Ibid.*, pp 682-3.
62 *Ibid.*, 8 April, 1972, p. 808.
63 Dáil debates, Vol 18, 23 February, 1925, p. 757.
64 *Ibid.*, p. 766.
65 *Ibid.*, 15 February, 1927, p. 468.
66 The Seanad had been abolished in 1936.
> Article 40.1.
> All citizens shall, as human persons, be held equal before the law.
> This shall not be held to mean that the State shall not in its enactments have due regard to differences of capacity, physical and moral, and of social function.
>
> The controversial section of Article 41 reads:
> 41.2.1°
> In particular, the State recognises that by her life within the home, woman gives to the state a support without which the common good cannot be achieved.
> 2° the State shall, therefore, endeavour to ensure that mothers shall not be obliged by economic necessity to engage in labour to the neglect of their duties in the home.

67 Dáil debates, Vols. 67-8, 11 May, 1937, p. 64.
68 Dáil debates, Vol. 18, 15 February, 1927, p. 489.
69 Critics in the Dáil included Deputies Costello, Lavery, McGilligan, O'Sullivan, Alton, Rice and Rowlette.
70 The campaign was led by the National University Women Graduates' Association in cooperation with the Irish Women Workers' Union, the Joint Committee of Women's Societies, and the Standing Committee on Legislation Affecting Women. Details of this campaign are in Mary McGinty, unpublished thesis, A Study of the Campaign for and against the enactment of the 1937 Constitution, (UCG, 1987). See also Dr Yvonne Scannell, "The Constitution and the role of women" in Brian Farrell (ed.) *De Valera's Constitution and Ours* (Dublin, 1988).
71 This was stated by Louie Bennett of the IWWU. De Valera's emphasis on woman's domestic role was attacked as reactionary by those engaged in the anti-Constitution campaign. One of his critics was Dorothy Macardle, author of *The Irish Republic* which contained a preface by De Valera.
72 See footnotes 14, 15 and 16.

Table 1

Women Deputies 1922-1937

(with political party, years elected and constituency)

Brugha, Caitlín (Republican/Sinn Fein)
1923 (A), June 1927*   Waterford
Clarke, Kathleen (Fianna Fáil)
June 1927   Dublin North
Collins-O'Driscoll, Margaret (Cumann na Gaedheal)
1923, June 1927, September 1927, 1932   Dublin North
Concannon, Helena (Fianna Fáil)
1933   N.U.I.
Lynn, Dr Kathleen (Republican)
1923 (A)   Dublin County
McSwiney, Mary (Republican)
1923 (A)   Cork City
Markievicz, Constance (Republican and, from 1926, Fianna Fáil)
1923 (A), June 1927   Dublin South
Pearse, Margaret (Fianna Fáil)
1933   Dublin County

Redmond, Bridget (Fine Gael)
1933, 1937   Waterford
Reynolds, Mary (Cumann na nGaedheal/Fine Gael)
1932, 1937   Leitrim-Sligo
(A) Indicates abstention
*June 1927: The Dáil which was elected in June was dissolved in August, and a general election was held in September, 1927.

Women Senators 1922 - 1937
(with year of election and year of departure)
Costello, Eileen	1922 - 1934
Countess of Desart	1922 (d.1933)
Stopford-Green, Alice	1922 (d.1929)
Wyse-Power, Jenny	1922 - 1936
Clarke, Kathleen	1928 - 1936
Browne, Kathleen	1929 - 1936

Fullness of Life: Defining Female Spirituality in Twentieth Century Ireland

Margaret Mac Curtain

If one were to speculate on the titles of the three or four most influential books that helped to shape the intellectual mind of Irish Catholic women in the final quarter of the nineteenth century, it might well prove a baffling and fruitless endeavour to arrive at the merest consensus. However, if one were to change the terms of reference and the geographical base, altering the emphasis from "intellectual" to "spiritual," then few would contest the mainstream influence of the Child of Mary manual, that sober guidebook to the spiritual life of the young Catholic Sodalist on admittance to the Confraternity of the Child of Mary. Wherever Jesuit-inspired schools at secondary level developed throughout western Europe, including Great Britain and Ireland, the initiation into, and practice of the Sodality, usually referred to as the E. de M. (*Enfant de Marie*), or the "Blue Ribbon" signified a mid-adolescent rite of passage into a position of leadership and responsibility in the upper school. Admittance to the ranks of the Sodality conveyed an aura of dignity and conferred status, even privilege, on a class educated into middle-class virtue. It was a serious consideration for a young person to accept the rules of the Sodality and be bound by its simple requirements, to live a chaste life and to perform its daily obligation of prayer.[1]

Equally daunting, as we learn from the young James Joyce, was the challenge of rejecting it and of accepting the consequences that followed the internal conflict set up by such a rejection.[2] It was not so much that the Sodalist became a member of an elite group in the school community and often combined its duties with those of a prefect. For the

Sodalist the touchstone of its membership was perceived to lie in its invitation to personal holiness at a period of life when young adolescents were making choices around their future, and with the help of the spiritual director of the Sodality, discerning vocations to the priesthood or to religious life.

For the Catholic girl, reception into the Sodality gave an added impetus to the deeply-rooted French traditions of girls' education, a tradition which regarded the societal role of the young girl to be within the family as daughter, wife and mother. Sissy O'Brien, in *The Farm by Lough Gur*, describes the experience with artless candour. Born in 1858, Sissy was about fifteen years of age when the event she narrates took place in her convent boarding-school belonging to the French Order of nuns, the Faithful Companions of Jesus, at Bruff, county Limerick.[3]

> In my third year I became a Child of Mary. I was promoted to the highest table. I was allowed to give lessons on Sundays in the Poor's School at the Convent gate. I slept in the Immaculate Conception dormitory, which had a small chapel at one end. In school I was in the highest form but I was still diffident, mistrustful of myself. Little was done by our teachers to encourage self-reliance and independence...our timorous outlook was intensified to such an extent that several of my schoolfellows chose to become nuns rather than face the danger and evil of life outside the convent. No direct effort was made to persuade the pupils to make this choice, certainly nothing was ever said to me, and though I was wholeheartedly religious, I had no wish to be a nun.

Sissy grew up to become the sensible, intelligent woman who married her neighbour, Richard Fogarty, a prosperous young farmer. Years later she gave Mary Carbery the memories of a farming childhood beside Lough Gur and unself-consciously produced a classic.

Increasingly over the last decade historians have suggested that religious practice in Ireland began to move from a populist, peasant-based native style towards a more disciplined and churchly observance in which there were gains and losses. The change accompanied the Great Famine, 1846-9 which in turn hastened the transition to town-based religious observances. Holy well patterns, wake customs and the superstitious rituals described by Sissy O'Brien disappeared. They were replaced by the new Roman devotions such as Benediction of the Blessed Sacrament, the Christmas Crib, and the annual mission given in the church by a visiting Redemptorist or Vincentian preacher. The laity were encouraged to make devotional visits to the Blessed Sacrament in the parish church. After the Famine, particularly during the period of Cardinal Paul Cullen's ministry as archbishop of Dublin (1852-78), the Catholic Church gained ascendancy over the minds of its flock. Devotions, more precisely "imported" devotions, became the familiar vehicle of prayer for the church-goer. In 1878 Ireland was formally consecrated to the Sacred Heart and to the older seventeenth-century devotion was added that of the Nine Fridays with the obligation of confession of sins followed by reception of Holy Communion and attendance at Mass on the first Friday of the month for nine consecutive months. The church-going laity devoutly made the Way of the Cross hung in fourteen pictorial representations along the walls of late Victorian churches and the chapels of boarding schools. The black-covered prayer book appeared, a sign of rising literacy. An anthology of prayers for all occasions, it was packed with invocations to continental saints. The Marian cult had deepened following the Apparitions of the Virgin Mary at Lourdes in the south of France in 1858. The Knock, county Mayo Apparition, 1879, added an Irish gloss to the yearly round of feast-days and May-day processions in Catholic schools.[4]

By the death of Cardinal Cullen in 1878, the fundamental changes in Irish society which made its general tone more "bourgeois" had taken place. For the Catholic population the dominant spirituality sprang from the middle class. It was town-based and centred on the "chapel." Convent schools for girls reflected these trends. Anne O'Connor in an essay "The

Revolution in girls' secondary education in Ireland, 1860-1910" remarks[5]

> The emphasis placed by many Irish convents on politeness, deportment, good conduct, order, regularity, and application was another striking aspect of the French convent tradition in education at work in girls' schools in Ireland in the nineteenth century... The Irish convent boarding schools supplied a certain status to their pupils which ensured the survival of these traditions until the mid-twentieth century.

Even more telling is O'Connor's analysis of the pervasiveness of French culture, including the spoken language, in girls' boarding-schools in Ireland. Moreover, the French character of the Irish School found approval from parents eager to promote the French virtues of *la politesse* and *le gout* (politeness and good taste) for their daughters. They enthusiastically endorsed the prevailing French objectives of girls' education: to prepare them for marriage or to become nuns. Refinement of manners was accompanied by character-formation. Training in self-discipline was set off by good handwriting and the cultivation of a literary style for the keeping of diaries and for letter-writing. A sound knowledge of the French language permitted the occasional use of a well-chosen phrase like Sissy O'Brien's *bonne tenue* and Nannie's comment to Sissy, "That's the French way of making a bed: all the rules are French."

In any consideration of the history of Irish spirituality, traditional Irish spirituality was, according to Diarmuid O'Laoghaire, S.J., an incomparable legacy from rural, Irish-speaking parts of the country.[6] It fuelled the devotional lives of the people even beyond Famine times. It continued to flourish in the Irish-speaking regions of the island as well as in the remote rural areas sealed off by lack of communication from Patrick Kavanagh's "clever villages that laughed at ancient holiness." We are fortunate in possessing the printed autobiography of an Irish-speaking woman, Peig Sayers (1873-1958), who lived most of her adult life on the Great

Blasket island off the coast of Kerry, where she became a noted story-teller. Elsewhere I have endeavoured to describe the spiritual resources on which Peig Sayers drew when, as a young bride, she left the mainland to dwell for over forty years on the Great Blasket as wife and mother.[7] She was part of an Irish-speaking community both on the adjacent mainland, the Dingle peninsula, and on the rocky island of the Blasket. Though she experienced several years of domestic service in the town of Dingle, she preserved the traditional spirituality which for her was connected with the roots of her essential identity. She could have chosen to emigrate to the United States and she was well aware of the freedom it offered; yet decisively, she accepted the offer of an arranged marriage and the hardship of living on a barren, wind-swept island. By mid-life she had lost husband and four children. "I remember bending to my work with my heart breaking. I used to think of Mary and the Lord—the hard life they had. I knew I had a duty to imitate them and bear my sorrow patiently."[8]

Peig Sayers was a convivial neighbour who enjoyed late nights of story-telling, a pipe of tobacco, and the company of men, including Oxford scholar Robin Flower. Yet the springs of her humanity were nourished by an intense sense of the presence of God and a delight in Creation, the core of Celtic spirituality, according to John McQuarrie.[9]

> The sense of God's immanence in his creation was so strong in Celtic spirituality as to amount sometimes to a pantheism... But perusal of typical Celtic poems and prayers makes it clear that God's presence was even more keenly felt in the daily round of human tasks and at the important junctures of life. Getting up, kindling the fire, going to work, going to bed, as well as birth, marriage, settling in a new house, death, were occasions for recognising the presence of God.

Peig Sayers tells us how she liked to withdraw into herself sitting in a solitary place overlooking the harbour out to sea, reflecting on life. There was a maturity inherent in the culture of the Irish-speaking Blasket Island, a kind of evening incandescence, to be observed also in the writings of her fellow islanders, Tomás Ó Criomhthain, and Tomas Ó Suilleabháin. The islanders had the capacity to confront their own isolation and to discover the truth behind the experience of living frugally and dangerously in such an exposed place. Bad weather and treacherous currents cut the islanders off from church-going, and from the comforting rituals of their religion for weeks on end.

Peig Sayers and her co-islanders were a segment of a society that had undergone revolution and civil war. They belonged to a country which had established its political identity as a democracy, the Irish Free State (Saorstát Éireann) in 1922. Their children were given elementary education on the island in a government school and continued to emigrate to the new world, or came to Dublin to work in areas created by the government in its aspirations to revive the Irish language. Wherever they scattered they embraced urban ways. Gradually throughout the thirties the old way of life of the Blasket declined. The school was closed and the last islanders left the island in the course of the next decade. Peig Sayers settled on the mainland in a secluded townland near Dunquin, where she was joined by her son Micheál, on his return from Cambridge, Massachusetts. From there she transferred to the Dingle hospital for the last few years of her life, dying in 1958 at the age of eighty-five years.

There are certain epochs when two separate worlds overlap, yet remain distinct, apart, with currents of communication flowing between them. Peig Sayers never travelled to a city. Even so, the bustling world of North American cities and the gossip of Dingle and Dublin reached her in letters and accounts of relatives and neighbours. In this study the writer has set herself the task of scrutinising the life-cycles of two Irishwomen drawn from those overlapping worlds in order to chart their paths of spirituality in the context of environment and life-style. Drawing on Peig Sayer's published writing and on the collection of stories and anecdotes that held her listeners enthralled over decades and which are now stored in the Archives of the Folklore Department, University College Dublin, it is possible to recognise that her spirituality drew on contemporary devotional practices such as that of having a lamp burning before an image of the Sacred Heart on her kitchen wall, and of invoking the help of Mary, Mother of Sorrows. It is also sustainable, though less demonstrably proofworthy, that the springs which nourished her spirituality reached back to a past unknown to her and to the islanders. Her life-cycles developed imperceptibly from each previous phase and were integrated and permeated by a spirituality that was unstudied, seemingly instinctive, even commonplace and in her own estimation, were she asked about it, unremarkable. In her own testimony, belief in God, in His will, *creideamh*, that elusive Irish word meaning faith or belief, was the rock of her soul.

The second woman, Edel Quinn, came from the other Catholic Ireland, a town-dweller from the business community in the first decade of the twentieth century. An intelligent, charming child, as is attested by the extant photographs of her at the ages of four and of eleven, she grew up to become a woman who, in the short span of thirty-seven years, encountered and kept at bay a fatal form of tuberculosis, travelled to East Africa as a lay-missioner, was regarded in her own lifetime as a person of great sanctity, and after her death in Nairobi, has been singled out by the Catholic Church as someone eminently worthy of being investigated for process of beatification.

Edel Quinn was born in Kanturk, county Cork, on 14 September 1907. She was born into the comfortable world of the banking community in provincial Ireland and she could have married into the pleasant provincial world of France twenty-one years later. The eldest of four children, three girls and a boy, her childhood was passed in a succession of towns to which her father was moved by the National Bank in which he was an official. Edel Quinn's family moved from

Clonmel to Cahir in County Tipperary, then to Enniscorthy in County Wexford. She was eleven years of age when the family arrived in Tralee, county Kerry. By then her father had been appointed manager of his bank in the chief town of the county, a well-to-do provincial centre with a brisk business community.

Wherever the Quinns moved they lived a town-life adjacent to bank, school and church. They were, as bank people, expected to live a reserved, well-mannered existence, keeping up the social position of a bank official. Those who recalled Edel Quinn in the first seventeen years of her life commented on her bright looks, "a good child, intelligent, full of life and fun and at the head of her class," according to one of her Tralee teachers in the Presentation convent school which she attended.[10]

The Quinn household was a kindly one with an unsophisticated religious atmosphere. Edel was close to her parents and recalled later in one of her letters the evening walks that her mother took with the children which invariably included a visit to the local church to pray before the Blessed Sacrament. When misfortune occurred, the Quinns met it with dignity and family loyalty. In Tralee, Mr Quinn infringed the rules of his bank by lending a sum of money injudiciously. It was 1923, in the immediate aftermath of the Civil War. The guidelines concerning the lending of money by a bank to a customer were inflexible; even a half-morning's latitude was not permitted. For the Quinns their loss of status was experienced immediately. Years of financial strain followed, plans for the children's future education disrupted. Edel was obliged to leave school in her seventeenth year. She was then boarding as a student in the convent school managed by the Faithful Companions of Jesus at Upton Hall, outside Liverpool. This was a period upon which she looked back with delight, when she was allowed to round off her education uninterrupted by the frequent removals of the household. Financed by one of her aunts, it gave her, among other skills, an opportunity to develop her talent for letter-writing.

Like Sissy O'Brien in Bruff, Edel was received into the Sodality of the Children of Mary. There, and in the general running of the school, she assumed a leadership role as a prefect. A serious student, she has left a record of her favourite books at this period in her school diary.[11] A promising academic career lay ahead of her, and, though she left the school before her seventeenth birthday, she had acquired the Cambridge School Certificate.

Edel returned home to a new environment, the sea-front at Monkstown, County Dublin, some seven miles from the centre of Dublin city. The family occupied a high, three-story house in Trafalgar Terrace, overlooking Dublin Bay towards Howth on the far side. Below the terrace, across the road close by the shore line, ran the railway. For the following eight years Edel caught the 8 a.m. train at the Monkstown station "invariably at the last minute," a familiar slim body which flung itself into a receding carriage. Edel was late because she took in morning mass on her way to the city, a not unusual practice in Catholic Dublin. In record time Edel had qualified herself in book-keeping and typing as a commercial secretary. She became a wage-earner, securing a position in the office of the Chagney Tile Works in Tara Street and bringing home her weekly pay packet to augment the family budget.

Frank Duff, founder of the Legion of Mary, a world-wide lay Catholic association, described her at this stage of her life. "When she became a self-supporting individual she did not give herself to devotion or to higher pursuits. She indulged in the usual after-work occupation with the extra one of helping in a girls' club". Frank Duff was making the point that it was the spirituality of the Legion of Mary that transformed Edel Quinn. His reference to "helping in a girls' club" dates back to her membership of the Sodality of the Children of Mary attached to the Loreto Convent in North Great George's Street which she joined on her return to Dublin. This Sodality operated a social club for working girls, and it was here in an area which was adjacent to the Dublin slums that Edel first encountered the poor of Dublin.

Edel's mother was unshakable in her testimony to her daughter's biographer Cardinal Suenens, that Edel, as a small child, was extraordinarily good-humoured and unselfish. Her sister Leslie, in her sworn testimony to the Process of Interrogation concerning Edel Quinn's Cause for Beatification (1963) revealed that the young Edel led a hidden life of prayer, was austere in her eating habits.[12] She had admitted to Leslie her attraction to religious life in a contemplative community. Yet Edel's close friend Mona Tierney was sceptical that Edel, at twenty, had the "makings" of a Legionary when Edel expressed her interest in joining the lay-organisation just seven years after Frank Duff had founded it. The energetic tennis-player who enjoyed dancing and was taking tuition in the French language from a young Frenchman, who had serious intentions of marrying her, concealed from most of her friends her spiritual quest.

Frank Duff, in founding the Association in 1921, released lay-people into a sense of their role and mission in the church of twentieth-century Ireland. The beginnings of the Legion of Mary were modest. A group of people came together in Myra House in Francis Street, in Dublin, Frank Duff being the convener and leader. Their intention, he recalled later, was to address the spiritual needs of the city using an organisational structure similar to that of the Conference of St Vincent de Paul which had spread from France in the previous century in a church-affiliated movement to assist the practical needs of the poor. Frank Duff's first group consisted of fifteen women, himself and a priest.

It was a time of grave national tension in the country. The War of Independence had just terminated in a Truce and the Treaty between the British Government and the Irish negotiators was in the process of being worked out in London. When the Treaty was subsequently put before the national parliament, Dáil Éireann, in December 1921, the House split on the issue of the oath of allegiance to the British monarchy, and the country found itself plunged in civil war between the pro- and anti-Treatyites. It was a shattering experience for all who had dreamt and fought for a new Ireland and its termination in 1923 left the pro-Treaty Free State government in control of a deeply divided country of twenty-six counties. For the official Catholic church, the hierarchy, who had acknowledged the significance of the reality of the Irish Free State with the signing of the Treaty, the civil war challenged them to declare their support for the will of the majority expressed in the Dáil and in the Provisional Government. In so doing they condemned the Republican cause and viewed the young men engaged in its defence as "unpatriotic." As for the civil war, in the words of Dr Margaret O'Callaghan, "the image of the fall, of a descent from heights of nobility was the prism through which the Church insisted on viewing the unfolding tragedy." O'Callaghan's thesis in her study "Religion and identity, the Church and Irish independence", that the hierarchy's revulsion against the anarchy and breakdown of social and familial bonds during the civil war was a strong element in determining the shape and ethos of the Irish Free State, leads her to conclude that in the years after the civil war the hierarchy asserted the immense authority of the Church of the majority in the Free State "in the area that was now their only real domain—the field of faith and morals." Moreover, their view of Irish human nature was pessimistic as a consequence of the civil war: they were "suspicious of their people's moral calibre, wary of their inclinations, determined to keep them under control."[13] Frank Duff's Association was lay-inspired and it had a head-start on the hierarchy's changed outlook after the civil war. Its distinguishing characteristics were its cultivation of the devotional life of the lay-Catholic through the cult of Mary as Mediatrix of All Graces, its emphasis on personal holiness, and an open-ended spiritual ministry to others to lift them out of their apathy, indifference or unawareness of God. As a lay Catholic organisation its self-confidence and autonomy were new experiences in Irish Catholicism. To Frank Duff's dismay, his Legion of Mary met with coldness, even suspicion from Dublin church authorities, the vicars of the archdiocese withholding formal approval for over two decades and two successive archbishops, Dr Byrne and Dr McQuaid, refraining from wholehearted support despite its enthusiastic reception into dioceses all over the world. Frank Duff's insistence that it was an organisation for men and women, and not women only as was suggested to him on one occasion by the vicars as a compromise, may have been a factor in withholding official approval in Dublin. Frank Duff more than once wondered if such was the case.

The full explanation for the success of the Legion of Mary abroad validates its intrinsic merits. In Dublin despite the lack of official approbation it attracted people of all classes. The names and occupations of those early groups reveal its populist character. By the mid-thirties a hundred groups or *praesidia* were functioning in Dublin. In addition to the weekly meetings for its members went the task of rehabilitating the marginalised, organising one-day retreats for all manner of people, and running hostels for the homeless. Frank Duff was accused of being "anti-clerical". He was "that fellow Duff" who was emancipating the paralysed tongues of the laity. Members of the Legion of Mary were sneered at for engaging on a spiritual level with a stratum of society which was demonstrably beyond redemption. Frank Duff was later to say in a fit of exasperation, "anyone who wants to work in Ireland will be cribbed, cabined and confined. Religion has become a routine. A terrible conservatism exercises relentless sway, and tells the Irish people they must walk in outmoded ways...plainly we are looking at Jansenism, and not true Catholicism." Those strictures were wrung from him in 1947.[14] In the first decade after the civil war, the sense of mission in the new state was tangible. The strains within Irish society were not strikingly visible for some time to come.

Frank Duff, in founding the association in 1921 that quickly became the Legion of Mary, created in Ireland a school of Marian spirituality. He found a society ready to accept a central devotion to Mary as developed by the French spiritual writer, Louis Marie de Montfort in the late seventeenth century, but only then gaining ground in Catholic devotional circles possibly because of the apparitions of Mary at Lourdes, La Salette and Knock. Frank Duff's *Handbook of the Legion of Mary* was based on a theology of the lay-apostolate not fully apprehended by official church authorities in Dublin though enthusiastically accepted elsewhere. Its influence in the middle decades of the twentieth century has never been fully appreciated though it is now acknowledged as a ground-breaking exercise for the theology of the laity that emerged from the deliberations of the Second Vatican Council, 1963-66.

Edel Quinn joined the Legion of Mary a few months before her twenty-first birthday, six years after it was founded. Her local branch, or *praesidium* (Frank Duff delighted in Latin titles) was bound to a weekly meeting consisting of prayers, spiritual reading and discourse, followed by the minutes of the previous meeting, a report on visitation work undertaken in pairs, and assignment of tasks for the coming week. Doubt had been expressed that the organisation would attract Edel. She persevered and in a short time she established herself as a person of perceived gifts. Soon she was spending most of her free time in the activities generated by her Legion undertakings, accomplishing demanding visitations after her own work was finished. At least two hours a week were required of Legion members. Edel went on to devote five evenings a week to hospital visitation, to the lonely in the slum tenements behind O'Connell Street, or, a task she found disagreeable, introducing herself at doors to families to promote devotion to the Sacred Heart. Her own preference was for isolated lonely people, for invalids and for the old. When she had served for two years as an ordinary member of the *praesidium*, she was appointed president of a group whose work was difficult and sensitive, making contact with prostitutes, offering them alternative living quarters, and restoring to them a sense of their own self-worth and spiritual identity. Despite objections to her youthful appearance and what seemed like her lack of experience, she won esteem and commendation for the manner in which she carried out her complicated assignments. It was through becoming an officer in the leadership cadre of the Legion of Mary that she came to the notice of Frank Duff.

"A process of ultra-refining" was how Frank Duff described the development of Edel's spirituality. She has left no autobiography behind her as did the remarkable Peig Sayers, author of two personal volumes of personal reflections. Edel Quinn, on the other hand, was an excellent letter-writer, and more than two hundred of her letters were kept by various people after her death, the bulk from East Africa between 1936-44, and some fifty to Pierre Jean François Landrin. Because of the singular scrutiny to which her life and actions have been subjected by church authorities in Rome as a potential candidate for beatification, the sworn testimonies of those who knew her comprise a large volume of 900 pages, *Summarium, super dubio, ad ejus Causa introducenda sit*, issued in Rome, 1982. There are also a considerable number of people still alive, or who have recently died, who gave oral interviews to Edel's distinguished biographer, Cardinal Leon-Joseph Suenens, Archbishop of Malines-Brussels, in the early fifties. His *Life of Edel Quinn* was first published in 1952 and has been translated into English, Dutch, Chinese, Japanese, Korean and Slavic. Still issuing in steady reprints, it is an important source for examining her life. Archbishop Antonio Riberi, Apostolic Nuncio to China, who has spent some time in the nunciature in Dublin, and later on in Nairobi in East Africa, was familiar with both the Legion of Mary and Edel Quinn's missionary activities. In his Preface to the Suenens' biography of Edel Quinn he wrote[15]

> I have always hoped that her wonderful life would find a pen capable of presenting it fittingly to the attentive examination of the Catholic world...It would be difficult to confide it to a person of greater authority, to a more brilliant writer, to a deeper thinker, to one with more expert knowledge of modern conditions.

Acquaintances who knew her in her early twenties describe her variously: "she had a distinctive personality...the extraordinary brightness of her face...exquisitely pretty...not robust...what she had to say carried weight...reserved..." Pierre Landrin had first met her when as a nineteen year old she arrived at the office of the Tile Company which he managed. For two years they saw each other once a week on a personal level, for tea in Jury's or the Savoy Hotel, and again at the weekends for a game of tennis. Pierre was well received at Edel's family home. Those who observed them commented on how compatible they were. Pierre began to teach her French which she had left aside after schooldays. He lent her works written in French and they enjoyed discussing books. She also gave him glimpses of the struggle she experienced at times in the Legion assignments. "I have to get in two visits to people, the second a horrible ordeal. I hate visiting, don't you?" she commented to Pierre on one occasion. To the surprise of Leslie, Edel's sister, one midday Edel arrived home, grieving, her distress obvious, and confessed to Leslie that she had finally not accepted Pierre's proposal of marriage.[16] Instead she was resolved to enter the Poor Clare contemplative community of Franciscan nuns in Belfast. Edel had entertained the idea for a long time. In a letter to Pierre she explained her delay in making her decision.

> I know you must wonder why I have not entered before, instead of holding on to office work. Well, when I left school, circumstances intervened which showed plainly that my duty, at the time and since, was to stay with my parents. About the beginning of this year, I believed I was free to follow my vocation. It was then I made arrangements. However, when I told Mother, she said I was still needed at home, and that it would not be right for me to go.
>
> After reflection and taking of advice, I saw my duty was for the present at home, and that being so, I could not conscientiously go away. So that is why I am still where I am. Please forgive, Pierre, this long writing about myself. I would not have spoken, and never have to anyone, about

this matter, which is so intimate. But I felt I owed it to you, who have been so frank with me.[17]

A religious vocation always implies choice and decision, and within that choice, a narrowing of choice, no matter how obvious the decision to the observer. The contemplative nun, enclosed and cloistered, is a metaphor of the archetypal symbolisations of the self. Religious life, so called, is a way of containing a developed sense of reflectiveness about the transcendent nature of reality. The individual responds to choosing a way of life that commits her to explore in a structured way what God has been calling her to in the particular mode designated by that impulse. Edel was, untypically, reticent about her selection of the Poor Clares of the Colletine Observance in Belfast and her decision came as a surprise to many who thought they knew her well. From the testimony of one of her closest friends, it emerges how carefully she had prepared for her entry into religious life.[18] She imposed upon herself a strict asceticism."She rose every morning at half past five, and Mass, Holy Communion, morning meditation and a very scanty breakfast were her preparation for the day's work." She also read widely the classics of the spiritual life, Juliana of Norwich, St John of the Cross, the French Carmelites, Thérèse of Lisieux and Elizabeth of the Trinity, Tanquerey's *A Treatise of the Spiritual Life, The Imitation of Christ* and the works of the contemporary Benedictines, Dom Marmion and Abbot Vonier. After essaying four chapters of *The Interior Castle* by the mystic Teresa of Avila, she returned it to its owner saying that a treatise of extraordinary graces was not for her. Increasingly she read daily the Scriptures, the Legion *Handbook* and de Montfort's *True Devotion to Mary*. Much later, in a letter to Cardinal Suenens giving his thoughts on Edel Quinn, Pierre Landrin wrote of "her irrevocable decision of entering the Poor Clare Convent in Belfast."

Edel planned to enter in the course of her twenty-fifth year. Early in February she became suddenly ill with a suspicious haemorrhage indicating the nature of the malady.

A medical examination confirmed that her lungs were in an advanced state of tuberculosis with little hope of permanent cure. On the 5 February 1932 she was taken to Newcastle sanatorium, county Wicklow, where she remained eighteen months. Tuberculosis in twentieth-century Ireland awaits its historian. It was for young and old "the dread disease," the only remedy at that time, quarantine in a sanatorium, preferably at a high, cold altitude. Edel was to become familiar with the clinical interior of the TB sanatorium, not once but several times in her life. Outwardly she remained a cheerful bright person who teased and bantered her way into the affections of her companions, and was called upon by the nurses in times of emergency. Inwardly the Newcastle interlude, one of intense cold and painful treatment, strengthened her will-power immeasurably. The perceptive Frank Duff stated that the experience "made her realistic." Years later, in answer to a question about Edel's ability to evaluate a situation while working in East Africa, he observed: "she was realistic in her comments, a critic, albeit a constructive one, sharp in her observations." Of her sojourn in Newcastle he said: "I do not know the details. She must have spent many sad moments in sanatoriums."[19]

An illness such as Edel got has more than one meaning. One must look at Edel's story in terms of life-cycle and endeavour to discover what made her succumb to tuberculosis, what levels of significance this may have for women's lives, and what the spectacular prolongation of her life for twelve more years might mean for the life-journeys of other casualties of tuberculosis. When her condition became known, friends remarked with concern how little she ate for years before, her seemingly tireless round of Legion activities, her athletic tennis-playing, the frequent wettings in the damp Dublin evening visits she undertook in the tenements. Concluded Muriel Wailes, a colleague and friend of Edel's: "though her family was a robust, athletic one, Edel abused her health, fasting, often missing her meals, abstaining from milk, butter and meat." While she has left no record of what conflicts may have been going on within her during those years or whether her struggle to repress the experiences of meeting Pierre took their toll, her descent into tuberculosis may have allowed her to economise on a psychical effort to have an undivided heart for her religious vocation. It was, on one level, a thwarting of her high purpose by closing off her entry into religious life. It was also a resolution of conflict in the manner in which she made it the prelude to a new life-cycle which was to be brimming with energy, unimagined travelled in Africa, and the period of her greatest achievements.

When Edel discharged herself from the Newcastle sanatorium in 1922 her lungs were not healed, but her health was much improved. One of the reasons why she left was the expense of the "gold injection treatment" which her family was financing and which had not healed the defective lungs. At that period there were no welfare benefits that Edel could draw upon and two of the younger members of the family were still school-going. The only ostensible change she made in her resumption of activities was her insistence that she occupy a room by herself always lest her tubercular state of health prove a hazard to others. This rule she maintained for the rest of her life. In Eastleigh, Nairobi, the little room she occupied behind the sacristy of the church is still used as a meeting place. It was in that room she died, rather suddenly, on 12 May 1944. She had chosen to live there instead of occupying a room in the small convent close by, lest her racking cough or her proximity to others in the house caused discomfort. The bareness of her little room, its isolation on the compound speak for her ability to encounter solitude and live with courage in the face of advancing death.

At first glance it seems far-fetched to suggest Edel Quinn as a study in survival strategies. When she was in the sanatorium she joked about her illness although it signified the end of her hopes for entering religious life, and dramatically altered her plans for her future. Pierre Landrin had returned to France and according to his own account had assumed she had departed to the Belfast monastery. She kept her own counsel, declining to be drawn on matters so intimate to her own life. She quickly found other work, this time as accounting secretary to Tallons Motorworks in Westland Row, close to the railway station. When Edel took the decision to discharge herself from Newcastle she was to demonstrate the qualities of a woman whose self-actualisation made her more confident and more authoritative in deciding how she would live the rest of her life. It was not a matter of time but of maturity. Instead of denying her tubercular state, Edel found acceptable outlets for her own deepest desires and following those deeper wishes, her religious aspirations were released and channelled creatively into the construction of a more humane society. Before we examine how she adapted herself to her changed condition, some consideration needs to be directed to the opinion Frank Duff held of her at this time. It was first expressed to Cardinal Suenens in preparation for the latter's study of Edel Quinn in the context of the lay-apostolate, undertaken five years after her death. Much later Frank Duff, under oath, testified to the Tribunal which was examining her Cause for Beatification and admitted to a friend, León Ó Broin, how meticulously he had endeavoured to be truthful.[20]

Frank Duff was a sound judge of character. A skilled civil servant, he largely drafted the Hogan Land Purchase Act of 1923. He acted briefly as personal secretary to Michael Collins, Chairman of the Provisional Government and Commander-in-Chief of the National Army, until the latter was killed. For over ten years he worked in the Finance and Supply Division of the Department of Finance and when he retired from the Civil Service in October 1934 to devote himself full-time to the Legion of Mary, he was probably even at that early stage the most influential layman in the Catholic Church in Ireland. His astute and energetic leadership of the Legion of Mary in its formative years was reflected in the kind of officer he personally selected for his organisation. It was a mark of his own standing among his colleagues in the Department of Finance that several of them joined his organisation and accepted responsibility in the leadership cadre. Thus León Ó Broin, distinguished man of letters and later secretary of the Department of Posts and Telegraphs, recounts how he met Frank Duff and became a life-long friend and associate of his in the work of the Legion, undertaking the quarterly editing of the periodical, *Maria Legionis,* for ten years as well as being an officer of the organisation. Seán Moynihan, secretary to the government and Maurice Moynihan, later to serve as secretary to the Department of Finance, remained, despite onerous public duties, devoted members of the Legion, assisting in the running of the hostels. Celia Shaw, who was recruited as a young graduate to the civil service, joined the Legion of Mary in 1924 and sixty years of close co-operation followed. Her collection of letters from Frank Duff form an important source of documentation for his life. He had no time for class or sectional interests. Among his first group of Legion officers, was the remarkable Elizabeth Kirwan, a New Zealander and an office cleaner, who later became a president of Concilium, the executive group of the worldwide organisation. Colette Gill from the heart of the Liberties in Dublin supplied much information on the early members of the Legion. There was Joe Gabbet, "the man with the fearsome moustache," and Jack Nagle, anchor-man for decades in the headquarters of the Legion of Mary in Myra House in North Brunswick Street. Like Sam Hughes, Jack Nagle was president of Concilium. Sam Hughes was a cycling companion of Frank Duff, from the civil service and was left, after Frank Duff's death, the task of steering the Legion of Mary into the late twentieth century.

There was no obvious strategy of recruitment, yet in a seemingly effortless way, Frank Duff attracted to his organisation in those early years men and women of unusual competence who were possessed of a genuine desire to minister to the spiritual needs of Dublin's numerous outcasts. Frank Duff's wholehearted devotion to the "down-and-outs" to whom he gave a refuge in the hostels off North Brunswick Street found an overwhelming response in a generation who understood his mission and who were themselves in the public life of the new state engaged in articulating and identifying the nature of the enterprise of that new state.

Frank Duff first met Edel Quinn in 1931 and became personally acquainted with her when she was appointed president of a *praesidium* shortly before her sojourn in Newcastle. On her return to active membership of the Legion, she was advised by him to take a less active position working with young people in a children's hospital close to the house her family had moved to in the same pleasant area of Monkstown. Though she had abandoned the idea of religious life, she kept her habit of early rising, morning mass and austerity. In those middle years of the thirties the Legion of Mary was rapidly expanding to America, to England and Wales, and to Africa. Frank Duff's concept of extension work to England, a system of short-term volunteering carried out during a legionary's holiday periods, was enthusiastically received by hierarchy and parochial clergy alike. The Legion Envoy was a bolder initiative. The notion of offering to a bishop of a diocese a lay-missioner who was prepared to work out a blueprint of which he had prior knowledge and to which he had given his approval proved to be a factor which won the Legion worldwide acclaim. The Legion Envoy, chosen and missioned by the Concilium of the Legion, undertook in whatever part of the world selected by Frank Duff and his executive committee, to establish a cohort of lay-people, bonded by the Legion structures, who functioned within the parish framework. It proved attractive in all missionary countries and in places where the clergy were scattered over a wide region. There was the communitarian element of assembling at a weekly meeting a group of lay-people who undertook the responsibility of spiritual ministry to their own people as well as developing their own spirituality. For a hard-worked missionary priest there was the availability of catechists, and visitors to the sick, the disease-ridden, and those who lived in remote inaccessible villages. The flow of information was invaluable and the reports of Legion Envoys to Concilium form a massive testimony to what León Ó Broin described as "Frank Duff's organisational genius."

Edel Quinn was singled out by Frank Duff to go to Wales on extension work. According to Muriel Wailes, her friend and longterm colleague of Frank Duff, he lifted down the map of Britain and pointed out the diocese of Minevia to Muriel and watching the expression on her face, "looked at her in that serene way he had and said 'Do your best, yes, it is a bleak part of the vineyard, but you can count on divine help.'" Edel had offered to use her 1936 holiday time on extension work and he sent her along with Muriel Wailes, secretly scrutinising her for other possibilities. According to Muriel Wailes, Edel was an astonishing success. Her *joie de vivre* and sense of fun, together with her sincerity and conviction brought to many a desire to be reconciled with their God and church.[21] On their return, Edel Quinn suggested to Frank Duff that she move to Chester, find an occupation there and spread the Legion of Mary from there to Wales and England. Hard on the heels of that proposal, Frank Duff recounts, came a request to develop the Legion of Mary in South Africa and he introduced Edel's name for consideration to Concilium. Then Bishop Heffernan of East Africa requested formally a Legion Envoy for his diocese. After serious consideration with the other officers of Concilium, Frank Duff invited Edel to consider Bishop Heffernan's request. She accepted.[22]

A storm of opposition ensued, dramatically described by Cardinal Suenens in his biography.[23] The ex-general of the Calced Carmelites, a man of considerable authority, shot to his feet. He enumerated in rapid-fire fashion the obstacles and perils that lay in wait there, arguing "to send Edel Quinn to Africa would be sheer folly, particularly for a woman travelling alone, the deadly climate, the vast distances to be covered under appalling conditions." And so he went on, "if someone must be sent, let it be a man of more than average strength, and not a fragile young girl." When he stopped for breath, Edel arose. "All those difficulties have been explained to me in detail," she interjected. "I know what is before me. It is exactly what I am looking for...I am going with my eyes open. I don't want to go on any picnic." Her unexpected vehemence disarmed her adversary and so won the consent of that experienced and shrewd assembly.

It was a critical decision and Edel was sensible of the responsibility placed not only upon her, but upon Frank Duff who had put forward her name. She wrote to him on board ship to Mombasa a few months later:

> I would like you to understand always, whatever happens, that I am glad you gave me the opportunity of going. I realise it is a privilege and also that only for you persisted I would never have been sent...Whatever be the consequence, rejoice you had to courage to emulate Our Lord, in his choice of weak things, in Faith. Any sorrow caused to others was worth it, remember; I know that you felt pretty badly the fact that others were suffering. Have no regrets...I am glad you let me go—the others will be glad later.[24]

On Saturday, 24 October 1936, Edel Quinn sailed away from Ireland never to return. *The Llangibby Castle* took her from Tilbury docks on Friday morning, 30 October and deposited her in Mombasa, the gateway to East Africa on 23 November. Awaiting her was Bishop Heffernan, there to welcome the new arrivals which included a group of Irish Loreto Sisters with whom Edel was always free to stay. On the bishop's suggestion, she made Nairobi her headquarters, travelling that same day the three hundred miles inland and uphill by train. Her remaining years, ones of spectacular success and of courageous travels into the interior of Africa, form a brilliant climax to her life.

In contrast to her declining health which forced her twice into TB clinics, the last eight years of her life were infused with energy and a richness of experience which lights up her weekly letters to Jack Nagle and Frank Duff. The log-book of her journey to Africa was published in the first numbers of *Maria Legionis*. Its publication brought her presence in Africa and her mission there to hundreds of readers. Her African letters were, in the main, factual reports, written on a typewriter which accompanied her, insofar as it was possible, wherever she travelled. Her correspondence with

Concilium in Dublin was extensive, full of information and sharp questions. She wrote with clarity but the reader senses that her letters were written in low-key, unemotional, predictable style which concealed many of her personal reflections.

In the thirties the relationship of Ireland to Africa was one of increasing geographical intimacy, all the more startling because it has never been articulated as a conscious extension of the Irish emigration experience. "The flight to Africa" in the middle decades of the twentieth century by hundreds of Irish men and women as missionaries intent on christianising that continent goes further than bridging a gap in the historical consciousness The earlier surge of religious orders to Africa at the end of the nineteenth century was arguably a following of the flag of empire and for the religious orders, Sisters like the Irish Dominicans, Christian Brothers and Irish branch of the Holy Ghost Order (C.S.S.P.), there was accommodation within British colonial Africa including South Africa. With the founding of the new missionary orders a different kind of impulse brought hundreds of young Irish missionaries to Africa. St Patrick's Society for African Missions, founded in 1932 from Maynooth College, followed the inspiration of Bishop Shanahan, C.S.S.P. in Nigeria 1902-43 in his strategy of development, schools, hospitals—but also farming, irrigation, road-making, tea and coffee plantations. For women the setting up of the Missionary Sisters of the Holy Rosary (Killeshandra) in 1924 also benefited from the inspiration of Bishop Shanahan's Nigerian endeavours. Earlier the Franciscan missionaries for Africa, under the leadership of Sister Kevin Kearney, pioneered nursing and midwifery skills in that part of the world. Her sisters were clustered mainly in Uganda with a major teaching hospital in Kampala. The founding of Mary Martin's Medical Missionaries of Mary in 1937 opened up a new phase by bringing professional medical services to remote regions of Africa. The rise in religious vocations in twentieth century Ireland overflowed to Africa in abundance. There was scarcely a townland or village in Ireland in the 1940s that had not some missionary working in Africa, nor a postman who could not locate some far-distant region of that continent by its postage stamp.

Edel Quinn's role was different. She was a young laywoman in a largely clericalised world of European missionaries. She was an accredited Envoy whose task it was to set up the Legion of Mary wherever a bishop or local priest invited it. According to the testimony of many who came forward to be interviewed for the process of beatification, she was much more. She proved herself a trainer of leaders, a resource person for the parishes, a tactful link between bishop and people. In the Legion archives are outlines of her formidable, highly efficient timetable. She showed the missioner when best to use a catechist, how to acquire an over-all plan of an area. She set goals for herself, she dealt expertly with masses of correspondence which awaited her on her return to Nairobi. She taught a non-literate society to run meetings.[25]

From the beginning Edel Quinn sensed that her core relationship was with the African people and tactfully she receded from the European and Goan communities in Nairobi and Mombasa to devote herself to getting in touch with the Kenyan, Ugandan and other African peoples. In the thirties East Africa was a segregated society. Yet Edel Quinn travelled simply in the matatoes packed tightly with African farm-workers. Most of the Europeans of the White Highlands of Kenya rode in motorcars or on horseback; Edel's simple mode of travel did not go unnoticed. John Omolo, who joined the Legion of Mary in 1939 as a result of meeting her and who later became the Chairman of the Senatus of the Legion in Nairobi, taking over the leadership of the Legion there after her death, believes that the secret of her success was her ability "to walk with us."[26] All recall her enthusiasm, the challenging, magnetic blue eyes, the clear face, the laugh, the husky voice, "bubbling with energy," the "tough tennis player." She worked at incredible speed, establishing the Legion securely, conscious that the Catholic

Church in East Africa was a developing one. She became the owner of a dilapidated Ford at one stage and, despite rationing and the hazards of World War II in East Africa, she journeyed through villages, the jungle tracks of Kenya, Uganda, Tanganyika, Nyasaland. A Missionary priest writing to Concilium after her death recalled her itinerary:

> At 11 a.m. she departed for a certain place about sixty miles away, returning the next day at 10 a.m. with a message for me from our Bishop. Immediately after this she went off on a trip of about 110 miles...On her way to our mission she got stuck in the mud and had to abandon the car. After walking ten miles she reached a hotel, where she had a little rest but she took no food. Early in the morning she went with the mechanic for the car...[27]

Her journeying brought her out to Mauritius where she had received a special invitation to set up the Legion. The alarming state of her health sent her to Johannesburg with a diagnosis of advanced pulmonary tuberculosis and a six month rest in bed in that cool bracing climate. That was 1941. She recovered and resumed her activities. By the beginning of 1943 she was back in Nairobi, directing her Envoy responsibilities through letters and the occasional short stay, invariably returning to her room in Eastleigh in the compound of the Precious Blood Sisters. Though she had not mastered Swahili, she studied it. East Africa was spread before her like an open book.

Edel Quinn died of a heart attack brought on by extreme exhaustion and weakness on Friday, May 12 1944, in the thirty-seventh year of her life. Frank Duff received the news by telegram almost immediately from Nairobi despite the war-situation. Unprecedentedly, by another telegram came from the Vatican Secretary of State to the Nuncio in Dublin formally announcing her death. Sadly Dublin heard the news filtered through on newspaper hoardings and in the daily papers. She had become a legend in her lifetime. Eight years later Cardinal Suenens produced his carefully documented biography of Edel Quinn in French. Dr Louise Gavan Duffy, the Irish educationalist and legionary, simultaneously translated it into English. In November 1956 Edel's Cause for Beatification was introduced in Nairobi. In effect it initiated the setting up of a Tribunal, and the process of interviewing witnesses under oath and collecting all manner of data concerning her life. No other Irish woman of the twentieth century has been so carefully documented, or so relentlessly revealed in the testimonials of her contemporaries and in her own letters as Edel Quinn. Her historical presence is assured.

Peig Sayers and Edel Quinn form a unique comparison in the context of Irish female spirituality. Peig Sayers inherited an archaic way of life and her religion, its beliefs and practices, were part of that life. Her spirituality never preoccupied her consciousness nor fired her imagination to achieve any heroic goal of sanctity. Her faith in God, in a life after death, in the humanity of Christ, in her closeness to his Mother Mary was deep and untroubled. Life, however, was destiny for her. Saying "yes" to God's will was to place trust in her father's and brother's judgment that the made "match" between them and her future husband was the right selection for her. Moreover, this world was a place of suffering in which she strove against the harsh poverty on a bleak island and became familiar with death which snatched her menfold early in life. She stands at the end of a tradition of christian living which, centuries before in the estimation of Professor James Carney "was perhaps the most ascetic that western Europe has known."[28] Like her Celtic ancestors of the ninth century Peig Sayers sought out and observed Nature in all its manifestations of changing moods. For her, as for them, Nature was the handicraft of God. She does not tell us of her moments of rebellion. She found relief by resorting to humour and drew upon a vast reservoir of stored tales. She celebrated life in the nightly story-telling (the scorafocht) in her house, in which she was both hostess and entertainer. Well might she echo the ninth-century Hag of Beare's great poem "Ebbing": she too outlived her loved ones and had passed through the seven ages. In her the natural life-cycles moved inexorably to her own encounter with death in old age. She survives in her two volumes of personal reflection and in the masses of folklore material that were collected by her friend Dr Robin Flower on his summer visits to the Great Blasket. Throughout the greater part of the twentieth century her *Autobiography* and her *Reflections of an Old Woman* have been standard textbooks for the Senior State examination in Irish language and literature.

Edel Quinn contrasts strongly with her older contemporary. She was urban as Peig was rural. There was a generational divide and an educational one. Her schooling with its French emphasis continued to influence her cultural and devotional interests. Her generation inherited "Independent" Ireland and there was present in her life goals that sense of dedication which women and men brought to the service of country, church and family after the civil war. Looking below the surface of her behaviour, her decisions were taken from somewhere inside and showed a steady inclination to move away from the patriarchal roles which Irish society in that period was bestowing on its womenfolk. The Legion of Mary, in the vigour of its first phase, supplied her quest for self-actualisation with an ideation content, largely of Frank Duff's making. Membership invited her to holiness. It intellectualised her simple piety by drawing her to the classics of the great spiritual writers. It was no accident that she chose as her guide Fr Eugene Boylan, the Irish Carthusian monk, whom she consulted. Central to the Legion spirituality were the writings of the French seventeenth-century Louis Marie de Montfort. Yet another clue to Edel's development, as we know from her letters to Pierre Landrin, was the autobiography of Thérèse of Liseux (given to her in French by Pierre), a volume underlined and pencilled with her own marginal notes. Suenens concludes that Edel was seeking the pure spirit of the Gospels, and at the end of her life the Scriptures had become her main daily reading.[29]

Saints, according to the psycho-analyst James Hillman, become transpersonal figures, ideal beings, beyond the human, "persons of the imaginal for the soul to remember." For the weak, the chronically ill, those with a terminal disease, Edel Quinn in that last period of her life demonstrates the ability of the human spirit to house the body and surrender it with courage and dignity. In the history of how women survive this was her greatest achievement, the possibility of inventing a life-cycle of amazing vitality in the face of advancing death.

Peig Sayers and Edel Quinn reflect two paradigms of religious culture in twentieth century Ireland. To both was given fullness of life and both developed, in quite different ways, strategies of survival. To be able to examine the elements that went into those modes of survival is intrinsically a satisfying intellectual exercise. But when we have acknowledged that contribution to understanding the life-cycles of twentieth-century women, something more remains. It is the reality of glimpsing lives lived to full capacity defying the boundaries of biography.

Notes

I would like to thank Professor Enda McDonagh for his valuable suggestions on the earlier draft of this article.

1 *Manual of the Child of Mary.* Rules of Membership.
2 Richard Ellman, *James Joyce* (Oxford 1983 revised ed.), pp 47-50.
3 S. O'Brien (Mary Carbery), *The Farm by Lough Gur* (Cork, 1973), p. 140.
4 P. J. Corish, *The Irish Catholic Experience* (Dublin, 1985), pp 229-30, 233; Kevin Whelan, "The Catholic parish, the Catholic chapel and village development in Ireland" in *Irish Geography,* xvi, (1983), pp 1-15.
5 A. V. O'Connor, "The Revolution in girls' secondary education in Ireland, 1860-1910" in Mary Cullen (ed.), *Girls Don't Do Honours* (Dublin, 1987), p. 39.
6 D. Ó Laoghaire, "Traditional Irish spirituality in modern times" in

M. Maher (ed.), *Irish Spirituality* (Dublin, 1981), pp 123-34.

7 Margaret MacCurtain, "Moving statues and Irish women" in *Studies,* vol. 73, no. 302, (1987), pp 139-46.

8 M. Ní Chinnéide (ed.), *Peig* (Dublin, 1963); B. MacMahon (trans.), *Peig, the Autobiography of Peig Sayers of the Great Blaskets* (Dublin, 1981). For evidence of the poverty of the inhabitants of the Great Blasket and of Peig's hardships, see Eibhlís Ní Shúilleabháin, *Letters from the Great Blasket* (Cork, 1978, reprinted 1988), pp 32-47.

9 Quoted in M. Maher (ed.), *Irish Spirituality* (Dublin, 1981), p. 7.

10 Interview by author with Presentation Sisters, Tralee, 9 March 1984.

11 Original sources written by Edel Quinn, and concerning her work, are now housed at the Concilium Headquarters, Legion of Mary, Dublin. The author brought back two substantial collections of her letters from Nairobi in the course of researching her life in Kenya, July through September 1983. These are now lodged in Concilium Archives, Dublin.

12 Sworn Testimony of C. Leslie Quinn, 15 November 1963 in *Cause of Edel Quinn, Summarium* (Rome, 1982), (proc. reg. Dublinen), pp 301-2.

13 Margaret O'Callaghan, "Religion and identity, the Church and Irish independence" in *The Crane Bag,* vol. 7, no. 2, (1983), p. 71.

14 Leon Ó Broin, *Frank Duff, a Biography* (Dublin, 1982), p. 9.

15 L. J. Suenens, *Edel Quinn, Envoy of the Legion of Mary to Africa* (Bruges, 1952; Dublin 1952).

16 *Summarium,* p. 300, Testimony of C. Leslie Quinn.

17 Edel Quinn to Pierre Landrin, 1931 (?), Suenens, *op. cit.*, p. 53.

18 Mary Wall, *I Knew Edel Quinn* (Dublin, 1966), pp 7-8. Mary Wall entered the Carthusian Order in Italy and wrote her recollections anonymously, describing herself in the title page as "an Irish Carthusian nun."

19 *Summarium,* p. 307, Testimony of C. Leslie Quinn.

20 Ó Broin, *op. cit.*, p. 43 ff.

21 Interview by author with Muriel Wailes, Dublin, 22 October 1983; Sworn Testimony of Muriel Wailes, 14 May 1964 in *Summarium,* pp 373-4.

22 Sworn Testimony of Frank Duff, 25 June 1964 in *Summarium* p. 382.

23 Suenens, *op. cit.*, p. 79.
24 Ó Broin, *op. cit.*, p. 54; Testimony of Frank Duff in *Summarium*, p. 383 (reference to the letter).
25 Sworn Testimony of: Miss Elizabeth Gannon, Sister Teresa Joseph O'Sullivan, S.L., Fr John Reidy C.S.S.P., Sister Servita Lembach, Sister Arsenia Ackfeld, Isabella de Mello, Fr Tom Maher C.S.S.P., in *Summarium* (ex Proc. Ord. Nairobien, 1963-9), pp 15-105.
26 Interview by author with John Omolo, Nairobi, 10 August 1983.
27 Suenens, *op. cit.*, p. 200.
28 J. Carney, *Medieval Irish Lyrics and the Irish Bardic Poet*, (Dublin, 1985), pp xxi, 28-41.
29 Suenens, *op. cit.*, p. 60; Sworn Testimony of Pierre Landrin, 28 May 1964 in *Summarium*, pp 503-07.

Suggestions for further reading: a select list

General:

Banks, Olive, *Faces of Feminism* (Oxford, 1981).

Berg, Barbara J., *The Remembered Gate: Origins of American Feminism: The Woman and the City 1800-1860* (Oxford, 1978).

Cott, Nancy F., *The Bonds of Womanhood: Women's Sphere in New England, 1780-1835* (London, 1977).

......, *The Grounding of Modern Feminism* (London, 1987).

Degler, Carl M., *Is There a History of Women?* (Oxford, 1975).

Delamont, Sara and Duffin, Lorna (eds.), *The Nineteenth-Century Woman: Her Cultural and Physical World* (London, 1978).

Elshtain, Jean Bethke, *The Public Man, Private Woman: Women in Social and Political Thought* (New Jersey, 1981).

Evans, Richard J., *The Feminists: Women's Emancipation Movements in Europe, America and Australasia, 1840-1920* (London, 1977).

Hartman, M. and Banner, L. W. (eds.), *Clio's Consciousness Raised: New Perspectives on the History of Woman* (New York, 1974).

Hellerstein, E. A. Hume, L. P. and Offen, K. M. (eds.), *Victorian Women. A Documentary Account of Women's Lives in Nineteenth-Century England, France and the United States* (Brighton, 1981).

Hewitt, Nancy A., "Beyond the search for sisterhood:

American women's history in the 1980s," *Social History*, no. 10 (1985), pp 299-321.

Kelly, Joan, *Women, History and Theory* (Chicago, 1984).

Lerner, Gerda, *The Majority Finds its Past: Placing Women in History* (New York, 1979).

Offen, Karen, "Defining feminism: a comparative historical approach," *Signs: Journal of Women in Society and Culture*, vol. 14, no. 1 (Autumn 1988), pp 119-157.

Rendall, Jane, *The Origins of Modern Feminism: Women in Britain, France and the United States, 1780-1860* (London, 1985).

.... (ed.) *Equal or Different: Women's Politics 1800-1914* (Oxford, 1987).

Rowbotham, Sheila, *Hidden from History: 300 years of Women's Oppression and the Fight Against It* (London, 1973).

Scott, Joan Wallach, "Survey articles: women in history: the modern period," *Past and Present*, no. 101 (November 1983), pp 141-157.

.........(ed.) "Gender: a useful category of historical analysis," *American Historical Review*, no. 91 (1986), pp 1053-75.

Tilly, L. A. and Scott, J. W., *Women's Work and the Family* (New York, 1978).

Vicinus, Martha (ed.), *Suffer and Be Still: Women in the Victorian Age* (London, 1980).

........., *A Widening Sphere. Changing Roles of Victorian Women* (London, 1980).

Welter, Barbara, "The cult of true womanhood, 1820-1860," *American Quarterly*, 18, (1966), pp 151-174.

Women's History in Ireland

General

Brady, Anne M., *Women in Ireland: An Annotated Bibliography* (Connecticut, 1988).

Cosgrove, Art (ed.), *Marriage in Ireland* (Dublin, 1985).

Cullen, Mary, "Some aspects of feminist studies," *Educational Matters*, no. 1 (Dec 1978).

........., "Women, history and identity," *The Maynooth Review*, (May 1980), pp 65-79.

Curtin, Chris, Pauline Jackson and Barbara O'Connor (eds.), *Gender in Irish Society* (Galway, 1987).

Doughan, David and Sanchez, Denise, *Feminist Periodicals 1855-1984: An Annotated Critical Bibliography of British, Irish, Commonwealth and International Titles* (Brighton, 1987).

Gallagher, S. F. (ed.), *Women in Irish Legend, Life and Literature* (Buckinghamshire, 1983).

Ní Chuilleanain, Eilean (ed.), *Irish Women: Image and Achievement* (Dublin, 1985).

Rose, Catherine, *The Female Experience: The Story of the Woman Movement in Ireland* (Dublin, 1975).

Scott, Liz Steiner (ed.), *Personally Speaking: Women's Thoughts on Women's Issues* (Dublin, 1985).

Images of the Irish Woman, *The Crane Bag*, vol. 4, no. 1, (1980).

Smyth, Ailbhe (ed.), *Women's Studies International Forum*, Special Issue Feminism in Ireland, vol. 11, no. 4 (1988).

Education:

Breathnach, Eibhlin, "Women and higher education in Ireland, 1879-1910", *The Crane Bag*, iv, (1980) pp 47-54.

Coombes, James, "Catherine Donovan (1788-1858) educational pioneer," *Seanchas Chairbre*, no. 1 (December 1982).

Cullen, Mary (ed.), *Girls Don't Do Honours: Irishwomen in Education in the Nineteenth and Twentieth Centuries* (Dublin, 1987).

O'Connor, Anne V. and Parkes, Susan M., *A History of Alexandra College and School, Dublin, 1866-1916* (Dublin, 1983).

O'Connor, Anne V., "Influences affecting girls' secondary education in Ireland, 1860-1910." *Archivium Hibernicum*, vol. xli, (1986).

O'Flynn, Grainne, "Some aspects of the education of Irishwomen throughout the years," *Capuchin Annual*, (1977), pp 164-79.

Walsh, Lorcan, "Images of women in nineteenth-century schoolbooks," *Irish Educational Studies*, vol. 4, no. 1, (1984), pp 73-87.

Social and Economic

Beale, Jenny, *Women in Ireland: Voices of Change* (Dublin, 1986).

Bolger, Pat (ed.), *And See Her Beauty Shining There: The Story of the Irish Countrywomen* (Dublin, 1986).

Bourke, Joanna, "Women and poultry in Ireland," *Irish Historical Studies*, vol. xxv, no 99 (May 1987), pp 293-310.

Boyle, Emily, "The linen strike of 1872," *Saothar*, vol. 2, (1976), pp 12-22.

Brophy, Imelda, "Women in the workforce," in David Dickson (ed.), *The Gorgeous Mask: Dublin 1700-1850* (Dublin, 1987), pp 51-63.

Carbery, Mary, *The Farm by Lough Gur* (Cork, 1986).

Daly, Mary E., "Women in the Irish workforce from pre-industrial to modern times," *Saothar*, vol. 7 (1981), pp 74-82.

de Montfort, S.L.M., "Mrs Pouden's experiences during the 1798 rising in county Wexford," *The Irish Ancestor*, vol. viii, no. 1 (1976), pp 4-8.

Devine, Francis, "Women in the Irish trade unions, a note," *Oibre: Journal of the Irish Labour History Society*, no. 2, (July 1975).

Diner, Hasia R., *Erin's Daughters in America: Irish Immigrant Women in the Nineteenth-Century* (Baltimore, 1983).

Fitzpatrick, David, "A share of the honeycomb: education, emigration and Irishwomen," *Continuity and Change*, vol. 1, no. 2, (1986), pp 217-34.

........., "Divorce and separation in modern Irish history," *Past and Present*, no. 114, (February 1987) pp 173-96.

........., "The modernisation of the Irish female," in P. O'Flanagan et al (eds.), *Rural Ireland: Modernisation and Change 1600-1900* (Cork, 1987), pp 162-80.

Jones, Mary, *These Obstreperous Lassies: A History of the Irish Women Workers' Union* (Dublin, 1988).

MacCurtain, Margaret and O'Corrain, Donncha, *Women in Irish Society: The Historical Dimension* (Dublin, 1978).

Messenger, Betty, *Picking Up the Linen Threads: Life in Ulster's Mills* (Belfast, 1988).

Moran, Mairead, "Women and the co-operative movement," *Co-op Ireland*, (May 1979), pp 37-8.

Murphy, Rev. J. J., "An Irish sister of Mercy in the Crimean war," *The Irish Sword*, vol. 5, (1961-2), pp 251-61.

O'Connell, T. J., *100 Years of Progress: The Story of the Irish National Teachers' Organisation, 1868-1968* (Dublin, 1968).

O'Leary, Eoin, "The Irish National Teachers' Organisation and the marriage bar for women national teachers, 1933-1958," *Saothar*, no. 12, (1987), pp 47-52.

Political:
Conlon, Lil, *Cumann na mBan and the Women of Ireland*, 1913-25 (Kilkenny, 1969).

Cullen, Mary, "How radical was Irish feminism between 1860 and 1920?" in P. J. Corish (ed.), *Radicals, Rebels and Establishments, Historical Studies XV* (Dublin, 1985), pp 185-201.

Did Your Granny Have a Hammer? A History of the Irish Suffrage Movement, 1876-1922 (Dublin, 1985).

Farrell, Brian, "Markievicz and the women of the revolution," in F. X. Martin (ed.), *Leaders and Men of the Easter Rising, Dublin 1916* (Dublin, 1967), pp 227-38.

Hazelkorn, Ellen, "The social and political views of Louie Bennett, 1870-1956," *Saothar*, no. 13, (1988), pp 32-44.

Hearne, Dana (ed.), Anna Parnell's *Tale of a Great Sham* (Dublin, 1986).

Hughes, Marie, "The Parnell sisters", *Dublin Historical Record*, vol. 20, no. 11, (March 1966), pp 14-27.

McKillen, Beth, "Irish feminism and national separatism 1914-1923," *Eire/Ireland*, xviii, no. 3, (1981), pp 52-67, continued in *ibid.*, xviii, no. 4, (1981), pp 72-90.

Moloney, Helena, "James Connolly and women," *Dublin Labour Year Book* (Dublin, 1930).

Murphy, Cliona, *The Women's Suffrage Movement and Irish Society in the Early Twentieth Century* (Brighton, 1989).

O'Neill, Maire, "The Dublin Women's Suffrage Society and its successors," *Dublin Historical Record*, vol. xxxviii, (Dec 1984-Sept 1985), pp 126-40.

Owens, Rosemary Cullen, "Votes for ladies, votes for women," organised labour and the suffrage movement, 1876-1922," *Saothar*, 9, (1983), pp 32-47.

........., *Smashing Times: The History of the Irish Suffrage Movement, 1890-1922* (Dublin, 1983).

Prison Letters of Countess Markievcz (London, 1986).

Scannell, Yvonne, "The Constitution and the role of women," in Brian Farrell (ed.), *De Valera's Constitution and Ours* (Dublin, 1988), pp 123-36.

Sheehy Skeffington, A.D. and Rosemary Owens (eds.), *Votes for Women: Irish Women's Struggle for the Vote* (Dublin, 1975).

Smyth, Ailbhe, "Feminism in the south of Ireland, a discussion," *The Honest Ulsterman*, no. 83, (Summer 1987).

Ward, Margaret, "Suffrage first—above all else! an account of the Irish suffrage movement," *Feminist Review*, 10, (1982), pp 21-36.

.........., *Unmanageable Revolutionaries: Women in Irish Nationalism* (Dingle, 1983).

Biography/Autobiography

Bayley Butler, Beatrice, "Lady Arbella Denny, 1707-1792," *Dublin Historical Record*, vol ix, no. 1, (Dec 1946-Feb 1947), pp 1-20.

Bayley Butler, Beatrice and Sr Katherine Butler, "Mrs John O'Brien: her life, her work, her friends," *Dublin Historical Record*, vol. xxxiii, (Dec 1979-Sept 1980), pp 141-56.

Cardozo, Nancy, *Maud Gonne: Lucky Eyes and a High Heart* (London, 1978).

Chambers, Anne, *Granuaile: The Life and Times of Grace O'Malley* (Dublin, 1979).

......, *Elinor, Countess of Desmond*, (Dublin, 1987).

Collis, Maurice, *Somerville and Ross: A Biography* (London, 1968).

Colum, Mary, *Life and the Dream* (New York, 1947).

Condon, Jim, "Elizabeth, lady Thurles," in W. Corbett and W. Nolan (eds.), *Thurles, The Cathedral Town* (Dublin, 1989), pp 41-5.

Cousins, James and Margaret, *We Two Together* (Madras, 1950).

Coxhead, Elizabeth, *Daughters of Erin: Five Women of the Irish Renaissance* (London, 1979, reprint).

Cummins, Geraldine, *Unseen Adventures* (London, 1951).

Fallon, Charlotte H., *Soul of Fire: A Biography of Mary MacSwiney* (Cork, 1986).

Fitzgerald, Brian, *Emily, Duchess of Leinster, 1731-1814* (London, 1949).

Fox, R.M., *Louie Bennett: Her Life and Times* (Dublin, 1957).

Haverty, Anne, *Constance Markievicz, An Independent Life* (London, 1988).

Hughes, Vera, *The Strange Story of Sarah Kelly* (Naas, 1988).

Levenson, Leah and Jerry Naderstad, *Hanna Sheehy Skeffington: A Pioneering Irish Feminist* (Syracuse, 1986).

Levenson, Samuel, *Maud Gonne* (London, 1977).

Levine, June, *Sisters: The Personal Story of an Irish Feminist* (Dublin, 1982).

Lewis, Gifford, *Eva Gore Booth and Esther Roper, A Biography* (London, 1988).

Linklater, Andro, *An Unhusbanded Life: Charlotte Despard: Suffragette, Socialist and Sinn Feiner* (London, 1980).

Marreco, Anne, *The Rebel Countess: The Life and Times of Constance Markievicz* (London, 1967).

MacBride, Maud Gonne, *A Servant of the Queen* (Suffolk, 1983 reprint).

McDowell, R. B., *Alice Stopford-Green: A Passionate Historian* (Dublin, 1985).

McNeill, Mary, *The Life and Times of Mary Ann McCracken 1770-1866* (Belfast, 1988 reprint).

Missing Pieces: Women in Irish History (Dublin, 1983).

More Missing Pieces: Her Story of Irish History (Dublin, 1985).

Mulvihill, Margaret, *Charlotte Despard, A Biography* (London, 1989).

Norman, Diana, *Terrible Beauty: A Life of Constance Markievicz* (Dublin, 1988).

O'Brien, Kate, *Presentation Parlour* (London, 1963).

......., "Memories of a catholic education," *The Stony Thursday Book*, no. 7, (1981), pp 28-32.

O'Cleirigh, Nellie, "Lady Aberdeen and the Irish connection," *Dublin Historical Record*, vol. xxxix, (Dec 1985-Sept 1986), pp 28-32.

Retrospections of Dorothea Herbert 1770-1806 (Dublin, 1988).

Sayers, Peig, *Peig* (Dublin, various editions).

Thomson, David and McGusty, Moyra, *The Irish Journals of Elizabeth Smith, 1840-1850* (Oxford, 1980).

Van Voris, Jacqueline, *Constance Markievicz: In the Cause of Ireland* (Amherst, 1967).

Religious

Clear, Caitriona, *Nuns in Nineteenth-Century Ireland* (Dublin, 1987).

......, "Walls within walls: nuns in nineteenth-century Ireland," in Chris Curtin et al (eds.), *Gender in Irish Society* (Galway, 1987), pp 134-51.

Bolster, Sr M. Angela, *The Sisters of Mercy in the Crimean War* (Cork, 1964).

......, *Catherine McAuley in Her Own Words* (Dublin, 1981).

......, *Mercy in Cork, 1837-1987* (Cork, 1987).

......, (ed.), *The Correspondence of Catherine McAuley, 1827-1841* (Cork, 1989).

Fahey, Tony, "Nuns in the Catholic church in Ireland in the nineteenth-century," in Cullen, *op. cit.*, pp 7-30.

Ffrench-Eager, Irene, *The Nun of Kenmare* (Cork, 1970).

Gibbons, Margaret, *The Life of Margaret Aylward* (London, 1928).

Kenneally, James J., "Sexism, the church, Irish women," *Eire/Ireland*, (Fall 1986), pp 3-16.

Lee, Joseph, "Women in the church since the famine," in MacCurtain and O'Corrain, *op. cit.*, pp 37-45.

Liguori, Sr M., "Presentation convent, Thurles, 1817-1917," in Corbett and Nolan, *op. cit.*, pp 213-21.

Lillis, Sr Mercedes, "The Ursulines in Thurles," in Corbett and Nolan, *op. cit.*, pp 191-211.

MacCurtain, Margaret, "Towards an appraisal of the religious image of women," *The Crane Bag*, vol. 4, no. 1, (1980), pp 26-30.

MacSwiney, P.M., (ed.), *Letters of Mary Aikenhead* (Dublin, 1914).

Member of the Congregation, *The Life and Work of Mary Aikenhead* (London, 1925).

Pauline, Sr. M., *God Wills It: Centenary Story of the Sisters of St Louis* (Dublin, 1959).

Savage, R. Burke, *A Valiant Dublin Woman: The Story of George's Hill* (Dublin, 1940).

Walsh, T. J., *Nano Nagle and the Presentation Sisters* (Dublin, 1959).

Contributors

Mary Clancy: graduated from University College, Galway with a B.A., H.Dip in Ed. and an M.A. She is currently employed as a tutor in the history department, UCG, and teaches women's history courses in the extra-mural Department and in the Peadar O'Donnell Unemployed centre, Galway. She is a national committee member of the Irish Labour History Society and secretary of the Galway branch.

Caitriona Clear: received her B.A. and M.A. degrees from University College, Galway and spent a year at the European University Institute in Florence. She has lectured in history in U.C.G. and the Institute of Public Administration, Dublin and is author of *Nuns in Nineteenth-Century Ireland*, (Dublin, 1987). She has also worked as a street-worker with Dublin Simon Community. Current research interests are women in Irish history and homelessness and subsistence strategies in post-Famine Ireland.

Mary Cullen: is a lecturer in Modern History in St Patrick's College, Maynooth. She has written a number of articles on women's history and edited *Girls Don't Do Honours: Irish Women and Education in the the 19th and 20th Centuries* (Dublin, 1987).

Mona Hearn: born in Dundalk and educated in St Vincent's School and Loreto College, Kilkenny. She trained as a domestic science teacher in St Mary's College, Cathal Brugha St., Dublin. She received a degree in social science in U.C.D. and was among the first group of graduates to be awarded an M.Ed. from T.C.D. in 1972. An interest in social history led to her spending approximately seven years investigating domestic service in Dublin and in the "big" houses of Ireland. In 1984 she was awarded a Ph.D from Trinity for this work. She is at present head of the School of Home and Social Sciences in Cathal Brugha St. College.

Maria Luddy: was awarded a B.Ed. from Mary Immaculate College of Education in Limerick and an M.A. and Ph.D. from the NUI. She teaches in a primary school in Tipperary. She is currently researching the history of prostitution in Ireland in the last century.

Margaret MacCurtain: lectures in Modern Irish History in University College Dublin. She is a Dominican Sister.

Dympna McLoughlin: received her B.A. from St Patrick's College, Maynooth. She was awarded an M.A. from the NUI and received a travelling studentship in geography. She completed her Ph.D. dissertation at Syracuse University, New York on "Shovelling out paupers: female emigration from Irish workhouses, 1840-1870." At present she is a Junior Research Fellow at the Institute of Irish Studies in Belfast working on infanticide in nineteenth-century Ireland.

Cliona Murphy: completed her B.A., H. Dip., and M.A. at University College Cork. She was awarded a fellowship in 1982 by the State University of New York Binghamton to undertake her Ph. D. in history which she completed in 1986. She has taught in London and at the Institute of Public Administration and School of Irish Studies in Dublin. She is currently lecturing in California State University Bakersfield in European history.

Index

abbesses, 19-20
Achonry diocese, 42
Addams, Jane, 186, 196
Addis, W and Arnold, T, 19
age of consent, 212-13, 215-16
Aikenhead, Mary, 28-9, 31, 32, 43, 70
Alexandra College, Dublin, 4
Antislavery Conference, 1840, 185
Antrim, Co, 109
Armagh Union, 125
Asquith, H H, 193
Association of the Ladies of Charity, 30
Athlone, Co Westmeath, 58
Aylward, Margaret, 30, 31, 36

Bagshawe, Dr, bishop of Nottingham, 39
Ball, Frances, 29, 32
Ballymony Union, 140
Bane, Liam, 38
Barry, Mary, 130
Beeton, Mrs, 152
begging, 86, 87
    survival strategy, 106-11
    women's work, 10, 113-14
Belfast, 189, 248
    domestic service in, 150, 157
    prostitution in, 52, 70
Benedictines, 248
Bennett, Louie, 184
Bicheno, J E, 112
Birmingham, George (O'Hannay), 183, 187
birth, concealment of, 141
Blackstone, Sir William, 91
Blasket Islands, 237-8, 260
Blythe, Ernest, TD, 217
Board of Trade, 155, 160
Bolger, Johanna, 123
Bottomly, Mr, MP, 163-4
Boylan, Fr Eugene, 260
Breen, Mary, 122
Brigidine Order, 23, 30-31, 34
brothels, 52, 57-9
Browne, Senator Kathleen, 209, 213, 214, 218, 221, 225, 232
Brugha, Caitlín, 231
Bryson, John, 129

Bundoran, Co Donegal, 22
Burke, Fr, 44
Burns, Lucy, 186
Butler, Dr, bishop of Limerick, 35
butter, sale of, 101
Byrne, Catherine, 123
Byrne, Dr, archbishop of Dublin, 244
Byrne, George, 137
Byrne, Lucy, 198

Cahill, Mary, 137
Carbery, Mary, 234
Carlow town, 22
Carmelites, 27-8, 248
Carney, Professor James, 259
Cashel diocese, 21
Castleisland, Co Kerry, 23
Catholic Church
    and Legion of Mary, 243-4
    pious observances, 234-5
    status of nuns in, 16-21
Catholic Emancipation, 27
Catholic Workers League, 208
Censorship of Publications Bill, 211-12
Chagney Tile Works, 241, 247
Charleville, Co Mayo, 23
children, 122, 128, see also illegitimacy
    abandonment of, 137-8, 140-1, 142
    childminding, 131, 139
    deserted, 132-6
    earnings of, 99
    links with parents, 132-6
    mortality rates, 138-9
    orphaned, 136-41
Children of Mary, 76, 233-4, 241-2
Christian Brothers, 256
Civil Service Regulation (Amendment) Bill, 1925, 217-19, 221
Civil War, 223, 242-3
Clare, Co, 102, 111
Clarke, Senator Kathleen, 209, 213, 214, 225, 231, 232
    on equal employment rights, 220-21
Cloyne diocese, 42
Cobh, Co Cork, 59
Coghlan, Michael, 130
Colby, Mrs, 189
Coleraine Union, 125-6, 140

Collet, Miss C E, 155, 157, 168
Collins, Michael, 251
Collins, Sally, 122-3
Collins-O'Driscoll, Margaret, TD, 207-8, 210, 211, 221-2, 231
   on equal employment rights, 217-18
Colthurst, Captain J C, 191
Colum, Padraic, 183
commission of enquiry into condition of poor, 86-91
Comyn, Michael, 220
Concannon, Helena, TD, 208, 212, 219, 224-5, 231
Conditions of Employment Bill, 1935, 219-21
Congregation of Mary, 42
Connolly, James, 220
Connor, Eliza, 126-7
Conservative and Unionist Women's Franchise Association, 196
Contagious Diseases Acts, 5, 59, 60, 69, 70
contraception, 128
   debate on, 211-14
convents, 15-46
   distribution of, 21-7
   education, 234, 235-6
   financial endowments, 22-3, 26
   projects of, 41-4
Cork city, 27, 189
   domestic service in, 150, 157
   prostitution in, 52, 58-9, 70
Cork Union, 131, 133, 138, 139, 141
   statistics, 119
Costello, Senator Eileen, 209, 218, 219, 222, 225, 232
Council of Trent, 20
Cousins, James, 183
Cousins, Margaret, 183
Criminal Law Amendment Act, 1855, 57-8
Criminal Law Amendment Bill, 1934, 212-18
Croke, Dr, archbishop of Cashel, 39
Cullen, Cardinal Paul, 19, 35, 38, 44, 235
Cumann na mBan, 210
Cumann na nGaedhael, 208, 217, 221, 222
Curragh, Co Kildare, 5, 59-60, 78
Curtis, Dr, 59
Cusack, Sr Mary Francis Clare, 38-40, 45, 46

Dail Eireann, 12
   censorship debate, 211-12
   Constitution debate, 224-5
   Criminal Law Amendment Bill, 212-13
   divorce debate, 210
   equal employment debate, 217, 219
   women deputies, 8, 206-26
D'Alton, 45
Daly, Mary, 150
Daly, Fr Peter, 37-8, 45
D'Arcy, Mr, 17
Daughters of Charity, 20, 28-9, 42
de Valera, Eamon, 180, 206, 208, 224
Degnan, Sr B, 45
Delaney, Dr, bishop of Kildare and Leighlin, 31, 34
Denny, Lady Arbella, 61-2
Desart, Countess of, 209, 232
deserted wives, 123-4, 127-30, 143
Deveraux, John, 122
d'Houet, Madame, 36
Dickens, Charles, 60
Digby, Margaret, 185
Dillon, John, 192, 193
Dingle, Co Kerry, 237, 238
divorce, debate on, 210-11
Dodd, Margaret Smith, 134-5
Domestic Servants' Bill, 164
domestic service, 11, 15-16, 78, 148-72, 237
   age of servants, 154-5
   board and lodging, 151, 160
   cooks, 153, 158, 162
   duties, 152-4
   hours of work, 165-6
   and marital status, 155-6
   mobility of servants, 168-9
   numbers employed, 148
   perquisites, 161-2
   relationship with employer, 166-70
   sources of servants, 148-52
   wages, 151, 156-63, 167
   working conditions, 163-6, 167
Domestic Training Institute for Protestant Girls, 152
Dominican Order, 27-8, 35-6, 256
Donegal, Co, 129
Donnelly, Mary, 123
Down, Co, 104
Down Town New York Ethical Society, 193

Doyle, Bridget, 126
Doyle, Julia, 122
Draper's Assistant, The, 162
Drogheda, Co Louth, 42
Dublin by Lamplight Institution, 66, 68
Dublin city, 42, 189
   domestic service in, 150, 153, 157, 171-2
   Magdalen Asylums, 70
   prostitution in, 57, 60, 78-9
Dublin diocese, 21
Dublin Female Penitentiary, 63-4, 66-8
Dublin Foundling Hospital, 61
Dublin Metropolitan Police, 52-5
Dublin Midnight Mission and Home, 62
Dublin Police Act, 1842, 56
Dublin South Union, 130
Dublin Women's Suffrage Society, 5
Duff, Frank, 260
   and Edel Quinn, 241, 246, 249, 253-4, 255, 258
   founds Legion of Mary, 242, 243-5
   organisational abilities, 251-3

Edgar, Dr, 52
education, 26, 27, 32, 42, 234, 235-6
Elizabeth of the Trinity, St, 248
Elphin, bishop of, 37
emigration, 66, 117-18, 131
   children left behind, 134-6, 142
   from workhouses, 120-1, 124, 134-6, 137, 140
employment for women, 8, 10, 15-16, 78, 148, 162-3. see also domestic service
   equal rights in, 217-21
   in factories, 15, 78, 150, 151, 162-3
   shop assistants, 162, 163
   wages, 160-61
Ennis, Co Clare, 22
Ennis Union, 139
Enniscorthy Union, 120, 123, 124, 126-7, 138
Ennistymon Union, 140
equal rights debate
   employment, 217-21
   jury service, 221-3
Evil Literature Committee, 211

Fagan, Michael, 132

Faithful Companions of Jesus, 23, 36, 234, 240
Female Penitent Asylum, 65
Female Penitent Refuge, Dublin, 63-4
Feminist History Forum, 1
Fermoy, Co Cork, 34
Fianna Fail, 208, 221, 225
Fitzgerald-Kenney, Mr, TD, 217
Flower, Dr Robin, 237, 260
Fogarty, Richard, 234
Foley, Peggy, 123
Folklore Department, UCD, 239
Frazer, Helen, 189-90
Free State Constitution, 1922, 217, 223, 226
Freeman's Journal, 17
   advertisements, 154, 158-60
Furlong, Dr, bishop of Ferns, 31

Gabbet, Joe, 252
Gaelic League, 210
Gallagher, John, 129
Galway, Co, 100
Galway town, 35, 70
Gavan Duffy, Dr Louise, 258-9
gender history, 6-7
Gill, Colette, 252
Gilman, Charlotte Perkins, 184, 187-8
Gonne, Maud, 2
Good Shepherd Orphanage, Cork, 152
Good Shepherd Sisters, 35, 36, 66, 74
   Magdalen Asylums, 61, 70
Grangegorman Female Prison, 56
Grimes, Mary, 138

Hackett, Thomas, 131
Hamilton, Nicholas, 122
Hanley, William, 108
Hanly, Patrick, 135
Harnett, Michael, 23
Hartnell, Anne, 130
Hartnett, Thomas, 137
Haslam, Anna, 5
Haslam, Mr and Mrs, 182
Heffernan, Bishop, 254, 255
Hillman, James, 260
Holy Ghost Order, 256
Home Rule
   and women's suffrage, 181-2, 184, 191-9

Home Rule Bill, 193
hospitals, 42
household budgets, 10, 85-115
   women's percentage contribution, 104-6
Hughes, Sam, 252

illegitimacy, 87, 113, 122, 168, 218-19
Illegitimate Children (Affiliation Orders) Bill, 218-19
Imitation of Christ, 248
income, see women's earnings
industrial schools, 149, 151
infanticide, 137, 141, 214
Inspection of Nunneries Bill, 17-18
Institute of the Blessed Virgin Mary, 28-9
Institute of the House of Mercy, 30
Irish Citizen, 167, 183, 186, 194, 198
   and USA suffrage movement, 186-9
Irish Constitution, 1937, 208, 223-5
Irish Countrywoman's Association, 185
Irish Ecclesiastical Record, 44-5
Irish Homestead, The, 164
Irish Parliamentary Party, 181-2, 192-3
Irish Times
   advertisements, 154-5, 158-9
Irish Women Citizens and Local Government Association (IWCLGA), 207, 212, 219
Irish Women Workers' Union (IWWU), 207, 219
Irish Women's Franchise League (IWFL), 183, 186, 191 and WSPU, 195-8
Irish Women's Suffrage and Local Government Association (IWSLGA), 182-3, 190

John of the Cross, St, 248
Joint Committee of Women's Societies and Social Workers, 218
Joyce, James, 233
Juliana of Norwich, 248
Juries Bill, 1924, 221-2
Juries Bill, 1927, 222-3
jury service, 221-3
Jus Suffragi, 184

Kavanagh, Patrick, 236
Keane, John, 212
Kearney, Sr Kevin, 256
Kells, Co Meath, 92, 100, 151
Kelly, Catherine, 137
Kelly, Joan, 3
Kelly, Patricia, 44
Kenmare Union, 119
Kennedy, Betty, 130
Kennedy's Agency, 159
Kenny, Mr and Mrs John, 153
Keogh, Dermot, 162
Kerry, Co, 102-3
Kildare, Co, 109
Kilkenny, Co, 28, 102, 104
Killaloe, bishop of, 22
Killarney, Co Kerry, 28, 34
Killarney School of Housewifery, 152
Killarney Union, 133
Kilrush Union, 137, 138-9
Kinvara, 22
Kirwan, Elizabeth, 252
Knight, Mary, 135
Knock, Co Mayo, 39, 46, 235, 245

La Salette apparition, 245
Labour Party, 220
labourers, see also seasonal labour
   household budgets, 10, 91-106
   women and household economy, 85-115
Ladies' Collegiate School, Belfast, 4
Ladies' Land League, 2, 39, 210
Lancet, The, 164
Land League, 39
Land Purchase Act, 1923, 251
Landrin, Pierre, 246, 247-8, 250, 260
Laois, Co (Queen's Co), 92, 94-5, 98, 107-8
Lawrence, Mrs Pethick, 198
Leahy, Dr, bishop of Dromore, 39
Legion of Mary, 246, 260
   foundation of, 242, 243-5
   organisation of, 251
Leitrim, Co, 100-01
Lemass, Sean, TD, 219
Leo XIII, Pope, 32-3
Lerner, Gerda, 2
Letterkenny, Co Donegal, 34
Lewis, G E Cornewall, 110
Limerick, Co, 103, 104

Limerick city, 22, 23, 36, 157
    prostitution in, 70
Limerick Union, 130, 131, 132-3, 135, 137
Local Government Act, 1898, 5
local government franchise, 183
Logan, William, 52, 59
Londonderry, Co, 129
Londonderry Union, 139
Longford, Co, 108-9
Loreto Abbey, Rathfarnham, Dublin, 29
Loreto Convent, Navan, 22
Loreto Convent, Nth Gt George's St, Dublin, 241
Loreto Order, 30, 42, 255
    decentralisation, 33-4
Lourdes apparition, 235, 245
Louth, Co, 92, 96-7
Lynn, Dr Kathleen, TD, 231

McAuley, Catherine, 29-30, 31, 37, 43, 45
McCabe, Cardinal, 39, 40
McCall, Mary, 123
McDonnell, Margaret, 122
McDonnell, Richard, 135
MacEvilly, Dr John, 38, 39, 45
McGarry, Daniel, 132-3
McGrath, Margaret, 130
MacHale, Dr John, 26
McMahon, Mary, 131
McMahony, Bridget, 130
McNamara, Pat, 108
McQuaid, Dr J C, archbishop of Dublin, 244
McQuarrie, John, 237
McSwiney, Mary, TD, 231
Magdalen Asylum, Cork, 74
Magdalen Asylum, Donnybrook, Dublin, 74-5
Magdalen Asylum, Drumcondra, Dublin, 70
Magdalen Asylum, Leeson St, Dublin, 61-2, 64, 65, 66
Magdalen Asylum, Limerick, 66, 67, 74, 75
Magdalen Asylum, Townsend St, Dublin, 66, 70
Magdalen Asylums, 63-4, 77
    funding, 67-8
    referrals to, 71, 74
    regime of, 64-5
    success rates, 66-7, 75-6
    voluntary entrance to, 71, 74
    work training, 64-5
Maria Legionis, 252, 255
Markievicz, Countess, TD, 2, 183, 231
Marmion, Dom, 248
marriage, 123-4, 127-30, 134-5
    age of, 105, 110
    and domestic servants, 155-6
    mobility of women within, 114, 120, 128, 142
    women's role in, 112-14
Martin, Mary, 256
Mary, devotion to, 244-5
Mason, W S, 58
Mayo, Co, 108, 109, 110
Mayo diocese, 42
Meath, Co, 92-3, 97-8, 100, 107
Medical Missionaries of Mary, 256
Men's League for Women's Suffrage, 195
Mill, John Stuart, 182
Missionary Sisters of the Holy Rosary, 256
missions, 256-7
Monaghan, Co, 34
Montfort, Louise Marie de, 245, 248, 260
Moskowitz, Mr, 193-4
Moynihan, Hannah, 135-6
Moynihan, Maurice, 252
Moynihan, Sean, 252
Mulally, Teresa, 28, 29
Munster Women's Franchise League, 196
Murphy, Anne, 123
Murphy, Bridget, 123
Murphy, Dominick, 17-18
Murphy, Mary, 123, 130
Murray, Dr, archbishop of Dublin, 28, 29, 30, 33

Naas Union, 140
Nagle, Jack, 252, 255
Nagle, Nano, 27-8, 29, 30, 31, 32
Nairobi, East Africa, 246, 249, 250, 254-8
Nally, Dr, bishop, 34
National American Women's Suffrage Association (NAWSA), 186, 189, 191
National Board of Education, 26
National Insurance Act, 1911, 167
National University Women Graduates Association, 224

Navan, Co Meath, 22, 34
New Ross, Co Wexford, 70
New Ross Union, 119
Nicholls, George, 112
Nun of Kenmare, 38-40
nuns, 8, 9, 15-46, 19, 26-7
   and bishops, 19, 26-7, 31, 31-2, 33-8, 37-8, 41
   centralised orders, 32-3
   istribution of, 21-7
   dowries, 26
   education, 26, 32
   enclosure, 18, 20, 27-8
   hospitals, 42
   Magdalen Asylums, 9, 69-80
   numbers of, 21
   socially conservative, 40-41
   status within church, 16-21, 27-46
   work of, 41-4

O'Beirne, Francis, 101
O'Brien, Sissy, 234, 235, 236, 241
O Broin, Leon, 251-2
O'Callaghan, Dr Margaret, 243
O'Connell, Daniel, 44, 180, 185
O'Connell, Dr, bishop of Galway, 38
O'Connor, Anne, 235-6
O'Connor, Frank, 152
O Criomhthain, Tomas, 238
Odette, Senator Ellen, Countess of Desart, 209, 232
Offaly, Co (King's Co), 102
O'Higgins, Kevin, 206, 221, 223, 224
Oireachtas. see Dail Eireann; Seanad Eireann
O'Laoghaire, Diarmuid, SJ, 236
Omagh, Co Tyrone, 34
Omolo, John, 257
O'Neill, Grace, 187
O'Riordan, 42
O'Shaugnessy, Jane, 130
O'Shea family, 138
O Súilleabháin, Tomás, 238
Oughterard, Co Galway, 23

Pankhurst, Mrs, 187, 189, 195, 197-8
Park, Alice, 186
Parnell, Charles Stewart, 180, 185
Paul, Alice, 184, 186, 198
paupers, 87, 124-7, see also workhouses
   women among, 113
Pearse, Margaret, TD, 207, 212, 219, 224
Penal Laws, 27, 28
pensions, 167
pigs, 98-9, 104, 106
Pius IX, pope, 35
Plunkett, Sir Horace, 185
Poor Clares, 27-8, 38-9, 40, 45, 247-8
Poor Enquiry, 86-91, 112
   local enquiries, 89-90
Poor Law, 11, 42, 43, 44, 110-11, 117-24, 182. see also workhouses
Poor Law Act, 1838, 117, 118, 121, 128
Poor Servants of the Mother of God, 42
poultry, 98-9, 104, 106
Presentation Convent, Castleisland, 22
Presentation Convent, Douglas St, Cork, 33
Presentation Convent, Limerick, 22
Presentation Order, 16, 22, 23, 32-3, 41
   education, 42
   enclosure, 18, 28, 31
Proclamation, 1916, 221, 224
Propaganda Fides, 18
prostitution, 5, 66, 210
   ages of prostitutes, 56-7, 79
   arrest statistics, 52-7
   case histories of prostitutes, 59, 62-3, 77-9
   convent asylums, 69-80
   extent of, 52-61
   garrison towns, 58, 59-60
   lay asylums, 61-9
   Oireachtas debate, 212, 213-14
   escue of prostitutes, 9-10, 61-80

Quakers, 182
Queen's Institute, Dublin, 4
Quinn, Edel, 12, 239-42, 245-51, 253-9, 260-1
   beatification process, 242, 251, 259
   biography, 242, 246, 251, 254, 258-9
   death, 250, 258
   in Legion of Mary, 245-6, 253-4
   in Nairobi, 254-8
   spirituality, 246-8, 260-1
   tuberculosis, 248-50
Quinn, Leslie, 242, 247

Rathdrum Union, 141
Reconstruction, Ministry of, 169
Reddan, Miss, 66
Redmond, Bridget, TD, 207-8, 212, 219, 224
Redmond, John, 180, 192, 193-4
Reed, Rev Henry, 59
Reform Bill, 1832, 3
Reform Bill, 1867, 3, 182
reformatories, 149, 151
Rescue Mission Home, Dublin, 62, 66
Reynolds, Mary, TD, 207
Riberi, Archbishop Antonio, 246
Roscrea, Co Tipperary, 23, 31, 108
Ross, Sir John, 163
Rowlan, Mary Jane, 139
Rowlette, Dr, TD, 214-15
Ruttledge, P J, TD, 213, 214
Ryan, Dr, bishop of Limerick, 36
Ryan, Mrs, 70
Ryan, Patrick, 122
Ryan, Sarah, 122
Ryan, Tom, 122

Sacred Heart Sisters, 23, 27
St John Gogarty, Oliver, 214-15
St Leger, Fr, 36
St Louis Convent, Bundoran, 22
St Louis Sisters, 34-5
St Patrick's College, Maynooth, 256
St Patrick's Society for African Missions, 256
St Vincent de Paul, Conference of, 242
Sayers, Micheal, 238
Sayers, Peig, 12, 236-9, 246
  spirituality, 237, 238-9, 259-60, 261
Seanad Eireann
  censorship debate, 212
  committee on Criminal Amendment Bill, 213-15
  divorce debate, 211
  equal employment rights debate, 218-19
  women in, 8, 12, 207, 209-10
seasonal labour, 104, 109, 110, 117-18
Seneca Falls meeting, 184, 185
Sex Disqualification Act, 1919, 217, 221, 222, 223
Shanahan, Bishop, 256
Shanahan, Michael Henry, 132
Shaw, Celia, 252

Shaw, George Bernard, 183
Sheehy Skeffington, Frank, 183, 187, 190-91, 196, 198-9
Sheehy Skeffington, Hanna, 183, 191, 197-8, 198
sickness benefit, 167
Sinn Fein, 210
Sinnot, Mary, 124
Sisters of Charity, 4, 29, 30, 43
  compared with Sisters of Mercy, 33-4
  Magdalen Asylums, 61, 66, 70-71
Sisters of Mercy, 16, 22, 23, 32, 41
  compared with Sisters of Charity, 33-4
  constitutions of, 18-19, 30
  Magdalen Asylums, 61, 70
  meeting of, 36-7
Sisters of Mercy convent, Baggot St, Dublin, 33
Sisters of Mercy convent, Carlow, 22
Sisters of Mercy convent, Galway, 37-8, 45
Sisters of Mercy convent, Limerick, 42
Sisters of Our Lady of Charity of Refuge, 70, 76
Sisters of Peace, 39, 46
Sisters of St John of God, 30-31, 42
Sisters of St Louis, 42
Sisters of the Charitable Instruction of the Sacred Heart of Jesus, 27
Sisters of the Holy Faith, 30
Sligo, Co, 101
social legislation, 210-17
Society of Friends, 182
Sodality of the Children of Mary. see Children of Mary
soldiers
  as deserting husbands, 129-30
  and prostitutes, 58, 59-60
South Dublin Union, 135
spirituality, female, 233-61
  Marian spirituality, 235, 244-5
Stephens, James, 183
Stopford-Green, Senator Alice, 209, 232
Suenens, Cardinal Leon-Joseph, 242, 246, 248, 252, 254, 258, 260
suffrage movement, 5, 8, 187-8, 209
  American influence on, 11, 180-99
  and English suffragists, 195-8
  and Home Rule movement, 191-9
  Irish suffragists in USA, 190-91
  overseas contacts, 184, 186
  in USA, 184-5

visits by American suffragists, 189-90
Sullivan, Michael, 134-5
Sullivan (pauper), 130
Swinford, Co Mayo, 22

Tallons Motorworks, 251
Teresa of Avila, St, 248
Therese of Lisieux, St, 248, 260
Thom's *Directory*, 171
Tierney, Mona, 242
Timmons, Jane, 122
Tipperary, Co, 103, 108
Tipperary town, 58
Tralee, Co Kerry, 70
Tralee Union, 137
Treatise of the Spiritual Life, A (Tanquerey), 248
Troy, Dr J T, archbishop of Dublin, 70
Troy, Mary, 141
Tuam diocese, 45, 270
Tullow, Co Carlow, 31

Ua Buachalla, D, TD, 211
'union-at-large', 125
United States of America
 and Home Rule movement, 193-4
 influence on Irish suffrage movement, 180-99
 Irish suffragists in, 190-91
 suffrage movement in, 184-5, 199
 women's history in, 2, 6
Ursuline Sisters, 22, 27

Vatican II, 46, 245
Vaughan, Fr, 43
Vere O'Brien family, 161
Vonier, Abbot, 248
Vote, The, 184
Votes for Women, 184, 193

Wailes, Muriel, 249, 254
Wallace, Miss, 22
Waterford, Co, 103

Waterford city, 28, 70
Waters, George, 101
Wexford, Co, 31
What Diantha Did (Gilman), 188
White, Thomas, 137
White Cross Vigilance Association, 57
Wicklow, Co, 92, 95-6, 108
Wilson, Mary Anne, 124
Wilson, President W, 191
Woman's Outlook, The, 184
Women's Advisory Committee on Domestic Service Problem, 169
women's earnings, 85-115
 percentage of household budget, 99-100, 104-6
 property of husband, 91
Women's Freedom League, 167
Women's Peace Party, 196
Women's Poor Law Guardian Act, 1896, 5
Women's Social and Political Union, 195-8
workhouses, 151-2
 administrative boundaries, 119-20, 124-5
 age of inmates, 123, 124
 children in, 136-41, 138-9
 and emigration, 120-1, 124, 134-6, 137, 140
 number of inmates, 118-19
 reasons for entering, 121-4
 women's use of, 10, 10-11, 117-43
Workman's Compensation Act, 1906, 167
World War I, 196-8
'Wrens of the Curragh', 59-60, 78
Wright, Eliza, 130
Wyse-Power, Senator Jenny, 12, 209-10, 222, 225, 232
 censorship debate, 212
 Criminal Amendment Bill, 213
 divorce debate, 211
 on equal employment rights, 218-19, 220-1
 on illegitimacy, 218-19

Yeats, W B, 183